A Country So

MW01013157

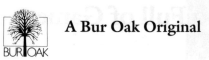A Bur Oak Original

A COUNTRY
SO FULL OF GAME
The Story of Wildlife in Iowa

By James J. Dinsmore

Illustrated by Mark Müller

UNIVERSITY OF IOWA PRESS  IOWA CITY

University of Iowa Press, Iowa City 52242
Printed in the United States of America

Design by Karen Copp

Printed on acid-free paper

Library of Congress Cataloging-in-
Publication Data
Dinsmore, James J.
    A country so full of game: the story of wildlife
in Iowa / by James J. Dinsmore; illustrated by
Mark Müller.
    p.   cm.—(A Bur oak original)
Includes bibliographical references and index.
ISBN 0-87745-453-1, ISBN 0-87745-454-X
(pbk.)
    1. Zoology—Iowa—History.   2. Hunting—
Iowa—History.   3. Animal populations—Iowa.
4. Game and game-birds—Iowa—History.
5. Man—Influence on nature—Iowa—History.
I. Title.   II. Series.
QL176.D56   1994
599.09777—dc20   93-34775
                                          CIP

98 97 96 95 94 C 5 4 3 2 1
98 97 96 95 94 P 5 4 3 2 1

Contents

Preface

The goal of this book is to present a comprehensive account of the status of wildlife in Iowa when Europeans first reached the state, describe how those people exploited and used the wildlife that they found, and explain what effect their actions had on the populations of the various species. I focus on events that occurred from the time the first explorers and settlers arrived until about 1900. It was during those years that both the exploitation of Iowa's wildlife and the changes in its landscape were most extensive. As will become apparent in the pages that follow, many species had disappeared from Iowa or their populations had reached their lowest levels by the turn of the century. I also include comments on developments during the twentieth century so as to provide a perspective on the species' current status both in the state and on the North American continent.

Wildlife was abundant and conspicuous in Iowa when Europeans arrived, and many pioneers mention their experiences with various species in their writings. Most encounters were with species that were used for food, that had valuable hides, or that were considered a threat to the settlers' livestock or crops. In this book, I discuss these interactions for sixteen species or groups of similar species that were native to Iowa. One other chapter discusses species that were introduced to Iowa in an attempt to augment or replace native species. All the species or groups discussed were either hunted or trapped. For a number of other such exploited species (e.g., rabbits, squirrels, and numerous less common furbearers), I have been unable to find enough information to cover them here. By writing only about the species that were hunted or trapped, I leave out the vast majority of Iowa's wildlife, the so-called nongame species. Again, for most of these, there is not enough information available to write a meaningful section.

Obviously, Europeans were not the first humans to occupy Iowa. There is a long history of occupation by Native Americans who were familiar with Iowa's wildlife and exploited it in a number of ways. A discussion of their interactions with Iowa's wildlife is beyond the scope of this book.

Information used in this book comes from a wide variety of

sources. Some of the first records are those written by explorers such as Lewis and Clark in 1804–6 and Thomas Say in 1819–20. Somewhat later, chroniclers of several of the early military expeditions across Iowa recorded their observations of Iowa's wildlife.

By the end of the 1800s, a scientific community was developing in Iowa, and its members began to publish their observations on Iowa's wildlife. In the late 1800s and early 1900s, comprehensive lists of both the birds and mammals of Iowa became available and provided a benchmark for later comparison. In the 1930s, comprehensive summaries of the birds and mammals of Iowa were published, and more recently new summaries for both groups became available. These publications along with literally hundreds of other recent papers provide us with a fairly broad understanding of the current distribution and status of most of Iowa's wildlife species.

Although less scientific, county histories provide another important source of information on Iowa's wildlife. Starting in the 1850s, several hundred county histories covering virtually all ninety-nine Iowa counties have been written. Some have whole chapters on the local fauna, while others contain only brief accounts of the wildlife that early settlers encountered. Often the wildlife is not mentioned at all, and some of the accounts probably are exaggerated or inaccurate. In total, though, these county histories provide a rich source of material about Iowa and its wildlife heritage.

Finally, many individuals have left behind personal accounts of settling and growing up in Iowa in the 1800s. Some of the individuals, such as Herbert Quick, would go on to careers as writers. More commonly, they were amateur historians who wanted to record their recollections so that future generations would appreciate their experiences. Examples include the simple diary kept by William Savage of Salem, Iowa; the stories of early duck hunters that were compiled by Jack Musgrove; the detailed account by H. Clay Merritt, who made his living as a market hunter; and many short notes published in the hunting magazine *Forest and Stream*. Whatever the source, our understanding of Iowa and its wildlife resources is richer because these individuals took the time to record their observations.

The landscape of Iowa has been changed more dramatically and completely than perhaps that of any other state. The extensive prairies and wetlands that once covered much of Iowa have largely disappeared, and even the woodlands that remain are much altered from their original state. The changes in natural habitat have affected many of our wildlife species: some species have disappeared from Iowa, others are much rarer now than they formerly were, and others are much more abundant now than they were in the past. Most present-day Iowans probably have no idea of the wide variety of wildlife that once lived in Iowa. I hope that this book will give them an appreciation of this rich heritage and a sense of what has been lost.

Acknowledgments

Many people and institutions have helped in various ways with this book. Much of the information compiled here was found in the libraries at Iowa State University and the State Historical Society of Iowa in Des Moines and Iowa City. Having their collections available for use was invaluable. In particular, workers in the microfilm room at Iowa State handled hundreds of requests for material under their care. A substantial amount of the work on this book was done during a faculty improvement leave from Iowa State University in spring 1987. I thank my colleagues and others who made that leave possible and also the staff at Manomet Bird Observatory in Manomet, Massachusetts, for allowing me to work there during my leave.

A number of others have helped by providing information, commenting on various sections of this work, and in other ways. These include Lou Best, Willis Goudy, Connie Mutel, John Pearson, Kevin Szcodronski, and Hank Zaletel. Mary Bennett, Jodi Evans, Chuck Greiner, Bill Johnson, Mike Meetz, and Lowell Washburn provided help in finding and preparing illustrations. A grant from the Iowa Science Foundation provided funds for the photographs and artwork. Paul Sievert and the late Joe Hickey helped provide access to A. W. Schorger's notes on passenger pigeons at the University of Wisconsin. Carolyn Brown patiently provided numerous suggestions of ways to make my writing more readable. The artwork by Mark Müller speaks for itself—it's great. I thank all of these people and groups for their help.

Finally, I thank my family for their patience while "Pop" was working on some mysterious book.

1. Wildlife and the Settlement of Iowa

Joseph Street said it well in 1833 when he described the Neutral Ground in northern Iowa as a country full of game. Street, an Indian agent stationed in Prairie du Chien, Wisconsin, had joined a group that was surveying land in the Neutral Ground, a forty-mile side strip of land in northeastern Iowa that was set aside in 1825 to separate two groups of Native Americans. This trip took him across the Turkey and Wapsipinicon rivers and to the Cedar River. On his return, Street wrote of his trip: "I had never rode through a country so full of game. The hunter who accompanied me, though living most of his time in the woods, expressed his astonishment at the abundance of all kinds of game except buffalo. . . ." Street's observations are consistent with those of explorers who preceded and followed him: Iowa had an abundance of wildlife.[1]

Fig. 1. Iowa as We Found It—1866. *This photoetching by noted cartoonist J. N. "Ding" Darling depicts the wealth of wildlife that early settlers found in Iowa. Courtesy University Art Collection, Iowa State University, Ames. Copyright held by J. N. Darling Foundation.*

Wildlife was a conspicuous feature of the land that Europeans encountered when they arrived and began settling in Iowa in the 1830s (fig. 1). The wealth that could be gained from trapping such furbearers as beaver was an attraction that brought trappers to Iowa, and the settlers that soon followed exploited a variety of animals for both their meat and fur.

The variety of life (or biodiversity) once found in Iowa is much greater than most Iowans would ever guess. Just among the backboned animals (the vertebrates), more than 450 species lived and bred in Iowa when Europeans arrived (table 1). Among the birds alone, another 190 or so species migrated through Iowa or occurred in the state occasionally, lengthening the list to more than 600 species. An even greater variety of insects, other

Table 1. Biodiversity of Vertebrate Species Native to Iowa

Group	Number of Species	Number Extirpated	Number Endangered	Number Threatened
Mammals	68	10	4	5
Birds	186	12	12	2
Reptiles	45	0	10	4
Amphibians	21	0	4	0
Fish	136	7	8	8
Totals	456	29	38	19

Sources: Bowles, J. B. 1981. Iowa's mammal fauna: an era of decline. Proceedings of the Iowa Academy of Science 88:38–42. Christiansen, J. L. 1981. Population trends among Iowa's amphibians and reptiles. Proceedings of the Iowa Academy of Science 88:24–27. Dinsmore, J. J. 1981. Iowa's avifauna: changes in the past and prospects for the future. Proceedings of the Iowa Academy of Science 88:28–37. Kent, T. H., and C. J. Bendorf. 1991. Official checklist of Iowa birds, 1991 edition, Iowa Bird Life 61:101–109. Menzel, B. W. 1981. Iowa's waters and fishes: a century and a half of change. Proceedings of the Iowa Academy of Science 88:17–23. State of Iowa. 1988. Iowa Administrative Code. Section 571, chapter 77.1, pp. 1–3.

nonbackboned animals, and plants were found in the state. Thus, several thousand species of plants and animals once occupied Iowa.[2]

A distressing number of those species either have been extirpated from Iowa or have become threatened or endangered. Among just the vertebrates, at least twenty-nine species no longer breed in Iowa, and the populations of another fifty-seven species have been reduced to such low levels that their future is in jeopardy (table 1). Dozens of other species, although not formally considered endangered, survive at population levels much lower than those of less than 200 years ago.

Rich soil, abundant water, and a favorable climate produced the extensive tall-grass prairies, rich wetlands, and lush forests that once covered Iowa—habitats which in turn supported a surprising variety of plants and animals. Ironically, the rich soil and water resources were also the reason for the loss of so many species and the decline in numbers of many others. Settlers soon discovered that Iowa's prairie soil was incredibly fertile and capable of producing abundant harvests of several crops. In a few short decades, much of Iowa's land surface was converted from its original natural landscape to a landscape dominated by only a few crops.

The face of Iowa has been changed more than perhaps any other state. The changes have in turn affected virtually all the state's native wildlife species. Some species have been extirpated, the populations of others have diminished, and in some cases their numbers have increased. Most amazing perhaps is the number of species that have survived and in some cases thrived with this vast alteration of the landscape. Thus, with the ever-increasing human population on our planet, the story of wildlife in Iowa may give us a window into the future and an idea of what we might expect to find happening as other areas of the planet are increasingly settled, developed, or altered by humans. The story of Iowa's wildlife is a mixed one, with both successes and failures. We can mourn the loss of such species as the bison and mountain lion, while we marvel at the recent success of wild turkeys and white-tailed deer. With the increasing concern over the loss of biodiversity on our planet, perhaps other states and countries can learn from Iowa's successes and failures.[3]

The story begins with a brief survey of Iowa's history, starting with the arrival of Europeans. Because the history of Iowa has been described in detail by several authors, I will not duplicate their narratives in this chapter.[4] Rather, I will emphasize the accounts of individuals who recorded their impressions of the wildlife that they found in Iowa.

Iowa, located near the center of the continental United States, was on the path of many North American explorers and travelers. Two major rivers, the Mississippi and Missouri, form all of its eastern and most of its western borders. These rivers provided a natural passageway for early explorers, traders, and adventurers, many of whom left written accounts of their journeys. However, most of the interior of Iowa was bypassed for many years, and little was written about much of the state until settlers arrived in the mid-1800s.

Early Explorers, Traders, and Statehood

As in most histories of Iowa, the expedition by Father Jacques Marquette and Louis Joliet is an appropriate starting place. After leaving Mackinac Island in Lake Huron in 1673, the two men made their way down the Wisconsin River and reached the Mississippi River near McGregor, Iowa. From there, they traveled downstream on the Mississippi River to the mouth of the Arkansas River, where they turned north and then returned home via the Illinois River. Although their journals are fairly brief, they do provide some information on the wildlife that they encountered. Especially notable is their description of bison, which they called wild cattle.[5]

After Marquette and Joliet, there is little record of the exploration of Iowa for the next 125 years. During that time, a number of trappers, traders, and explorers visited the state. Some were in the state only briefly, while others set up temporary quarters in an area for a year or two, traded with the Indians, and then moved on. Most of these people were poorly educated, and thus there is little written record of what they saw or found. This is unfortunate, since at least some of them spent considerable time in Iowa and probably had a good knowledge of what wildlife was found in the state before the arrival of permanent European settlers.

In the late 1700s and early 1800s, a number of trading posts were established along the Mississippi, Missouri, and other rivers. These outposts served as centers for trappers and Indians to exchange furs for various trade items. One of the most important was at Prairie du Chien, Wisconsin, just across from Marquette, Iowa. The trading post established there in 1781 served as a trading center for many years. Other trading posts that were important to Iowa include Fort Madison in southeastern Iowa, Fort Armstrong at Rock Island, Illinois, and several posts in the Council Bluffs area.[6]

In the late 1700s, the Spanish governor of Louisiana gave tracts of land in present-day Iowa to several men. The first tract went to Julien Dubuque, who was the first European to reside permanently in Iowa. He established a trading post at the lead mines at Dubuque in 1788 and remained there until he died in 1810. Similar land grants were given to Louis H. Tesson at Montrose in 1799 and to Basil Giard at McGregor in 1800.[7]

Although most Europeans in Iowa before 1830 recorded little about their encounters with wildlife, they probably did have an effect on the populations of such species as white-tailed deer, beaver, and perhaps bison, especially near trading posts. Thus,

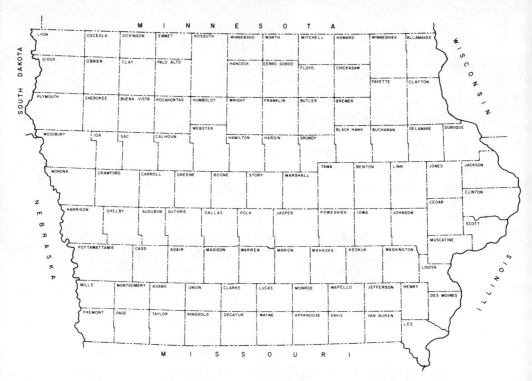

Map 1. Counties of
Iowa.

the abundance of wildlife that permanent settlers found when they started entering Iowa in the 1830s was probably somewhat reduced from that of truly presettlement times.

Iowa became part of the United States in 1803, when the Louisiana Territory was purchased from France. At first the area now known as Iowa was administered as part of the Louisiana Territory. Later, it was part of the Missouri, then the Michigan, and finally the Wisconsin territory. Other than the three Spanish land grants, Iowa was closed to settlers until 1833, when parts of eastern and southeastern Iowa were opened for settlement. In 1838, the Iowa Territory, with a territorial capital in Iowa City, was established. Settlers from the East rapidly moved into Iowa, and the population grew from 22,859 in 1838 to 96,088 in 1846. In 1846, Iowa was admitted to the United States as the twenty-ninth state. At that time the boundaries of the state were set; other than minor adjustments due to changes in the Mississippi and Missouri river channels, Iowa's boundaries have remained the same to the present day (map 1). At statehood, southeastern and eastern Iowa were somewhat settled, but central and western Iowa were largely unsettled and unknown lands.

6   *Wildlife and the Settlement of Iowa*

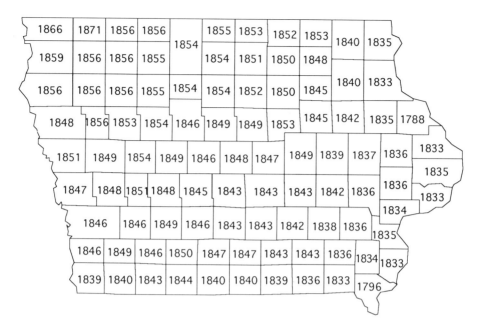

1866	1871	1856	1856	1854		1855	1853	1852	1853	1840	1835
1859	1856	1856	1855			1854	1851	1850	1848		
1856	1856	1856	1855	1854	1854	1852	1850	1845		1840	1833
1848	1856	1853	1854	1846	1849	1849	1853	1845	1842	1835	1788
1851	1849	1854	1849	1846	1848	1847	1849	1839	1837	1836	1833 / 1835
1847	1848	1851	1848	1845	1843	1843	1843	1842	1836	1836	1833
1846	1846	1849	1846	1843	1843	1842	1838	1836	1834	1835	
1846	1849	1846	1850	1847	1847	1843	1843	1836	1834	1833	
1839	1840	1843	1844	1840	1840	1839	1836	1833	1796		

Map 2. Year of first permanent settlement in each of Iowa's ninety-nine counties.

Statehood encouraged even more settlement, and increasing numbers of land-hungry people entered Iowa and claimed land. The pace of settlement across the state was very rapid, especially for the next fifteen years, and the human population grew rapidly. By the time the Civil War started in 1861, nearly all of Iowa's ninety-nine counties had at least a few settlers (map 2), and most counties had set up some form of local government. In much of the state, however, there was still land that had not been claimed. The last county in the state to be settled, Osceola, finally had its first permanent residents in 1871, thirty-eight years after the state was opened to settlement.

For most of the settlers, wildlife was not something to be admired or studied; rather, it was fresh meat to supplement the diet, hides that could be used or sold, or a competitor to or predator on the settlers' domestic animals and crops. Thus, most settlers shot, trapped, or in some other way killed or drove off the wildlife that they encountered.

Early Chroniclers of Wildlife

During the settlement of Iowa, a number of explorers, scientists, and others left at least some record of the wildlife that they found

Joel Asaph Allen,
1838–1921

One of the few
eastern scientists
to study wildlife
in Iowa in the
1800s, Joel Asaph
Allen was born
in Springfield,
Massachusetts.
Allen worked
and studied with
Louis Agassiz
at Harvard
University from
1862 to 1885. In
1867, he spent
several months in
central and
western Iowa
collecting birds
and mammals.
The collections
resulted in several
papers that were
the first scientific
lists of Iowa's birds
and mammals
since the Stephen
Long expedition
in 1819–20. In
1885, Allen
moved to the
American
Museum of
Natural History
in New York City,
where he spent the
rest of his career.
Allen was one of
the leading

in the state. The first important such record comes from the journals of Meriwether Lewis and William Clark. Their expedition was sent to explore the newly acquired Louisiana Purchase of 1803. Starting out in St. Louis, they arrived in southwestern Iowa on 18 July 1804 and spent thirty-four days as they moved north along the Missouri River, finally leaving Iowa's border on 21 August 1804. They passed through Iowa again on their return trip in early September 1806. Lewis and Clark left behind fairly detailed descriptions of what they saw, although at times it is difficult to tell whether their observations occurred in Iowa or Nebraska. They saw many deer, which provided them with fresh meat. The only bison they mention seeing along the Iowa border were found eighty miles from the river (probably in Nebraska), and they rarely saw elk. They saw many beaver and mention wolves a number of times. Canada geese and their young were common along the river.[8]

About the same time, another well-known explorer, Zebulon Pike, passed through Iowa. In late August and early September 1805, he explored the upper Mississippi River valley from Keokuk to the northeastern corner of Iowa. His journals provide some description of the landscape, but he says little about wildlife other than that he hunted passenger pigeons several times.[9]

After Lewis and Clark, the next detailed description of the wildlife of presettlement Iowa comes from Edwin James's description of the Stephen Long expedition to the Rocky Mountains in 1819–20. This group traveled up the Missouri River and entered Iowa in September 1819. They established a winter camp, Engineer Cantonment, north of present-day Council Bluffs near the mouth of the Boyer River. Their winter camp actually was in Nebraska, but much of the information James recorded must also pertain to Iowa. The zoologist in the group, Thomas Say, wrote detailed notes on some wildlife, including descriptions of the coyote and a new subspecies of the wolf and an account of the frustrations they had in trying to trap coyotes. Say wrote extensive descriptions of how the various Indian tribes hunted and trapped. He also compiled lists of the birds and mammals he saw at Engineer Cantonment, the first such faunal lists for Iowa.[10]

The leader of the expedition, Stephen Long, went back east for the winter and then returned in spring 1820. On this return trip, Long traveled overland from central Missouri through extreme southwestern Iowa to the Missouri River near the mouth of the Platte River. He said that elk were common, and he also saw quite a few wild turkeys. However, bison already seemed to be gone from that part of Iowa.[11]

One of the most interesting naturalists to visit Iowa was the German Prince Maximilian of Wied. Maximilian visited North America with a goal of seeing and exploring the Rocky Mountains. In spring 1833, he traveled up the Missouri River by steamboat and spent a few days along the western border of Iowa. His journal provides a glimpse of western Iowa at that time.[12]

Despite the frequent travel along the two major rivers, for many years there was almost no description of the interior of Iowa. Three army expeditions helped fill that void. In 1820, Stephen Kearny led a United States Army party up the Boyer River, starting near the present-day town of Missouri Valley. They proceeded north to near Ruthven, then east past Britt and Northwood, and eventually entered Minnesota. They often saw elk and also saw a herd of 5,000 bison, the largest group of bison that is mentioned by any explorer in Iowa.[13]

In 1835, Kearny made a second trip through interior Iowa, this time starting at Fort Des Moines in extreme southeastern Iowa. He traveled northwest between the Skunk and Des Moines rivers and ultimately entered Minnesota north of Osage. On his return, he reentered Iowa north of Algona and followed the Des Moines River back to Fort Des Moines. He again found elk plentiful but seldom mentioned seeing bison.[14]

A third trip was made by Captain James Allen in 1844. He started from Fort Des Moines and traveled north, passing east of the Iowa Great Lakes region and entering Minnesota near Estherville. He continued on through southwestern Minnesota and southeastern South Dakota before reentering Iowa along the Big Sioux River in the northwestern corner of the state. He then traveled southeast, generally following the Raccoon River back to Fort Des Moines. Like Kearny in 1834, he saw many elk but few bison in Iowa.[15]

In 1843, John James Audubon, the famous artist and naturalist, visited Iowa briefly on his way to and from the upper Missouri River region. Audubon was aging and no longer had the enthusiasm and energy that had characterized his earlier work, so he seldom ventured far from his boat. He did mention seeing many geese, deer, and turkeys, as well as a number of species of smaller birds along the river.[16]

scientists of his day. He was a founder of the American Ornithologists' Union, the society's first president, and editor of its journal for many years. He published extensively on both birds and mammals, including a monograph on the bison.

Source: Chapman, F. M. 1922. In memoriam: Joel Asaph Allen. Auk 39:1–14.

From Audubon's trip in 1843 until about 1870, there was little formal study of wildlife in Iowa. Most scientists from major museums and universities on the East Coast were more interested in exploring new areas and finding new species, and Iowa had little to offer them. Iowa's wildlife was similar to that of most states to the east, while the Great Plains and Rocky Mountain regions had new and undescribed species waiting for scientists to discover. Thus, Iowa was largely neglected by scientists for several decades. About 1870, the reports of visiting and local naturalists, university scientists, and others began to appear. These records were more complete in their coverage of the wildlife, but already some species had been extirpated from Iowa. Joel Asaph Allen of Boston visited parts of central and western Iowa in July–September 1867 and later published notes on the birds and mammals he saw, as well as a list of the birds of Iowa.[17]

The founding of the Iowa Academy of Sciences in 1887 and the establishment of its journal in 1890 provided an impetus to publish articles on the fauna of Iowa. Since then, most of the scientific work on Iowa's fauna has been published by Iowans. By 1910, two fairly complete lists of Iowa's mammals and a comprehensive survey of Iowa's birds had been published. Thus, by 1910 both the exploration and settlement of Iowa as well as the basic foundations of our knowledge of Iowa's wildlife had been completed. As the pages that follow will show, the years up to that time had a dramatic effect on much of Iowa's wildlife.[18]

2. Bison

Bison (or buffalo, as they are more commonly called), the largest hooved mammal in North America, is a species that many people closely associate with the exploration and settlement of the Great Plains by Europeans. In the mid-1700s, bison were found across most of the United States except along the Atlantic and Pacific coasts. They also were found in northern Mexico and in the Prairie Provinces of Canada. Bison were also very abundant; one authority estimated that when Europeans reached North America, there were 50–75 million bison on the continent.[1]

Bison had long been important to the Native Americans living in what is now Iowa and elsewhere on the Great Plains. Valued for their meat, hides, and a variety of other body parts, bison were also an important part of the religious ceremonies of many tribes. As European explorers and traders moved west from the Atlantic seaboard, they soon encountered bison and recognized the value of their meat and of their hides, which were used for robes or tanned for use in leather products; much later, bison bones were used for fertilizer. Besides their direct economic value, many bison were killed for "sport" and to reduce competition with domestic livestock on range land.[2]

Because of the value of bison to humans, they were heavily exploited. The slaughter of the bison in North America in many ways is similar to the story of the passenger pigeon, although in the case of the bison, the species managed to survive. The herds east of the Mississippi River were not nearly as large as those in the West, and most of the eastern animals were gone by 1820. The last bison reported east of the Mississippi River seem to have been two killed in southwestern Wisconsin in 1832.[3]

It first seemed that the large western herds could never be killed off. However, as railroads were built across the Great Plains, bison herds no longer were isolated from settlers and hunters from the East. With railroads providing access to the bison herds and a way to ship the hides east, many men made a living by hunting bison. In the 1860s, the Union Pacific Railroad across Kansas and Colorado divided the Great Plains bison into southern and northern herds. The southern herd was the first to disappear. From 1871 to 1874, huge numbers of bison were killed on the southern plains. Often the hunters cut off only a few choice parts of the body to eat, stripped off the hide, and then left the rest of the carcass to rot. By 1880, the southern herd was essentially gone. The completion of the Northern Pacific Railroad across North Dakota and Montana provided access to the northern herd, and, from 1876 to 1883, it, too, was slaughtered. By 1883, only a few scattered individuals from that once huge herd survived. By about 1895, fewer than 1,000 bison were thought to survive, and the only wild herd remaining was in Canada. In the United States, bison were confined to zoos, private holdings, and a few parks, most notably Yellowstone National Park. The survival of the species was in doubt.[4]

Bison in Presettlement Iowa

Bison once were found throughout Iowa, although the greatest numbers were in the northwestern and north-central parts of the state. The first mention of bison from Iowa is from the journals of Marquette and Joliet. They describe the species as large wild cattle and indicate that they saw herds of as many as 400 animals near the Mississippi River in 1673.[5]

Before Europeans settled Iowa, various Indian tribes occupied Iowa and commonly hunted bison. Although few accounts of these hunts are available, one of the most detailed involves Keokuk, a Sauk chief. In 1833, he and a number of Sauk and Fox Indians traveled to the headwaters of the Iowa River (probably to Franklin or Wright county), where their hunting trip was delayed by a fracas with a party of Sioux. Eventually, they found a herd of 300 bison, of which they killed 80.[6]

Most early explorers of Iowa followed either the Missouri or the Mississippi river valleys. Thus, before settlement, we have few descriptions of the prairie landscape of interior Iowa where bison were most abundant. These glimpses, notably Stephen Long's return trip to Iowa in 1820, the passage of Stephen Kearny across northwestern Iowa in 1820, Kearny's and Albert Lea's trip through central Iowa in 1835, and the travels of Captain James Allen's dragoons through northwestern Iowa in 1844, generally suggest that bison were less common than elk and in fact were almost uncommon on the prairies of Iowa.

In spring 1820, Stephen Long returned to Engineer Cantonment, the camp he had established near Council Bluffs in 1819. In north-central Missouri he left the Missouri River and traveled up the Grand River to its source in south-central Iowa and then headed west to the Missouri River. He saw the trail of only one bull bison and thought that bison no longer were found in what is now southwestern Iowa. During his absence, a hunting party from Engineer Cantonment killed twelve bison from a herd of several hundred they found near the (Little?) Sioux River in February 1820, indicating that bison were still present in northwestern Iowa. Three years later, Paul Wilhelm also said there were no bison in southwestern Iowa, although they had been there a few years earlier.[7]

Also in 1820, Stephen Kearny spent sixteen days traveling from Council Bluffs to the Minnesota border near Northwood. He reported seeing bison on four of those days: a bull shot near Peterson in Clay County, a herd of 5,000 in Clay or Palo Alto county near Ruthven, a herd of one hundred and later another herd east of Emmetsburg, and a cow and calf near Britt in Hancock County.[8]

In 1835, Kearny returned to Iowa and spent twenty-four days there with his troops. He traveled north from Keokuk, staying between the Skunk and Des Moines rivers and eventually entered Minnesota near Osage. He reported seeing bison on only two days: five or six killed on the upper reaches of the Cedar River and several more killed near Osage in Mitchell County.[9]

In 1844, a company of United States Army Dragoons, commanded by Captain James Allen, traveled from Fort Dodge through northern Iowa into Minnesota and South Dakota and returned through northwestern Iowa. Allen saw bison on only one of the thirty-seven days he spent in Iowa, a bull shot in Lyon County. He said that bison were common in southern Minnesota and southeastern South Dakota, and he thought that the land from the source of the Des Moines River west to the Big Sioux River was the prime range of the bison.[10]

One other report from this era, with no details, says that a convoy passing north of Clinton County in 1839 was stopped for two days by a herd of bison. Only this record and the 5,000 reported by Kearny suggest that large herds of bison lived in Iowa. It seems more likely that Iowa had modest numbers of bison scattered across the prairies and that they soon moved away or were killed off as the state was settled. H. Arnold Bennett arrived at the same conclusion about the number of bison found in Iowa but suggested that hunting by Indians and natural causes, including predation by wolves, prairie fires, deep snow cover, inferior food, and falling through ice on rivers were major factors in the decline of bison in Iowa. Although such factors may have contributed to the decline of bison, I think hunting by settlers clearly was the major cause of their demise in Iowa. The bison herds were small to begin with, and, with thousands of settlers pouring into Iowa between 1833 and 1860, the bison simply could not reproduce fast enough to replace those that were killed by hunters.[11]

Disappearance of Bison from Iowa

In the 1840s and 1850s, the stream of settlers arriving in Iowa eventually spilled out of the woodlands and wooded river valleys of eastern and southern Iowa onto the prairies of north-central and northwestern Iowa, where the very early arrivals usually were familiar with bison. Although there are relatively few specific accounts of bison hunts from this era, most describe some sort of a chase resulting in the animal being killed. Bison had a reputation of having good meat and lots of it, and anytime one could be killed, it was an economic bonus for those settlers lucky enough to be there for the partaking. For example, a lone bison that was chased and killed in Denison in 1857 was estimated to weigh 1,800 pounds. The small size of the bison herds meant that the market hunting that was common further west on the Great Plains never developed in Iowa; in fact, bison were largely gone from Iowa by the time market hunting really flourished to the west.[12]

Many records of bison in Iowa come from north-central Iowa near the headwaters of the Iowa, Cedar, and Des Moines rivers. This area apparently was traditionally used by bison for calving, and thus hunters often went there to shoot or capture bison. Most of the reports are of fairly small numbers of bison, but a few involve fair-sized herds. In 1849, M. P. Donahey saw hundreds of bison at the head of the Iowa River, at Twin Lakes in Hancock County, and in Hardin County. Hunters camped near Clear Lake took large but unspecified numbers of bison in 1851, and one hundred bison were reported in Franklin County in 1852. Further east, twenty-eight were seen near Hudson in Black Hawk County in December 1852; two were shot immediately, and at least three more were killed in the ensuing days. A herd of 300 was reported near Tama in winter 1852–53, but all reports after that mention much smaller numbers. In August 1854, a surveyor's party saw forty-seven bison in Kossuth County just after a terrifying encounter with Indians. Forty to fifty bison were reported in Kossuth County the next year, the last reported for that county. One hunter killed nine in Wright County in 1854, seven were seen in Hancock County in 1855, five were killed in Calhoun County in 1862, and two herds of about fifteen to seventeen were reported in the Dallas-Guthrie county area about 1864, but otherwise nearly all other records after 1855 involve only one or two bison, most of which were promptly killed. The report of five in Washington County in southeastern Iowa in February 1865 seems highly questionable because bison had largely disappeared in southern Iowa at least twenty-five years earlier. A bison killed in Fremont County in 1858 was said to be the last bison in southwestern Iowa, but another was killed in Harrison County in 1863. Even that one was considered an oddity, and it was noted that the bison's usual range was well to the west in Nebraska.[13]

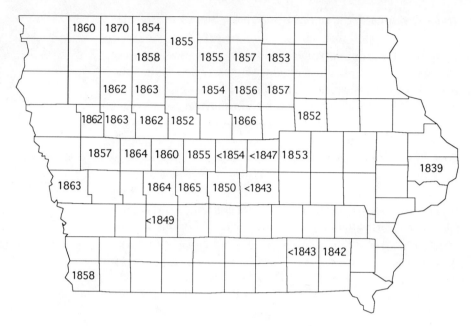

1860	1870	1854	1855						
		1858		1855	1857	1853			
	1862	1863		1854	1856	1857			
1862	1863	1862	1852		1866		1852		
1857	1864	1860	1855	<1854	<1847	1853			1839
1863		1864	1865	1850	<1843				
		<1849							
							<1843	1842	
1858									

Map 3. Bison distribution in Iowa. Date indicates year of last record of bison in each county.

Virtually all the reports of bison in Iowa after 1860 involve an immediate chase by whoever found the animal and end with the killing of the bison. Some examples include two bison chased from near Sac City to near Jefferson, where they were killed in 1860; two chased from Newell to Ida Grove, where they were killed in 1862; two found in Okoboji Township, Dickinson County, in August 1863 and chased to the Little Sioux River, where one was killed; and single bison that were seen in Sac and Pocahontas counties in 1863. Single bison were reportedly seen near Panora on the 4th of July in both 1863 and 1864. Two bison seen at the fork of the Little Sioux River in Dickinson County, west of West Okoboji Lake, in 1870 appear to have been the last sighted in Iowa.[14]

In most parts of Iowa, bison disappeared within a few years after the first settlers arrived (map 3). The average interval between the date of the first permanent settlement in a county and the last record of a bison there is only six years. Of the original large mammals found in Iowa, bison either were the easiest to hunt or were one of the most intolerant of humans. Most settlers, unless they were in the very first wave of pioneers in the area, never saw a wild bison in Iowa.

Long before Europeans reached North America, the Indians of the Great Plains hunted bison. One of the most detailed descriptions of how Native Americans hunted bison comes from the notes made by Thomas Say, who accompanied Stephen Long's expedition up the Missouri River. He spent the winter of 1819–20 at Engineer Cantonment near Council Bluffs and made extensive notes on the Omaha tribe. Although most of what he recorded probably refers to Nebraska tribes, Iowa tribes are likely to have hunted in a similar manner. Say describes how they hunted bison from horseback, using only a bow and arrow to kill the animal. After the hunt, virtually all parts of the bison were used for food, leather, or various other purposes.[15]

Bison hunting by European settlers in Iowa was not the organized commercial business it was further west. Virtually all bison that were taken were used for their meat, and there is no evidence that any appreciable hide industry ever developed in Iowa. The closest Iowans came to having a role in the bison-hide industry was as bystanders watching shipments of hides going east. Newspaper accounts tell of huge loads of bison hides from the Yellowstone River area of Montana passing by Sioux City on Missouri River steamboats in 1880. To be sure, some settlers probably embarked on hunting trips to take bison, but most of these were once-a-year trips that did not provide a way for settlers to support themselves. The original settlers of Cerro Gordo County were hunters seeking bison and other big game near Clear Lake in 1851. The area was apparently a favorite hunting place. Hunters from Black Hawk County went there in 1847 or 1848 and returned with several bison calves. For most of the kills, the hunting pattern included a chase on horseback, repeated shots at the animal, and, finally, the death of the exhausted, wounded bison. These kills hardly matched the bison-hunting feats of Buffalo Bill Cody or other storied western heroes on the Great Plains, for whom seemingly every bison was dropped with a single shot.[16]

A few examples provide an idea of how bison were hunted in Iowa. Probably the most "sportsmanlike" of the hunts that we have a record of is one by William H. Ingham, A. L. Seeley, and Thomas C. Covel near Titonka, Kossuth County, in August 1855. These three hunters had good horses and guns, and were hunting for the "sport" of it. On an earlier hunt, they had turned down the chance to shoot bison when no chase was involved. On this particular hunt, they chased a herd of forty to fifty bison until the bison jumped into a small creek and became mired down in the soft stream bottom. The hunters fired seventeen shots into the mass of bison without downing any, although several were wounded. The herd then left the creek for the solid ground of the surrounding prairie. The three hunters followed them and succeeded in killing one bison, although it took at least nine more shots to do so. In the process, Seeley lost a spur (which was found thirty-two years later) and Covel broke the cinch fastening on his saddle. Three other bison they had wounded were eventually killed by other hunters.[17]

A more typical story involves the last bison reported from Pocahontas County. When a large bull was seen near Pocahontas in August 1863, four men took chase, although they had only one horse that could keep up with the bison. For guns, they had a revolver and several old Springfield muskets for which they had only small cartridges. The lead man finally caught up with the bison and fired several shots from his revolver. In response, the bison charged the man, who retreated until his companions caught up. When they arrived, each shot at the animal. The bison attacked each of them in turn, and one man lost his gun while retreating. Finally, the bison retreated to a nearby slough, and the hunting strategy changed. Under the new plan, the men approached the bison, shot at it, and then withdrew when it attacked them. The bison then retreated to another slough while the men reloaded and then attacked again. This strategy continued through several sloughs until the men finally drove the bison out onto dry land, where they were able to kill the exhausted animal with several well-placed shots. The hunt had taken three hours and had covered nine miles, and at least twenty rifle balls were required to kill the 1,400-pound bison. To top it off, when the men returned with a team of horses to carry off the meat, at first they could not find the bison's body in the tall prairie grass and only relocated it after a lengthy search. From such stories legends are made. The location of this kill is marked now with a small commemorative sign near the town of Plover (fig. 2).[18]

The only bison known to have been killed in Harrison County is one that showed up along the Boyer River near Woodbine in 1863. Several men chased it on horseback and followed it for five

COMMEMORATIVE SITE

IN A SLOUGH ON THE S.W. QUARTER OF THIS SECTION THE LAST BUFFALO SEEN IN THIS TERRITORY WAS KILLED ON AUGUST 20, 1863.
ARMED WITH THREE MUSKETS AND A REVOLVER, W.H.HAIT (WHO KILLED THE BUFFALO), ORLANDO SLOSSON, ROBINSON GORDON AND ABIEL STICKNEY STARTED THE CHASE AT OLD ROLFE, 5 MILES S.E. OF HERE.
THE 1400 POUND ANIMAL FURNISHED THE SETTLERS OF OLD ROLFE WITH MEAT AS LONG AS THEY WERE ABLE TO KEEP IT IN THE HOT WEATHER.

Fig. 2. This sign, commemorating the last bison killed in Pocahontas County, is located along a country road near Plover, Iowa.

or six miles. Finally, it approached the house of George W. Pugsley, who had been watching the chase. The bison approached him and stopped to rest, and Pugsley shot it dead on the spot. At least he was a better shot than some of the earlier hunters.[19]

A somewhat different kind of hunt occurred in north-central Iowa in 1850, when a surveyor named Grey was charged by a bison while working near Rockford. When the bison got close, Grey struck it on the forehead with an axe, killing the animal. Later, he found that the bison had been burned in a fire and was blind.[20]

On the Great Plains, a common method of hunting bison was to approach a herd stealthily until it was within rifle range and then quietly pick off the animals one by one. If done properly, the animals were slow to flee, and many could be killed from one stand. The only Iowa story that tells of shooting bison from such a stand is that of Hiram Ludington. In December 1852, he encountered a herd of twenty-eight bison along the Black Hawk River near Hudson in Black Hawk County. He crawled up close to the bison and succeeded in downing two bison, although it took twenty-eight shots to do so. He later found that he had been shooting too high and had missed the vital organs. Eventually, the herd moved toward him, and he had to climb a tree to escape them. He returned the next two days and killed two more bison. Those were the last bison reported from that county.[21]

Bison in Captivity

There are a number of stories of settlers' capturing bison and trying to domesticate them. In general these attempts were not a big success. The first settlers in Cerro Gordo County were attracted to the area by the bison they found there. They followed the bison herds, waiting for the young calves to fall behind the herd, and then lassoed them. Cows were also caught, although how is not described. Little is recorded of what eventually became of these animals, but at least some were sold and shipped east. In 1837, W. A. Delashmutt saw twelve captive bison calves in Burlington. They had been caught along Lizard Creek northwest of Fort Dodge and were being readied for shipment by boat to Covington, Kentucky.[22]

Some of the early settlers in Buchanan County traveled west to hunt bison and elk, sometimes going as far as present-day Ackley. In spring 1844, Rufus Clark and several others set out with several horses, ox teams, and cows on such a hunt. The cows were taken to provide milk for any young bison and elk that were caught. The men brought back eleven bison, but only one survived; the others died from the heat. The next year Clark's group started earlier in spring, were gone seven weeks, and brought back four bison. Clark kept one bison for three years. By then, it had become too boisterous, and he killed and ate it. In 1848, Clark sold his herd of seven bison and seven elk to Asa Blood for $500. Blood took this herd to Milwaukee and Chicago, where they were put on display, and at least some were killed and eaten. In Milwaukee, the bison were fed malt from a brewery, and one cow bison became intoxicated. She broke out of her pen and into another that held elk, three of which she killed before she was captured and returned to her own pen.[23]

M. P. Donahey of Keokuk County also had a bison-hunting

adventure. In spring 1849, he and six others set out from Washington, Iowa, on a hunting trip to north-central Iowa. They took with them two wagons, two yoke of oxen, and twelve milk cows. They saw their first bison in Hardin County but found bison most common at the head of the Iowa River in Hancock County. The group went on to Clear Lake and eventually into Minnesota, although they did not find any bison there. They caught bison calves by chasing the herd on horseback and lassoing any calves that fell behind. The trip lasted two months, and they caught fourteen bison calves and three young elk. Six of the bison died before they returned home. Donahey's share of the profits was two bison calves, which he sold for fifty dollars each. Three of the bison they had caught were still alive in Sigourney in 1851.[24]

There are other similar stories. Tjernagel tells of a bison calf caught in the early 1850s and held near Roland in Story County. The calf was eventually crossbred with cows, but the offspring produced little milk and the experiment was terminated. Likewise, hunters from Benton County traveled to near Mason City in 1847 or 1848, their outfit including several milk cows. When they returned, they had captured several bison calves that were nursed by the cows. These bison were raised near Vinton, but what eventually happened to them is not recorded. In the 1840s or 1850s, two buffalo hunters from Jefferson County caught four bison calves and raised them with their cattle. These four and their descendents were kept for about forty years before they were sold to a farmer in Henry County.[25]

Not all such trips were a success. In 1845, three Wapello County men took a lengthy trip to northwestern Iowa in search of bison and other big game. They ranged as far west as Ida County and north to near Storm Lake and Fort Dodge. They caught eight or ten young elk but saw no sign of any bison. Their travels covered much of the same area that Captain James Allen had covered the preceding year. Neither group found bison there, suggesting that bison already were uncommon in that region.[26]

In 1874, E. A. Collins obtained two young bison and an elk and put them in with 200 cattle on his 1,000-acre farm in Shelby County. The dominant bull in his cattle herd attempted to dominate the smaller bison bull but was soon put in its place. It is not recorded how long Collins kept the bison, nor what became of them. Presumably they eventually were killed and eaten.[27]

John F. Lacey, 1841–1913

Born in West Virginia, John Lacey moved to Oskaloosa in 1855. He served in the Civil War and after the war served in the Iowa legislature. Lacey was elected to the United States House of Representatives in 1888 and, except from 1891 to 1893, served there until 1907. Lacey's work in Congress established him as a pioneer in conservation legislation. Besides his 1894 bill protecting wildlife in Yellowstone National Park, another more enduring bill made interstate transportation of wild game that was taken illegally a federal offense. This precedent-setting bill, commonly called the Lacey Act, was passed in

The Lasting Impact of Bison

Although bison no longer are part of the fauna of Iowa, they have left behind numerous reminders. At least two towns (Buffalo, Buffalo Center), five townships, and several creeks and streams carry the name "buffalo," reminding us of the bison that once lived in the state.

Because of their large size, bison had a physical impact on their surroundings. Some buffalo wallows, the depressions in the ground in which the bison habitually rolled to escape the heat or pesky insects, remained evident long after bison disappeared from Iowa. By the 1870s, a one-acre wallow in Jones County was still largely bare of vegetation, although grasses were gradually invading it. Another wallow near Kellerton in Ringgold County was worn down to a depth of twenty feet and covered two acres. Wallows were still visible in Black Hawk County until 1918. Another less obvious feature that bison left on the landscape was their trails. These paths, worn by years of use by bison, often were converted into roads by the earliest settlers.[28]

Finally, bison left behind their skeletal remains. Loren Hart, who moved to Dickens in Clay County in 1869, claimed that although bison were gone when he arrived there, he could walk a mile and always be standing on bison bones. Hundreds of bison bones have been discovered, and more are still being found throughout Iowa. Some are found at old Indian campsites, but most are found along streambeds and in old bogs, the result of natural deaths. Some of the animals may have broken through thin ice and drowned, while others fell in creeks with steep banks and were unable to get out of the water. Many probably got mired down in soft ground along a stream or in a bog and could not free themselves. Some of the bones are of relatively recent origin, while others probably date back hundreds or even thousands of years.[29]

Epilogue

With the disappearance of wild bison from Iowa in 1870, one of the most important native mammals of North America was removed from the Iowa scene. The few bison now found in Iowa are confined to zoos or private collections, and there seems to be no possibility that they will ever again roam free in the state. In 1970, only about sixteen small captive herds remained, most of them numbering fewer than ten individuals. In 1993, there were about 1,000 bison on about sixty ranches in the state. Several attempts to raise bison or a bison-cattle cross commercially have met with mixed success. Although the animals still retain some of their wild spirit, they are a far cry from the true wild bison that once roamed over Iowa.[30]

For the continent as a whole, the story of the bison has been more encouraging. From a low of fewer than 1,000 bison in the late 1890s, bison have gradually made a comeback and now number more than 40,000. Most of these are on private ranches. Iowans are probably most familiar with the herds at Wind Cave National Park and Custer State Park in South Dakota, Fort Niobrara National Wildlife Refuge in Nebraska, and Yellowstone National Park. Other herds are located in South Dakota, Kansas, Oklahoma, and Wyoming. Some of these herds live on sizable ranges and give the visitor some feel for what it must have been like to encounter herds in the wild. Still, on most of the Great Plains, the animal that perhaps better than any other exemplified that region of North America is no longer found. The loss was perhaps inevitable, but it still is a loss.[31]

Ironically, three men with ties to Iowa played a significant role first in the destruction and later in the eventual protection of bison. William F. (Buffalo Bill) Cody was born in Le Claire near Davenport in 1846 and went west while still a young boy. He was the most famous of the buffalo hunters who supplied meat to the railroad builders. John Lacey, a congressman from Oskaloosa, Iowa, had a lead role in legislation to protect bison. In 1894, he learned that authorities could not prosecute poachers who had killed bison inside Yellowstone National Park. A bill introduced by Lacey and passed by Congress that same year called for both a fine and a jail sentence for such poaching. The act finally gave the Yellowstone Park bison herd some protection and assured its survival. The third Iowan was William T. Hornaday, who attended Iowa State College in 1873. Hornaday was one of the leading spokesmen of the early conservation movement in North America. The preservation of bison was one of his favorite projects, and he played a leading role in making people aware of the plight of the species. His actions helped to insure the survival of bison in North America.[32]

1900 and is still one of the most powerful pieces of federal wildlife legislation. In 1926, Lacey-Keosauqua State Park in southeastern Iowa was renamed to honor him.

Source: Gallagher, A. 1981. Citizen of the nation: John Fletcher Lacey, conservationist. Annals of Iowa, 3rd series, 46:9–24.

3. Elk

$\mathbf{A}$lthough less familiar to most Iowans than the white-tailed deer, a second member of the deer family, the elk (or wapiti), once was common in Iowa. Many people now associate elk with mountain meadows in the Rocky Mountain states and do not realize that their range was once much more extensive and included several different habitats. Elk were found over most of the United States except for the Atlantic coastal region, the Deep South, and desert regions of the West. They also occurred over much of Manitoba, Saskatchewan, Alberta, and southern Ontario.[1]

When the first European settlers arrived, there may have been as many as ten million elk in North America. Their large size and good-tasting meat made them a favorite target of hunters. Thus, they were heavily exploited and disappeared rapidly from much of their range. By the mid-1800s, they were largely gone from east of the Mississippi River, although a few survived in the mountains of Pennsylvania until 1867 and in northern Wisconsin until 1868. The herds west of the Mississippi disappeared just as rapidly, and by the early 1900s, because of heavy hunting and loss of habitat, there were perhaps only 50,000–100,000 elk remaining in North America.[2]

In Iowa, elk were most common on grasslands in the western two-thirds of the state, although they occurred in eastern Iowa, too. Iowa elk spent the summer in loose groups scattered across the prairies, while in winter they often congregated and formed larger herds. In winter storms, they took shelter in tall stands of rushes in marshes or in groves of trees. Elk disappeared soon after settlement and were largely gone from Iowa by the 1860s. The last record of elk in Iowa was a herd seen in northwestern Iowa in 1871.[3]

Elk in Iowa

Several military expeditions that traveled across Iowa reported on the abundance of elk in presettlement days. The reports give the impression that elk were more abundant than bison at this time. During his sixteen-day journey in 1820 from Council Bluffs to the Minnesota border north of Northwood, Stephen Kearny saw elk on five days, including 200 cows on 10 July near Sioux Rapids. His comments suggest that elk were common on the prairies he passed through. In 1833, Joseph Street, who spent seventeen days surveying the Neutral Ground in northeastern Iowa, found that elk were abundant on the prairies, whereas he saw few bison. In 1835, Kearny explored the country between the Skunk and Des Moines rivers from Keokuk to the Minnesota border north of Osage. An account of that trip makes little mention of big game; elk are mentioned only once and bison twice.[4]

Finally, in 1844, Captain James Allen led a troop of army dragoons from Des Moines north into Minnesota. They reentered Iowa in Lyon County and eventually returned to Des Moines. Allen saw many elk on 16 August, including a herd of one hundred south of Lizard Creek, probably in Webster County. Allen called the country north of there to the source of the Des Moines River the range of the elk. Overall, he saw hundreds of elk and killed many. In contrast, the only bison he saw in Iowa were in northern Lyon County.[5]

Many of the county histories of Iowa also indicate that elk were common, even plentiful, at the time of settlement. Numerous settlers mention seeing elk, whereas only the very earliest pioneers mention bison. The elk's tendency to scatter during the summer could have given the impression of greater abundance than was actually the case. Major Mintor Brassfield, who hunted along the Boone River in Hamilton and Wright counties starting in 1851, claimed that he killed 150 elk in his lifetime and as many as six in one day, an indication that elk once were very common in Iowa. Thus, the overall impression that emerges is that at least on the prairies of north-central and northwestern Iowa, elk were more widespread and abundant than bison at the time of settlement. Likewise, they survived in Iowa for a few years longer than did the bison.[6]

The severe winter of 1856–57 was disastrous for elk and other wildlife. A blizzard on 1 December 1856 left much of Iowa covered with deep snow. A few days later, freezing rain formed a crust on the snow. Many wildlife species, including elk, were hard-pressed to survive and sought food and shelter along the wooded rivers and streams, where they often came in contact with humans. In a number of areas of Iowa, herds of elk were slaughtered that winter. In Butler County, they had been common near Bristow but were not seen again. Many were killed in Cerro Gordo County, and the last elk seen in Adair, Hamilton, and Harrison counties were killed that winter. In Montgomery County, sixteen or seventeen were killed, and no more were seen. A herd of twenty-five to fifty elk was killed in the deep snows in Shelby County, but few were seen in subsequent years. The report of thousands of elk in Cass County in the winter of 1858 may be a mistake and may really refer to 1856–57. In general, after 1856–57 elk were much rarer in Iowa.[7]

Last Elk

As settlers moved westward across the state, the range of elk in Iowa retracted rapidly (map 4). They were apparently gone from extreme eastern and southeastern Iowa by 1850. Elk were still very plentiful along the Wapsipinicon River in Jones County in 1837, but there are no later records from there. The last records in eastern Iowa include one elk shot in Linn County in 1838, the report of only a few still present in Wapello County in 1843, and a large female shot in Independence in 1848.[8]

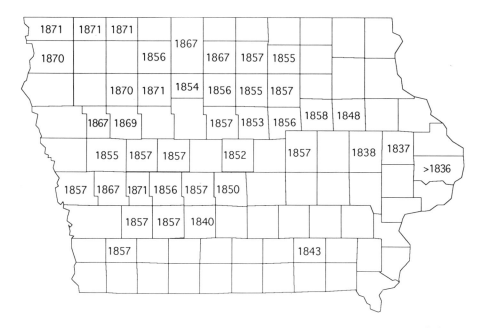

1871	1871	1871		1867							
1870			1856		1867	1857	1855				
		1870	1871	1854	1856	1855	1857				
	1867	1869			1857	1853	1856	1858	1848		
	1855	1857	1857		1852		1857		1838	1837	
1857	1867	1871	1856	1857	1850						>1836
		1857	1857	1840							
	1857						1843				

Map 4. Elk distribution in Iowa. Date indicates year of last record of elk in each county.

The severe winter of 1856–57 brought about the demise of elk from much of north-central, west-central, and southwestern Iowa. Thus, by 1860 elk persisted in numbers only in northwestern Iowa. The few records of elk in Iowa after 1860 include seventy-five seen between Cherokee and Spirit Lake in 1862, one shot in Carroll County in June 1864, one killed near Wesley in Hancock County in 1867, two near Irwin in Shelby County in 1867, a herd that passed near Ida Grove in the fall of 1867, some in Audubon County in the winter of 1867–68, a large one killed in Pocahontas County in fall 1868, a herd of forty in Sac County in October 1869, and one killed in Pocahontas County in January 1870. Passengers on a train near Storm Lake were treated to the sight of eighteen elk passing nearby in October 1870; they shot at them but did not kill any. The last elk in Iowa were the 200 or more that lived in unsettled lands near the headwaters of the Rock and Little Sioux rivers in and around Osceola County. As settlers started to move into the region, the elk moved to the Ocheyedan River valley. In July 1871, the herd was harassed and driven south, and broke up into several smaller herds. Most or all of these elk were killed before they reached the Missouri River. The fragments of the herd were responsible for a number of elk records in 1871, including thirty in southwestern

William H. Ingham, 1827–1914

Born in New York, William Ingham moved to Cedar Rapids in 1851. In 1854, Ingham traveled over much of Iowa searching for a place to settle. When he reached what is now Kossuth County, he immediately was attracted to the wooded ravines along Black Cat Creek north of Algona. The land had already been claimed, but the next year Ingham took over another person's claim and settled there. He farmed for several years and in 1865 moved to Algona, where he was in the banking business. Ingham thrived on outdoor adventure and emphasized the sporting aspects of his hunts. In the 1850s, he

Dickinson County, eighteen in Pocahontas County, and unspecified numbers in Lyon and Osceola counties. The claims that a few were present in Buena Vista County in 1873 and that a herd was seen near Jefferson in the winter of 1875–76 seem questionable. The last elk in the state can safely be considered those that were driven from northwestern Iowa in 1871.[9]

Hunting Elk

Like many other large mammals, elk were mainly sought out for their meat. It was considered delicious, and the steaks were often used for banquets. Some said that elk meat tasted better than mutton or beef. Elk are much larger than deer and provide much more meat. The weights of a few Iowa elk were recorded, including a 600-pound female shot in Independence in October 1848, an 800-pound male killed in Hancock County in 1867 (its antlers are still in the Kossuth County courthouse in Algona), a 400-pound one shot in Pocahontas County in 1868, and three killed in Lyon County in 1871 that weighed 349, 360, and 398 pounds. One killed in Grundy County in 1856 weighed 600 pounds after being dressed. Elk hides were also valuable. They were tanned and used to make cattle whips and whip crackers.[10]

There are few descriptions of elk hunting in Iowa. Because elk generally inhabited the open prairies, they were usually hunted from horseback and were chased until the hunters were close enough to shoot the elk. Sometimes dogs were used, but usually not. The best description of an elk hunt in Iowa is an account of one undertaken by William Campbell, Thomas Covel, and William Ingham of Kossuth County (the last two also had an exciting bison hunt in 1855). In November 1856, an elk with very large antlers had been seen in the county, but no one had been able to kill it. In February 1857 (this was the famous winter of 1856–57), the three set out from northeast of Algona on snowshoes, each pulling a sled loaded with supplies. During the first afternoon they were overcome on the open prairie by a blizzard. Before they lost all sense of direction in the blowing snow, they took a compass reading on the nearest grove of trees, some seven or eight miles away. Fortunately, they reached the grove and found a deserted cabin where they took shelter.

The next day, Covel dropped out of the hunt, but the other two kept on, hunting east of Burt. They soon found a large bull elk and released their dog, which brought the elk to bay. Campbell's first shot wounded the elk, which then charged him. At the last second, Campbell ducked behind a tree, and the elk's antlers crashed into the tree. The elk then saw Ingham and charged him. He, too, ducked behind a small tree. The elk's head struck the tree, and Ingham found he had antlers within his reach on each side of him. By then Campbell had recovered from his close call and shot the elk a second time, and then decided it was Ingham's turn to shoot. The bull was badly wounded by now, and Ingham finally killed it with a revolver shot. As it was late in the day, they cleaned the elk and hung the quarters of meat from a nearby tree. Throughout the night they saw and heard wolves (probably coyotes), foxes, and lynx (bobcats?) in the area and shot at them to try to drive them away. However, the scavengers were able to reach the meat, and in the morning all of it was gone. The two men continued their hunt and killed another elk near Armstrong, were caught in a second snowstorm, and saw many elk tracks in the area before they returned home. They never did find the large elk that was their original quarry. The uncertainties of the weather were not the only dangers they had to face. Only three weeks later, more than thirty settlers were killed by a band of Sioux at Spirit Lake, twenty-five miles to the west. This was truly an adventurous frontier elk hunt.[11]

A less organized and perhaps more typical elk hunt occurred in Franklin County in September 1855. Two men who were loading hay saw an elk and pursued it on horseback, each armed with a pitchfork. They both wounded the animal with their primitive weapons but did not kill it. A third man, who was hunting prairie-chickens and had a shotgun, joined the hunt. However, he was so excited that his first shot missed the elk, even though he was only ten feet from the animal. His second shot wounded the elk, and the third, at six inches, finally killed it. With such skill, one wonders whether he ever hit any prairie-chickens.[12]

Peter Lloyd, an Ida County hunter, used a more traditional method to hunt elk. He stalked the animals and approached the elk herd upwind, crawling if necessary, to get close enough to shoot the animal of his choice.[13]

During the winter of 1856–57, when elk movements were limited by the deep snow, less sporting means were used to kill elk. Elk were killed with clubs and knives as well as guns. Near

participated in several elk and bison hunts on the prairies near Algona. His descriptions of these hunts provide a detailed record of early "gentlemanly" hunting on the prairies. Ingham was looked upon as one of the fathers of Kossuth County, and Ingham Lake in nearby Emmet County was named for him.

Source: Reed, B. F. 1913. History of Kossuth County, Iowa. S. J. Clarke Publishing Co., Chicago, volume 2, pp. 5–11.

Hudson, one was even killed with a sled stake. Presumably, the same methods were used other times when elk were hindered by deep snow.[14]

In 1857, the Iowa legislature established a closed season for elk extending from 1 February to 15 July. A fine of fifteen dollars was set for each elk taken or possessed illegally. The next year, the closed season was extended so that it ran from 1 January to 15 August, and in 1862, to 1 September. The season was altered slightly several times, but there is no evidence that the laws were ever enforced in Iowa. Since elk were extirpated in Iowa by the early 1870s, the laws could not have done much good. Interestingly, in 1898 elk were given complete protection in Iowa, some twenty-seven years too late. At least animals that have wandered into Iowa in recent years have had some protection.[15]

Large Herds of Elk in Iowa

Most reports of Iowa elk were of small groups, and big herds were unusual. Most of these reports come from northwestern and north-central Iowa, the heart of the species' range in Iowa. The biggest herd of elk mentioned for Iowa is the thousands seen at Lost Island Lake in Palo Alto County in fall 1856. Several writers indicate that thousands of elk were seen along the Raccoon River valley in Dallas and Greene counties in the winter of 1856–57. Although these animals may have been somewhat scattered, certainly many elk were present in the area. One of the few records of a large herd in eastern Iowa is the report of herds of up to 100 between the Wapsipinicon and Maquoketa rivers. Other reports of large herds include up to 500 near Fonda in Sac County in the early days, 100 in Humboldt County in 1854, 200 in Kossuth County in August 1854, 200 in Palo Alto County in fall 1855, more than 195 in Franklin County in fall 1855, about 500 in northwestern Franklin County in fall 1855, more than 100 near Exira in 1856–57, and more than 100 in Sioux County in 1869.[16]

Elk in Captivity

One of the most fascinating aspects of the history of elk in Iowa is the number of times settlers attempted to domesticate them. This was done by catching young elk and then raising them in captivity. The area from Greene County north to around the headwaters of the Raccoon River was a favorite elk hunting ground. Some of the hunts were well organized and not just casual forays. John Wright, a well-known hunter from Dallas County, spent as much as a month on a single elk-hunting trip. His hunting outfit included supply wagons, horses, and cows to provide milk for the young elk on the return trip. Rufus Clark of Quasqueton in Buchanan County made several hunting trips to the Ackley region and was gone for as long as seven weeks. In 1844, he returned with eleven bison and seven elk, but only one bison and two elk survived, the others dying from the stress of the chase and the heat. The next year he brought back seven elk and four bison. Three men from Wapello County hunted elk and bison in Ida County and near the headwaters of the Raccoon River in spring 1845. They saw many deer and elk but no bison; they brought back eight to ten young elk.[17]

Several methods were used by these elk hunters. In early summer, they looked for adult elk with young calves. Once the hunters had located adult elk, they then searched nearby areas for young hiding in thick cover. Dogs were often used in these searches. After a calf had been found, it was usually chased from horseback until it tired and could be caught by hand. The Buchanan County hunter, Rufus Clark, used a lasso to catch the elk calf. Another method used to catch young elk was to sneak up on a calf and throw a blanket over it. When the adult elk left, the calf would follow the humans.[18]

Once caught, a few were kept as pets, but most were held and broken to a harness. Their temperamental disposition and the long antlers of the bulls probably kept most settlers from considering them good pets. The danger was real: a young boy in Des Moines was badly gored but not killed by an elk.[19]

Elk were easy to domesticate but were not a success as a beast of burden. In 1855, the first Floyd County settler, Joseph Kelly, caught and trained four young elk to pull his wagon. However, they frightened any horse that came near them, so Kelly ended up selling his elk. Kelly bought another tame bull elk for sixty dollars. Its antlers were so large that they towered over any horse. This frightened his horses, so he could not use the elk with the rest of his team. In spring 1856, some dogs chased it, and it ran into a house, terrifying the occupants. Kelly finally let the animal go and never tried to recapture it. Other attempts to capitalize on elk as a domestic animal generally were failures. In Adel in 1851, Elisha Morris broke some young elk to the harness. He finally decided that they were too hard to handle, so he hitched the pair of two-year-old bucks to a buggy and drove to Oskaloosa. He could not sell them there, but he was able to swap them for a horse, which he then sold for eighty dollars. Thus, he did get a little return for the time he spent breaking the elk.[20]

Others, however, were more successful in their efforts to domesticate elk. In 1848, Asa Blood of Buchanan County purchased seven elk and seven bison for $500. These animals had been caught by Rufus Clark near Ackley two or three years earlier. Blood tamed them so they would pull a sleigh, and he took them to Milwaukee to put them on exhibit. As noted earlier, he made the mistake of feeding the animals malt from a brewery. One female bison ate too much of this, broke out of its pen, and got into the elk pen, where it killed three elk before it was caught. Still, Blood made money from the exhibit and sold the rest of his animals for $1,100. In 1851, Jeremiah Bradshaw of Cass County had a menagerie of wild animals that included seven elk, two of which he had trained to work like horses. He had a harness made to fit them and used them to pull a sleigh. He eventually sold the pair for $100. In June 1855, the noted hunter William Ingham and three other men found many elk near present-day Emmetsburg. They succeeded in catching four calves, which they sent back east in a pen they built on their wagon. In 1860, a captive bull elk was shipped from Bradford, Chickasaw County, to Williams College in Massachusetts, but its price and fate are not recorded. David Haggard of Kossuth County sold elk at an auction for ten to twelve dollars apiece, probably in the 1860s or 1870s.[21]

A somewhat different approach was used by a few settlers in an attempt to get some economic gain from elk. One year an Audubon County man killed nine elk around Christmas and captured another adult alive. He held the latter animal until the next summer, fattened it up, and then killed and ate it. In the 1870s, E. A. Collins of Shelby County kept an elk and two bison with his herd of 200 cattle. He apparently just had them graze with his cattle and made no attempt to domesticate them further. Presumably, he eventually killed and ate them.[22]

Epilogue

There is little hope that wild elk will ever be reestablished in Iowa. The blocks of suitable habitat are not large enough to support a truly wild herd, and any animals wandering out of those areas would probably not be tolerated by adjacent landowners. Thus, we have to be content with the numerous place names, such as Elk River, Elk Horn, and Elkhart, to remind us of this magnificent animal's past role in the state. Occasionally, an elk is seen wandering freely in Iowa. Most of these have probably escaped from one of the captive herds held at some parks or by individuals in Iowa. That was probably the source of an elk seen in Wright, Franklin, and Butler counties in north-central Iowa from November 1981 to September 1982, one in Lee County in November 1984, and one near Nora Springs in October 1988. However, one seen in Sioux and Lyon counties in late November 1978, another near Rock Rapids in September 1983, and individuals killed near Denison and Riverton in December 1986 and near Ida Grove in the fall of 1989 may have wandered east from the Black Hills of South Dakota, where wild elk are still found.[23]

Nationally, the outlook is more optimistic. From the low of fewer than 100,000 elk in the early 1900s, elk numbers increased to about 500,000 in the late 1970s. Elk populations are concentrated in the Rocky Mountains from British Columbia and Alberta south to northern Arizona and New Mexico. Two coastal forms survive from California north to British Columbia, and other populations are scattered across southern Canada and various states. Many of the elk herds live on federal land, such as national forests, wildlife refuges, or national parks. Elk are hunted in several states, and about 100,000 were taken yearly in the late 1970s. In some areas, such as Yellowstone National Park and the nearby National Elk Refuge, adequate winter range is a problem. This has led to a controversy over whether the animals should be artificially fed or allowed to starve if the range will not support them. Still, with proper management of the elk and their habitat, their future should be secure.[24]

4. White-tailed Deer

White-tailed deer were the most abundant large game mammal settlers encountered in eastern North America. White-tails were once found over all of the eastern United States and southern Canada west to the Rocky Mountains. Deer were eagerly hunted for their meat, which supplemented the settlers' usual diet. Tens of thousands were killed for food or for their hides, which were used as a trade item. As a result, the number of deer declined rapidly as settlers moved west. The deer population was estimated to number at least 40 million east of the Great Plains when Europeans arrived in North America, but by 1908 perhaps only 500,000 deer remained.[1]

White-tailed deer were common over most of Iowa when early explorers and traders reached the state. They were still commonly encountered when settlers arrived. Deer probably were most abundant in the wooded regions of eastern and southern Iowa, but they also were found on the prairies, especially along river valleys. Like the bison and elk, deer provided a welcome supply of meat for trappers and settlers and were avidly hunted. Most early writers mention the severe winter of 1856–57 as a disaster for deer in Iowa, just as it was for elk. During that winter, perhaps thousands of deer were killed by humans or wild predators or died from the extreme weather. Afterward, they were absent or rare in many parts of Iowa. By the mid-1860s, deer were almost gone from eastern and central Iowa. However, in a few sections of Iowa, such as Kossuth and Sac counties, the number of deer increased after settlement and probably peaked in the late 1860s or early 1870s. In parts of Kossuth County in the 1870s, deer often fed on farmers' crops and were considered a pest. The remaining deer rapidly disappeared, however, and by the 1880s deer were largely gone from the state; by the end of the century they were considered extinct in Iowa.[2]

Deer in Iowa

There are numerous records to show that deer were abundant in Iowa when settlers arrived. Many early Iowans described the groups of deer that they saw. A sample includes more than one hundred seen by a man hunting in Scott County, forty together in Delaware County, fifty-two near Ames in the 1850s, forty-five in sight at one time near Atlantic in Cass County in the 1850s, and the claim that you could see forty to fifty within one mile of the town of Washington. Several settlers said that one could often see 200–300 deer at one time in the early days in Harrison County. Even on the prairies of extreme northwestern Iowa, 200 deer could be seen in the early 1870s. These reports, together with records of the number of deer that were killed, clearly indicate that deer were abundant in the state.[3]

Weather seems to have been an important factor determining the year-to-year fluctuations in the number of deer in Iowa. Deep snow in the winter of 1848–49 led to the loss of many deer in south-central Iowa. Like the elk, deer from many parts of Iowa died during the severe winter of 1856–57. Many more deer were killed by settlers during another severe winter in 1880–81. For much of the state, it has been only recently that deer numbers have approached those present before that winter.[4]

After 1857, deer numbers generally declined throughout Iowa, but few specific dates are given for their disappearance from various parts of the state. In southeastern Iowa, they were common in Monroe County until 1870 but rare in Washington County by 1885. In southwestern Iowa, some of the last reported were eleven killed in Shelby County during the winter of 1876–77; tracks of three were seen near Exira in Audubon County in 1880. One killed near McPaul in Fremont County in 1881 seems to be the last report from that part of Iowa. In northeastern Iowa, one was killed in Buchanan County in 1871; they were still present near Postville in Allamakee County in the late 1890s. Although northwestern Iowa had the poorest natural deer habitat, it was one of the last strongholds for the species in the state because it was the last area of Iowa to be settled. The last deer in Buena Vista County was killed in 1876, and deer were last seen in numbers in Dickinson County in 1881–82. One was shot in Pocahontas County in 1882, and another was found in northern Sac County about 1890, the last record for that section of the state. Thus, except for perhaps a few individuals that survived in some isolated areas, most likely in the wooded regions of northeastern Iowa, deer were extirpated from the state by 1900. Put another way, in about seventy years, an animal that was once abundant disappeared from Iowa.[5]

Deer did not disappear without some efforts to protect them. In 1856, the state legislature established a closed season for deer from 1 February to 15 July. The length of the closed season was changed slightly in 1868 and 1872. Despite these efforts, deer numbers continued to decline. In general, there was little enforcement of game laws, and people continued to hunt whenever they pleased. Finally, deer were given complete protection in 1898. By then, they were essentially gone from Iowa, so the law had little effect.[6]

Hunting Deer

Among the variety of methods used to hunt deer in Iowa, shooting was the most common. Numerous reports indicate that at times deer were either common enough or tame enough to be shot from the front steps of a settler's cabin. Probably more often, the hunter either happened upon a deer in the woods, stalked the deer, or had a deer wander near enough to be shot. There are many stories of the hunting exploits of early Iowans.

One of the earliest deer-hunting stories from Iowa involves the Englishman Charles Murray, who hunted deer and other big game along the Turkey River in eastern Iowa in 1835. His hunt was not a big success, as he failed to kill a single deer in six days although he saw several. One man in Butler County shot twelve deer (and a bison) in one day soon after settlement of that area. In the fall of 1850, Joseph Kelly killed eight deer in one day near St. Charles in Floyd County, and Jordan Whitacre of Mahaska County claimed to have shot seven deer from one spot without moving. Sarah Brewer-Bonebright, who lived along the Boone River near Webster City, said her father killed twenty-seven deer in two days, probably in the 1850s. One man said he killed more than 600 deer in Montgomery County, including 105 in the winter of 1851–52. Another man shot ninety-six deer (plus six elk and a bison) in the winter of 1859 along the Des Moines River in Pocahontas County, and two men claimed to have killed 300 deer in Winnebago County, although the time period is not indicated. One of the largest deer reported from Iowa was a buck said to weigh more than 400 pounds that was killed near Fairview in Jones County soon after settlement. A sled pulled by a yoke of oxen was used to bring the carcass home. Clearly, deer must have been fairly easy to find and kill during the early days of settlement.[7]

Besides shooting deer, settlers sometimes killed them with knives or by other means if they could approach close enough. In the winter of 1868, Mrs. Samuel Sands, who lived near Bancroft in Kossuth County, saw a deer near her house taking shelter from a blizzard. Since she was out of food, Mrs. Sands saw the animal as a fresh supply of meat. She sent her two dogs out to attack the deer, and once they had grabbed it, she ran up to it and cut its throat with a butcher knife. Under similar circumstances, two deer were killed with an axe in Mahaska County in 1844.[8]

One of the more exciting deer kills in Iowa involves thirteen-year-old Jasper Bell in Hamilton County. In late fall, Jasper was sent outside to gather kindling wood for the morning fire. When he saw a buck deer nearby, he quickly forgot that he was dressed only in his nightclothes. Jasper returned to his house and released his two dogs, a hound and a bulldog. The hound chased the deer into a nearby river, whereupon the bulldog jumped into the freezing water, grabbed the deer by the throat, and dragged it to the edge of the ice, where the boy's father killed it and pulled it from the water. We are not told whether young Jasper ever did get a fire started that morning.[9]

*The winter of
1856–57 was
perhaps the most
disastrous of any
winter for Iowa's
wildlife. The bad
weather started
early when heavy
snow fell across
most of Iowa
for three days
beginning on 1
December. Shortly
after the snow
ended, it rained
and a heavy crust
formed on the
snow's surface.
The snow's crust
was too thin to
support large
animals like deer
and elk, while
wolves, coyotes,
and humans
could walk on it.
As a result, the
large mammals
were helpless in the
snow and were
easy prey for both
wild predators
and humans.
Many elk and
deer sought food
and shelter along
wooded streams
and other
protected areas.*

The greatest slaughter of deer in Iowa took place during the winter of 1856–57. A great snowstorm in early December forced deer and other wildlife into river valleys, frequently near towns, where they were easily killed by settlers. Often hunters did not even have to shoot the animals but could walk up to them and stab or club them to death. A fifteen-year-old boy in Guthrie County killed one with a knife that winter; the deep snow kept the animal from escaping, and the boy was able to sit on it and kill it. Because of the severity of the winter, settlers were short of food, and the deer probably saved the lives of many. Dick Chamberlain killed seventy-eight deer in Montgomery County during the winter of 1856–57, and a father and his son shot forty-one deer in Clayton County. In Cerro Gordo County, thirty-two were killed along the west fork of the Cedar River; few were seen there after that winter. Hundreds or perhaps thousands of deer were killed in Black Hawk, Butler, Fayette, Floyd, Harrison, Sac, Woodbury, and other counties. Wolves and coyotes probably killed many deer that winter, too.[10]

Markets for Deer

The most obvious value of deer was their meat. Usually the deer was eaten by whoever shot it, or else it was given to neighbors or relatives. Generally, there was a market for any excess venison, even though the lack of refrigeration made storage difficult. One writer says deer were so abundant in Madison County before 1844 that their meat had little value except to new settlers who did not know how to hunt. For four or five years after settlement of that area, venison was hauled to riverside markets, presumably in eastern Iowa. In the winter of 1847–48, Ann Dickens of Clayton County delivered 2,000 pounds of venison to McGregor; from there it was taken by wagon to Fort Atkinson in Winneshiek County. In the 1850s, venison was so plentiful in Muscatine that at times it could not be given away.[11]

Although deer were valued for their meat, few details about prices have been recorded; the accounts that are available indicate that in general the prices were low. In the late 1830s, venison sold for two or three cents a pound in Scott County; two men killed 110 deer in less than two months and sold them for one dollar each. Saddles (the two hindquarters) sold for fifty cents each in Sioux City in the 1850s, while in the winter of 1856–57 whole deer sold for $2.50 each. At that time, the skin alone was worth one dollar. In 1857, William Savage of Salem, Iowa, sold one deer for $4.50 and three quarters of a young buck for $3.18, indicating a price of about $1.05–$1.15 per quarter. In 1868, H. F. Andrews took thirty saddles of venison from Audubon County to Des Moines for sale there.[12]

Deer hides were also very important commercially. In the 1800s, the synthetic fibers that we now take for granted were not available, so leather was used for footwear, clothing, riding saddles, and a host of other products. Deer hides were therefore in high demand and were an important part of the early fur trade in North America. In Iowa, much of the early trade was centered along the Mississippi River. In 1809, the inventory at Fort Madison in Lee County included 3,000 pounds of whole deerskins worth $601.20 (twenty cents per pound) and 25,021 pounds of shaved deerskins worth $6,255 (twenty-five cents per pound). As a measure of the importance of deer, the value of the deerskins was twice that of all the other furs then on hand.[13]

Dealers away from the Mississippi River also commonly dealt in deerskins. A story that is repeated in several county histories tells of a dealer in Iowa City who made a profit of $150 one winter by buying deerskins locally for eighteen cents per pound and selling them for thirty-one cents per pound. In Delaware County, skins sold for fifty cents, again indicating a healthy market for deerskins. The relative importance of hides is shown by a story from Winnebago County. There, some hunters killed deer just for their skins and left the carcasses to rot.[14]

Often this forced them to move close to human settlements. The settlers were having a tough winter, too, and the herds of deer and elk were an easy-to-obtain food supply. Many deer and elk were killed that winter, and both species eventually disappeared from Iowa. Only in the past fifty years have deer numbers come back to match those found in Iowa before the winter of 1856–57.

Source: Brainard, J. M. 1894. The great blizzard of 1856. Annals of Iowa, 3rd series, 1:391–394.

The Return of Deer to Iowa

It is hard for many present-day Iowa citizens to realize how much the deer's status has changed in the twentieth century. The species was absent from the state at the turn of the century but is now so abundant that it is considered a pest in some parts of Iowa.

The deer now found in Iowa are probably descended from three captive herds and from individual deer that moved in from neighboring states. About 1885, William Cuppy of Avoca in Pottawattamie County in southwestern Iowa started a captive herd with deer he purchased in Nebraska. In 1894, the gate to his deer pen was left open and about thirty-five deer escaped. Twelve years later, it was estimated that the wild deer descended from the escapees numbered about 200. Around 1915, as many as 150 could be seen at a time, and the herd was estimated to number 400–500 head. In November 1911, the game warden and some local citizens attempted to round up the deer, which then numbered about 200. They eventually succeeded in driving thirty to fifty deer into a large corral. Some of the deer were sold for twenty-five dollars each, but others escaped when someone cut a hole in the fence. Although the local farmers at first welcomed seeing deer in the area, some soon grew tired of the crop damage, and in 1914 a deer was shot in defiance of a law forbidding the killing of pest deer. The offender was arrested, and the case eventually went to the Iowa Supreme Court, where the farmer won. This decision was a setback to wildlife conservation, as it allowed landowners to kill game out of season. Nevertheless, the deer herd survived and in 1937 was thought to number about 140, although it had split up into several herds, including some in Shelby County.[15]

In central Iowa, a second herd of deer was kept at the state game farm near Ledges State Park south of Boone. Some of the deer were caught near Avoca, while two were bought in Minnesota in 1928. By 1933, fourteen deer had been released, and twenty more were released the next year. Others may have escaped from the enclosure. By 1937, a number of these deer were living in the wooded areas along the nearby Des Moines River.[16]

The third herd had its origin from the captive Singmaster herd that was held near Keota in Washington County in southeastern Iowa. In the early 1920s, about sixty deer escaped and established a wild herd along the nearby Skunk River. In 1937, the herd numbered about sixty individuals.[17]

In all three cases, the deer gradually populated the nearby countryside. The original escapees often were very tame, and local people protected them. Thus, they survived and gradually spread out over Iowa. In some cases, the Iowa Conservation Commission moved deer from these herds to repopulate other parts of the state. Besides the deer that originated from these captive herds, wild deer from herds in Minnesota and Wisconsin entered the northeastern corner of Iowa and established herds there. Other deer may have wandered in elsewhere along the borders of Iowa, populating other parts of the state.[18]

Few people realized how well these deer would adapt to the

heavily farmed landscape. Although it was often thought that deer needed relatively large woodlands to survive, the deer in Iowa thrived in small woodlots and farm groves as well as in larger stands of timber. They found an abundant supply of food readily available in the nearest cornfield, and thus winter starvation was not the problem that it was and still is in states to the north. In Iowa, female deer often breed during their first fall of life, and older does commonly have twins. Thus, the population has the capacity to increase rapidly.

Iowa's deer herd was conservatively estimated to number about 500–700 individuals in 1936. A statewide survey in 1947 estimated that Iowa had a total of 1,650 deer in fifty-eight counties. By 1950, deer were established in eighty-nine counties, and the population was estimated at 4,530. By 1953, the population had grown to 13,000, and legislation was passed allowing deer hunting again after fifty-five years of closed seasons. Hunting was allowed in forty-five counties, and about 4,000 deer were taken. Since then, hunting has been allowed every year, and the area open to hunting has gradually been expanded so that now virtually all of Iowa has some deer hunting. Besides a shotgun hunting season, there are special seasons for bowhunters and muzzleloaders. Even with liberalized hunting seasons, the Iowa deer population has continued to grow. In 1989 and 1990, almost 100,000 deer were taken in Iowa, and the population showed no sign of stabilizing. The posthunting season deer population in fall 1989 was estimated to number about 200,000.[19]

The success of white-tailed deer has not been limited to Iowa. Nationally, they have recovered and returned to their position as the top big-game mammal in North America. They have reoccupied nearly all their original range and perhaps have even expanded it in some places. They currently number an estimated fourteen million, down from their original numbers but probably near the limit their habitat can support in many areas. Deer are hunted over most of this range. About two million were killed by legal hunters in 1978, and yet the population seems stable. In many areas they are so numerous that they are sometimes considered a nuisance, causing damage in collisions with cars and feeding on gardens and croplands. Still, on balance, deer are one of the favorite wildlife species in the eyes of the North American public.[20]

5. Wild Cats

The various wild cats are the epitome of a predator, using a combination of strength, speed, stealth, and agility to capture their prey. Two or perhaps three species of wild cat were found by early settlers in Iowa. Both the mountain lion and bobcat (or wildcat) definitely were found in Iowa, while the lynx probably occurred here. Many writers seem to have used the name "lynx" carelessly to describe the bobcat, and most reports of the lynx probably really were bobcats. Bobcats were fairly common, while mountain lions were probably quite rare in Iowa. All three species were considered threats to settlers' livestock and poultry, and they usually were shot whenever they were encountered. Most records of these cats provide few details, and often all that is said is that the species was present in an area.

Throughout the history of Europeans in Iowa, there usually

has been an economic incentive for humans to kill various predators, including the wild cats. Bounties for killing wild cats date back to 1817, when Iowa was still part of the Missouri Territory. At that time, a bounty of two dollars was paid for each mountain lion and fifty cents for each wildcat killed. That law was repealed in 1818 and not until 1834 were bounties for mountain lions reestablished. In 1836, Iowa became part of Wisconsin Territory, which had no bounties. However, in 1858, the state of Iowa established a bounty of $1.50 for wildcat and lynx; the claimant was required to present the scalp of the animal to a justice of the peace or county judge within ten days of killing the animal. The bounty was reduced to one dollar in 1860 and remained at that level until it was dropped to fifty cents in 1933. Currently, no bounty is paid for killing any of the wild cats. Bounties certainly encouraged people to kill wild cats and reinforced the notion that, by doing so, the individual was helping society. Only in recent years has there been much appreciation of these predators and an understanding that they, too, have a place in nature.[1]

Bobcats

Bobcats occurred over most of the United States, southern Canada, and Mexico when Europeans first arrived. They lived in a variety of habitats ranging from thick woods to desert scrublands. Bobcats were found throughout Iowa (map 5). Many of the animals that early Iowa records refer to as "wildcats" were probably bobcats rather than lynx, and I shall treat them as such unless the writer clearly indicates that there were two species present or describes the animal in some detail. Several writers speak of seeing bobcats quite often, and they must have been the most abundant of the three cats in Iowa. They are described as being numerous in the early days (ca. 1850) in Hamilton County; one writer says that a conservative estimate would be that hundreds were killed near Webster City, probably in the 1850s. Charles Babbitt said that they were common in the Council Bluffs area, also in the 1850s. Bounty records also suggest that they were fairly common. Bounties were paid for ten bobcats in Muscatine County in 1867, and, in Allamakee County, for thirty-seven in 1871 and forty-three in 1881. Ellison Orr said that bobcats were common in the rough parts of Allamakee County, although they were seldom seen. By the late 1800s, there was little mention of bobcats in Iowa. The last one in Sac

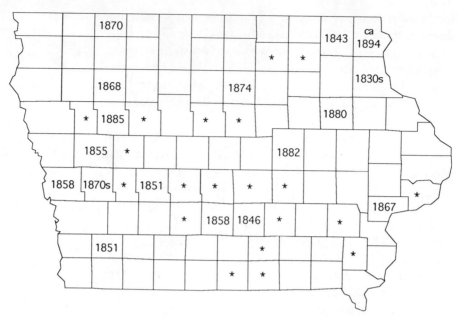

County was found in 1885, and three were killed along the Yellow River in Allamakee County about 1894.[2]

Despite the abundance of bobcats, there are few stories about
encounters between settlers and bobcats. Bobcats certainly were
shot, trapped, and sometimes even poisoned. Their skins also
had some value, selling for fifty cents each in Des Moines in
1866, but they were not as valuable as those of most other furbearers. About 1856, R. W. Williamson was hunting bobcats in
Warren County. His dogs drove a bobcat into a large hollow log
and killed it there. Since Williamson wanted the cat's scalp, he
crawled into the log to retrieve it. He reached the cat but had
trouble backing out and got stuck. It took both his hunting part-
ners to drag him out with his quarry. During the winter of
1869–70 or 1870–71, a trapper named Frank Mead was trapping near West Lake Okoboji. One night he heard an animal
feeding on the muskrat carcasses he had thrown out near his tent.
He looked out of his tent to find a bobcat six inches away and
promptly shot it with his revolver. Another hunting story involving a bobcat is Ellison Orr's mention that one treed during a
raccoon hunt in Allamakee County eventually escaped. In 1846,
a man found an adult bobcat with three young in a hollow tree

in Marion County. His dogs killed the adult, and he took the three young home with him. He kept them in captivity for a short time but soon decided that they were poor pets and got rid of them.[3]

By about 1900, bobcats seem largely to have disappeared from Iowa, and there is almost no mention of them for a number of years. Emmett Polder's summary of bobcat records from the 1930s and 1940s lists reports from all four corners of the state, although most were from northeastern Iowa. Several bobcats were taken in eastern Iowa in 1946 and 1947, indicating their continued presence in that part of the state. Bobcats are still found infrequently throughout Iowa, but because of their secretiveness, their numbers are hard to assess. They have been reported in about twenty counties during the past fifty years, especially along the state's eastern and western borders. They are considered an endangered species in Iowa, a status that supposedly gives them special protection. However, several of the recent reports involve bobcats that were caught in traps set for other animals. Others undoubtedly are shot when encountered by hunters who are unaware of the species' protected status. Thus, the chances are slim that the species will ever regain much more than a small fraction of its former numbers in Iowa.[4]

Mountain Lions

The mountain lion (or puma, panther, cougar, and various other names) is the largest of the three wild cats reported in Iowa. When Europeans reached North America, mountain lions had perhaps the widest distribution of any land mammal in the New World. They were found across southern Canada, throughout the United States, and south through Central and South America to Chile and Argentina. In Iowa, they probably occurred throughout the state, but nowhere in great numbers (map 6). The few definite records from the state include a report of six— including one that was nine feet long (its hide sold for five dollars)—that were shot by Ned Dickens in Clayton County in 1838, one killed in a cave in Delaware County about 1845, one killed in Montgomery County in 1851, one or two seen in Madison County in 1861, and one that was hunted but not killed in eastern Adair County in spring 1864. One shot near Cincinnati in Appanoose County in 1867 seems to be the last record of a

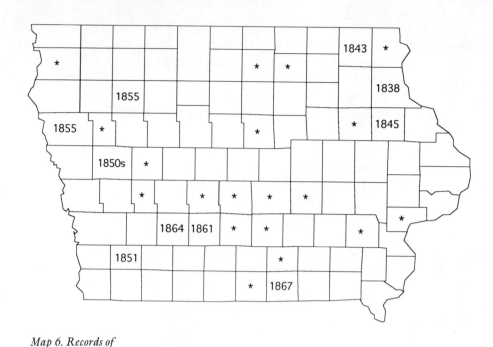

Map 6. Records of mountain lions in Iowa. Date indicates year of last record in each county. An asterisk indicates a county with a record of mountain lions present but with no specific date for the record.

mountain lion in Iowa. Thus, resident mountain lions probably disappeared from Iowa in the 1860s, sharing with the bison and elk the dubious honor of being the first of the native wildlife to be extirpated from Iowa. The report of a 160-pound mountain lion killed on an island in Rush Lake, Osceola County, in April 1909 seems to be secondhand, and since Rush Lake has no islands on it, the report seems dubious. At best, this must have been a stray animal rather than a representative of a permanent population.[5]

The rarity of mountain lions in Iowa is reinforced by the scarcity of stories that have been recorded in county histories or in the accounts of early explorers. Several stories describe attacks on livestock and attempts to trap the large cats. A mountain lion was reported taking a calf in Monroe County, and one in Adair County in 1864 was said to have killed colts, calves, sheep, and about forty hogs. In Washington County, they took pigs and poultry. A trapper in Ida County said he trapped mountain lions by hanging part of a dead deer from a tree and setting a double-spring trap underneath the carcass. When the mountain lion jumped up to get at the meat, it would land on the trap and be caught.[6]

46   *Wild Cats*

Other stories refer to chance encounters between settlers and mountain lions. In 1843, two boys wandering in the woods of Winneshiek County encountered a panther that their dogs had treed. They were so interested in watching the cat that they became lost in the woods for several days before they found their way home. In 1854, a Woodbury County man was following the trail of a deer he had wounded when he encountered two cougars. He said that the cougars followed him all the way to a neighbor's home before he managed to scare them away. The next year, another man saw two cougars in the same area. In the winter of 1855–56, a boy who was tending livestock along the Boyer River in Crawford County was attacked by a panther. The boy's bull terrier came to his rescue and the cat fled, leaving the boy scratched but not seriously hurt. In Sioux County, a small panther was killed along the Rock River. Eighteen-year-old Allison Brewington surprised the animal and just managed to wound it with a shotgun blast before it leaped on him. Brewington finally managed to push the cat away long enough to get another shot off, killing the cat. It was three feet long and weighed more than fifty pounds.[7]

Mountain lions still are fairly common in parts of the Rocky Mountain states, especially in isolated areas where they are not heavily hunted. A few survive in Florida, and there are recurring stories of their existence elsewhere in eastern North America. Occasionally, there are reports that someone has seen or heard a mountain lion or found their tracks in Iowa, but none of the recent reports have been verified (e.g., reports from Council Bluffs in 1978 and 1979 and near Deep River, Poweshiek County, in 1980). The nearest wild population is in the Black Hills of South Dakota, and it is unlikely that one from there would wander so far east. The slim chance of mountain lions' reaching Iowa, the lack of enough suitable habitat, and the likelihood that any such animal would be promptly shot make it unlikely that the species will ever be reestablished in Iowa. If indeed any of the recent sightings have been mountain lions, it is more likely that they were pets that escaped.[8]

Lynx

The lynx currently is found mainly in the coniferous forests of Canada and extreme northern United States. In the early 1800s,

Bounties

The concept of paying a reward for the killing of an unwanted animal dates back to at least the 1500s, when Henry VIII ordered a bounty paid for killing crows and related birds. The first bounty in the United States was established in 1630, when the Massachusetts Bay Colony paid a penny for each wolf killed. Bounties were established in Iowa in territorial days and were paid for several predators up until recent years. The concept has long been controversial. While some argue that bounties help keep populations of unwanted predators and other "varmints" under control, others argue that there is no evidence

though, its range extended further south, and it apparently was a rare resident in northern Iowa. Many writers confused this species with the somewhat similar bobcat, and bobcats were commonly called bay lynx. Probably most Iowa reports of lynx really refer to misidentified bobcats. Still, several early writers who seem to have known the difference between the two species note that both were found in their area. These records include one shot in Crawford County in the 1850s, bounties for two in Muscatine County in 1867, one killed in Warren County in 1868, bounties for two in Montgomery County in 1869, the last one in Calhoun County in 1869, three trapped in Sac County in 1869, and one trapped there in 1875. C. H. Babbitt says that they occasionally were seen in the Council Bluffs area, apparently in the 1850s. A few said to have been present in Dickinson County in 1882 seem to be the last of the original lynx in Iowa. Thus, lynx were gone from the state by the mid-1880s.[9]

Currently, lynx occur no closer than northeastern Minnesota, and even there they are considered uncommon. However, if their usual prey of rabbits and hares becomes rare, they may wander widely. In 1962–63 and 1972–73, several individuals were found in southern Minnesota, south of their normal range. Such wanderers probably were the source of a lynx shot in Shelby County, Iowa, in July 1963. Another lynx reported from near Muscatine in January 1906 also must have been a wandering individual. Like the mountain lion, this species has little chance of being reestablished in Iowa.[10]

Epilogue

In 1979, the Iowa Conservation Commission developed plans to augment the few bobcats remaining in the state. They made arrangements to obtain ten pairs of bobcats from Oklahoma, which they planned to release in the loess hills of western Iowa. Word of this plan got out to the general public, and some livestock owners became concerned that the bobcats would be a threat to their domestic animals. A bobcat usually weighs only about fifteen to twenty-five pounds, with few weighing more than thirty-five pounds. Generally, they feed on rabbits, and other than taking an occasional lamb, they really are not a threat to the livestock industry. Still, the complaints were heard, and in the end plans for the bobcat release were squelched. Thus,

48   *Wild Cats*

for the present at least, the bobcat must make it on its own in Iowa.[11]

On a continental basis, bobcats and other wild cats face another threat. In recent years, the furs of various spotted cats, including lynx and bobcat, have been highly coveted, and prices for them have skyrocketed. In 1982–83, about 81,000 bobcats were taken in the United States and Canada, and an average of $142 was paid per pelt. Bobcat pelts have sold for as much as $300 apiece. In the early 1980s, the number of lynx pelts sold annually in North America varied from 15,000 to 50,000. Lynx pelts sold for an average of $650 in 1984–85, and an especially fine pelt might bring more than $1,000. With prices that high, there has been much interest in trapping bobcats and lynx.

Although the two species are closely related, their populations have responded differently to the intrusions of Europeans in North America. Lynx populations historically have shown cyclic highs and lows that are correlated with the population cycle of their main food, the snowshoe hare. Heavy trapping pressure when lynx numbers are low could extirpate them from an area. In North America, from a population low around 1940, lynx numbers increased during the mid-1900s, but in the last ten years or so, they seem to have declined again. Trapping and perhaps continued habitat loss seem to be involved in this decline. Although it is unlikely that lynx will be considered endangered in the near future, their dependence on snowshoe hares for food and the high trapping mortality they often suffer mean that they require continued attention from wildlife managers. In contrast, bobcats seem to be more adaptable and tolerant of human activities. Their reproductive potential is also fairly high. Still, with fur prices so high, there is the danger that trapping could extirpate them in parts of their range. Thus, both species certainly deserve close attention and management to ensure their survival.[12]

that predator populations are reduced to any great extent and that bounties are a waste of money. In 1993, the state legislature considered restoring a bounty on coyotes in Iowa.

Sources: Leopold, A. 1933. Game management. Charles Scribner's Sons, New York, p. 9. Shaw, J. H. 1985. Introduction to wildlife management. McGraw-Hill Book Co., New York, p. 5. Waller, D. W., and P. L. Errington. 1961. The bounty system in Iowa. Proceedings of the Iowa Academy of Science 68: 301–313.

6. Black Bears

Black bears were one of the most recognizable and noticeable mammals encountered by Europeans as they settled North America. Besides the familiar black phase, black bears may also be brown or gray in color. Bears once occurred across much of North America and were usually found in wooded areas. As settlers moved west, they generally killed any bears they encountered. Thus, bear numbers declined rapidly in many areas, and bears disappeared from much of their former range. The larger grizzly bear was once found on the Great Plains and the Rocky Mountains, where a small population still persists. It is possible that grizzlies may have occasionally wandered into Iowa, but I know of no documented records of such an occurrence.

Most present-day Iowans probably associate black bears with some of our large national parks and do not realize that they once occurred in Iowa. Black bears were widespread but not especially common over most of Iowa at the time of settlement. They were reported most often from the woodlands of eastern Iowa. Several writers mention finding them in caves, which presumably served as dens, in northeastern Iowa. There are fewer reports from western and northwestern Iowa, where the prairie habitat was less suitable for them.

As the largest predator found in Iowa, black bears attracted considerable attention. There are three reports of bears in Iowa that weighed 300 pounds or more: one killed in Harrison County in the winter of 1857–58, another killed near Hardin in Allamakee County in January 1858, and a third shot in Buchanan County in 1859. Most bear stories refer to someone hunting and eventually killing the animal. Some of the stories have been published several times, each version differing slightly, so it is not always possible to sort out truth from fiction. At least a few stories indicate that bears harassed or killed livestock, and early settlers certainly saw them as a threat to their domestic animals. Bears also could damage crops and, in general, be a nuisance. Thus, settlers usually killed any bears they encountered.[1]

Bears were also killed because they were valuable both as food and for their hides. In 1843 or 1844, a Dr. Brewer in Buchanan County served bearmeat to his father, who was visiting from the East. His father at first thought he had eaten pork. However, when he was told what he had eaten, he asked for another slice, an indication that he found it quite edible. Bearskins were also valuable in commercial trade, although few details are available. The inventory of the trading post at Fort Madison on the Mississippi River in Lee County in 1809 included twenty first-quality bearskins worth $1.50 each and forty-four second-quality skins worth one dollar each. By the mid-1800s, prices were much higher. About that time, bearskins sold for ten dollars in Delaware County, while a bear killed in Delaware County in 1859 was sold for twenty dollars. In 1847, A. H. Mallory captured a young bear in Delaware County and kept it in captivity. All went well until Mallory joined the Gold Rush and left for California in 1849. The bear refused to eat, became vicious, and finally was killed.[2]

Arlie W.
Schorger,
1884–1972

Perhaps the most
thorough wildlife
historian of this
century, Arlie
Schorger was born
in Ohio. He
attended Wooster
College, where he
studied chemistry.
Schorger received
a doctorate in
chemistry from the
University of
Wisconsin and
held several
positions in
government and
private industry,
specializing in
cellulose chemistry.
Long interested
in birds and
mammals,
Schorger began in
1930 to search
through early
Wisconsin
newspapers for
information on
wildlife. It took
him about twenty
years, but he
eventually looked
at virtually every
page of every
Wisconsin
newspaper
published before

Hunting Bears in Iowa

As would be expected, several stories of the exploits of early-day "Davy Crocketts" in Iowa have been recorded. Some are short and direct. Moses Van Sickel killed seven bears single-handedly in a cave near Garnavillo in Clayton County in the winter of 1840, and Ned Dickens killed four in the same county in 1838. Other stories are more detailed. A bear found in Mahaska County in 1844 had attacked some pigs. It was treed and shot but only wounded. The wounded bear fell to the ground, where the hunter's dogs jumped on it. In the excitement, the hunter tried to strike the bear with a club but hit one of his dogs instead, removing the dog from the battle. Soon another man got a clear shot and killed the bear.[3]

A 300-pound bear found on the prairie near Brandon in Buchanan County in 1859 was such an oddity that forty unarmed men and boys along with a pack of dogs chased the animal. The bear was fat and slow-moving and finally was cornered, but no one had a weapon to kill it with. After a three-hour wait, a Joel Allen arrived with a rifle and killed the bear with three shots.[4]

Another story involves a large bear that had attacked a hog near Bevington in Warren County in 1865. The bear was chased and finally treed. The pursuers fired at least fifteen shots from assorted shotguns, rifles, and revolvers at the animal, most of them missing it, before they finally killed the bear.[5]

About 1849, Jacob Hoover, a new settler near West Union in Fayette County, had a close encounter with a bear. One day, while hunting deer, he saw the bear. Hoover forgot about deer and, with his dog, took off after the bear. The dog soon annoyed the bear enough that Hoover was able to shoot the bear twice. The second shot wounded the bear badly enough that Hoover thought that it was dead. Hoover remained on his horse and approached the bear to admire it. Suddenly, the bear reared up and grabbed Hoover's legs, knocking his gun away at the same time. Hoover's dog proved to be the hero: it attacked the bear, distracting it long enough for Hoover to get free, grab his gun, and finally kill the animal.[6]

Probably the best Iowa bear story involves Thomas Bearse of Winnebago County. In May 1855, he saw two bears near his home east of Forest City. Bearse hid behind a tree, and when one bear got close to him, he shot it. The wounded bear continued to approach him and then climbed the tree Bearse was hiding behind. Eventually, the wounded animal dropped to the ground. Bearse drew his knife and was trying to cut the bear's throat when a second bear came up behind him, grabbed him, and squeezed him in a bear hug. Bearse clubbed that bear with a branch, and it ran away. The story may have been exaggerated a bit, but it certainly must have been an exciting encounter.[7]

Another colorful story involves John Wright, who was hunting elk near the source of the Raccoon River in northwestern Iowa, a favorite hunting ground in the mid-1850s. Wright saw a dark lump on the prairie and, when he approached it, discovered that it was a bear. He chased it on horseback and, coming alongside the animal, jumped from his horse onto the bear. His timing was wrong, though, for the bear chose that instant to turn toward him, and Wright ended up in the embrace of a bear. How he escaped is not reported, but he supposedly captured the animal and returned to civilization, where the captive bear was put on display in Adel. Evidently, Wright soon moved west, but what became of the bear was not recorded.[8]

The only bear reported from Harrison County was killed by George Caywood near Modale in the winter of 1857–58. Caywood was hunting wildcats when his dogs scented an animal. Caywood thought they had cornered a wildcat, and he was within fifteen feet of the bear before it stood up in some willows and then charged him. Caywood fired one shot at the bear and then dropped his gun and ran for home two miles away. He waited until the next day and then, with help, returned to see what had happened to the bear. They found the 300-pound bear dead, shot through the heart.[9]

One of the most unusual Iowa bear episodes occurred near Webster City, probably in the 1850s, when a small bear raided a settler's beehives. The bees counterattacked and soon had the bear's full attention. In the midst of this melee, a young boy, armed with a bow, shot the bear with several of his arrows. One arrow wounded the bear in the ear, disabling it enough that the boy's mother could kill it with an axe. Obviously, child care in those days was different from modern times.[10]

An indication of the abundance of bears in the early days comes from the tale of two Delaware County men. While hunting near Greeley, they surprised two bears sleeping near a spring. They killed one bear with an axe and shot and wounded the other. The wounded bear attacked the men and knocked their gun away. The bear then fought with their dogs for several min-

1900. This information was summarized in a series of papers on wildlife in early Wisconsin and later in books on the passenger pigeon and wild turkey. Schorger's attention to detail makes these articles classics on the changes in wildlife populations in Wisconsin and the Midwest.

Source: Hickey, J. J. 1973. In memoriam: Arlie William Schorger. Auk 90:664–671.

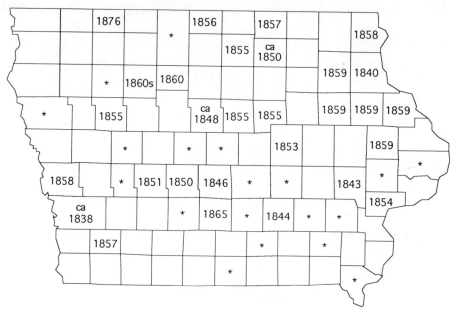

Map 7. Records of black bears in Iowa. Date indicates year of last record in each county. An asterisk indicates a county with a record of black bears present but with no specific date for the record.

utes. Finally, the hunters got a clear shot and killed the bear. They continued their hunting trip and killed two more bears before they returned home. Thus, they killed four bears on a single hunting trip.[11]

Distribution of Bears in Iowa

There are pre-1900 records of black bears from forty-eight Iowa counties, two-thirds of them from counties in the eastern half of the state (map 7). The eastern half of Iowa was originally the most heavily wooded, so the abundance of records there is not surprising. Still, there are several records from northwestern Iowa, indicating that bears did wander out onto the prairies. Nineteen of the forty-eight records indicate only that bears were present but give no date. The other twenty-nine give a date and probably are more reliable records. More than half of the records with dates are from the northeastern corner of the state, again suggesting that the area was the most important for bears. Many of these are the last record for that particular county, and thus they provide at least an approximation of when the species disappeared from Iowa. By decades, the twenty-nine records include one from the 1830s, five from the 1840s, nineteen from the 1850s, three from the 1860s, and one from the 1870s. Thus, bears disappeared soon after settlement, and for all practical purposes the species was extirpated from Iowa by about 1860. The last reported bear from the 1800s was one found near Spirit Lake in November 1876.[12]

There was a flurry of reports of bears in northeastern Iowa in the fall of 1859, somewhat after bears had largely disappeared from that area. In that year, bears were reported in Buchanan, Delaware, Dubuque, Fayette, and Jones counties. Wildlife historian Arlie Schorger noted that periodically black bears in Wisconsin emigrated to areas where they normally were not found. One such emigration occurred in 1859, when bears moved south to the southern border of Wisconsin. It seems likely that the bears seen in Iowa were part of that emigration.[13]

Epilogue

In recent years, bears have occasionally been reported in Iowa. All seem to have wandered in from another state or to have escaped from captivity. Presently, there is no established wild population of bears in Iowa. Recent records include one shot near Tipton in Cedar County in May 1965 after it had raided a beehive. This may have been the same individual that was tracked from Wapello to Mahaska county earlier that year. One was reported in Allamakee County in 1968; bear tracks were seen in Tama County in 1970; and an adult and cub were reported near Decorah in Winneshiek County in 1970. One reported near Gilmore City in October 1987 was thought to be an escaped pet.[14]

The lack of any large wilderness areas and the likelihood that any bears seen in Iowa will be shot mean that there is little chance that bears will again be part of our fauna. Currently, the nearest established wild populations of black bears are in northern Wisconsin, northern Minnesota, and southern Missouri. Presumably, wanderers from any of those populations could occasionally reach Iowa. The eighteen Bear and four Little Bear creeks in Iowa provide a hint of how widespread bears once were in Iowa and the attention settlers gave them. In addition, the Maquoketa River takes its name from an Indian word for bear. The name "bear" was also given to several townships and other landmarks and thus reminds us of its former presence in Iowa.[15]

Nationally, more than 200,000 black bears are estimated to live in the lower forty-eight states; healthy populations also occur in Alaska and much of Canada. Although their numbers dwindled with the European settlement of North America, bear numbers have increased somewhat in recent years. The establishment of numerous publicly owned parks, refuges, and forests and the abandonment of many farms in parts of their range have provided black bears with the forest habitat they prefer. Although black bears are fairly adaptable, some of the smaller and more isolated populations will probably gradually dwindle and die out. However, as long as habitat is provided and human disturbance is minimized, the future survival of the larger populations is probably secure.[16]

7. Wolves and Coyotes

Two large wolflike mammals were frequently encountered by early explorers and settlers in Iowa. These two, the gray wolf and the coyote, were frequently confused or simply called "wolves." Because it is often impossible to be sure which species writers were referring to, I will treat reports as indefinite (and probably referring to coyotes) unless there are further details or the author indicates some familiarity with both species. What is certain is that both species once were found in Iowa, both were greatly persecuted, and only the coyote still occurs in Iowa.

The gray wolf and the coyote once had extensive ranges in North America. Gray wolves were found over much of the continent, ranging from central Mexico north to the Arctic Ocean. In Iowa, the gray wolf was found statewide, inhabiting both the prairies and wooded regions. Two different types or subspecies

57

of gray wolf occurred in Iowa. The Great Plains wolf (a name that causes considerable confusion because the coyote was often given a similar name, the prairie wolf) was found over roughly the western two-thirds of the state. This type of wolf typically followed the bison herds, feeding on stragglers from the herd as well as on other prey. Because bison were most abundant in north-central and northwestern Iowa, the Great Plains wolf also was probably most abundant in those regions. The other type of gray wolf found in Iowa was the timber wolf, the subspecies that currently inhabits northern Minnesota. Timber wolves were found in eastern Iowa, especially in the wooded northeastern corner of the state.[1]

Coyotes were found in the western half of the United States, southern Canada, and northern Mexico. Since the settlement of North America, they have expanded their range and now occupy much of the continent. In Iowa, coyotes were once common to abundant throughout the state.[2]

Food Habits

The gray wolf and the coyote are carnivores and feed primarily on mammals, birds, and other animals. Both species are opportunistic and will feed on domestic animals if the opportunity exists. These food habits have long given both species a bad reputation and have led to numerous stories about them, some greatly exaggerated. The only information on gray wolf food habits in Iowa is anecdotal. Presumably, those that lived on the prairies followed the bison herds and fed on young, weak, or lame bison. Gray wolves often fed on the domestic animals that settlers brought into Iowa, and there are numerous reports of their killing chickens, pigs, and sheep in Iowa.[3]

Coyote food habits probably were similar to those of the wolf, but because the coyote is a smaller animal, it generally fed on smaller prey. Like wolves, coyotes also took domestic animals. They were known to occasionally kill chickens, sheep, pigs, and calves, but their main prey was cottontail rabbits. A recent study of coyote food habits in Iowa showed that in winter about half their diet was rabbits, a quarter was livestock (cattle, pigs, and sheep), a fifth other mammals, and the remainder various birds and plants. Although coyotes do kill and eat some sheep, cattle, pigs, and poultry, they will also feed on animals that have died of disease or other natural causes.[4]

There are numerous stories of real and supposed wolf attacks on settlers in Iowa. Most people who traveled in the state before about 1860 were probably aware of the species, and if they had not encountered a wolf in person, they had at least heard stories about them. Despite all these stories, there are few that record an actual attack by a wolf on a human in Iowa and none that report a human death due to a wolf attack.

One story involves a young man in Guthrie County who, in the winter of 1853–54, walked ten miles (!) to visit his girl-friend. At midnight, he was given his choice of staying for the night in the tiny cabin and sharing a bed with three others (but definitely not including his girlfriend), sleeping on a pallet in the loft, or walking home. He chose the latter but soon found his lone companions on the open prairie were coyotes that seemed to howl from every hill he passed. He made it home safely but vowed that next time he would either keep his girlfriend up all night or sleep on whatever accommodation he was offered.[5]

There is a similar story from Hamilton County. In 1857, six young people from Saratoga were on their way to a Christmas Eve dance. When they were near Kamrar, their sleigh was sur-rounded and followed by a pack of coyotes that they estimated numbered one hundred animals. Some approached as close as five to ten feet from the sleigh, where they snarled at the young people and in general scared them out of their wits. Although one of the men had a revolver, he decided that there were too many coyotes and did not use it. They finally made it to the dance safely, but they remembered the ride for years.[6]

One of the more humorous stories comes from Tama County. In 1856, the settlers held a dance to celebrate the completion of their new schoolhouse near Redman. The dance was delayed when the entire orchestra, consisting solely of one Fiddlin' Jim, did not show up. A search party soon found Jim nearby, perched on the roof of an empty shed and playing his violin to six wolves. Jim explained that whenever he stopped playing, the wolves came closer, so he kept playing. Whether this was because they did or did not enjoy his playing is not clear, but Fiddlin' Jim commented that at least he "sure got tuned up good" for the dance.[7]

A somewhat different story involves a Captain Willard Glazier, who was traveling across the country in 1876. One October eve-

Fig. 3. A circle hunt for wolves, a common social event in the early days of Iowa. Courtesy State Historical Society of Iowa, Iowa City.

ning, while on his way to Anita in Cass County, he stopped for the night some distance from any town. Having nowhere else to sleep, he slept in a haystack. However, Glazier soon found that he had a pack of coyotes for company. The coyotes began to howl and make life unpleasant for him. Glazier shot several of the coyotes with his revolver, but they continued to threaten him. Just then he found he had additional company, a dog. The friendly dog helped keep the coyotes at bay for the rest of the night, and Glazier continued on his way in the morning.[8]

Hunting and Trapping Wolves and Coyotes

Because of the widespread interest in trying to eliminate wolves and coyotes from Iowa, settlers developed methods to hunt or trap them. Since both species had the reputation of being very intelligent and hard to fool, this was a difficult task. Still, over the years several methods were perfected. The hunting method that is mentioned most often is the circular wolf hunt. In such a hunt, a large number of people gathered on the designated day and spread out to surround the section of land to be hunted (fig. 3). On a large hunt, this might involve several hundred hunters and cover several square miles. At the starting time, the hunters, on foot or on horseback, together with their dogs, gradually started closing the circle. Generally, they tried to make as much noise as possible to drive the wolves, as well as any other game, into the ever smaller area in front of them. The idea was to confine the wolves in a small area, where they could be killed by the dogs or with clubs. Because of the large number of people involved, guns were considered too dangerous and usually were not used. On some hunts, ten or more wolves were killed. Besides serving as a way of ridding an area of wolves and other varmints, circle hunts were also a social event, drawing many people together for a day of hunting, visiting, and eating.[9]

The other way that wolves were often hunted was to run them down on horseback. Dogs were frequently used on these hunts. This was most successful on the open prairie, where there were few hiding places and it was possible to tire the animal out after a long chase. If there was a light snow cover, the wolves would sink in it and were easier to catch. In a wolf hunt on the prairie near Osage in the 1870s described by Hamlin Garland, a noted writer of life on the frontier, the hunters were all on horseback, and each rider in turn cut the animal off whenever it attempted to turn from a straight course. Finally, the hunters got close to the exhausted animal and either shot it or ran it down.[10]

Several hunters noted that coyotes, when they were exhausted and finally overtaken, often would "play possum" and feign death (a habit that hunters usually attributed to their cowardice). A hunter in Warren County in 1856 caught a coyote that he thought his dogs had killed. He turned away to get his rope to tie the animal to his saddle, when he heard his dogs running away from him. The coyote had "come to life" and was already far down the road, the dogs in hot pursuit. He caught it again but this time made sure it was dead before he tried to tie it up. He was thankful that he had not tied the live coyote to his mule. If he had, his mule probably would have given him an exciting ride home.[11]

Many Iowans tried to trap wolves, although they were considered a very difficult animal to capture. Although they often would approach the bait in a trap, they seemed to sense the danger and would not take the bait. In the winter of 1819–20, members of the Stephen Long expedition encamped near Council Bluffs tried both box and steel traps but had little success in trapping wolves. In 1844, a Mr. A. Covey of Keokuk County devised a wolf trap that was very successful; that February he caught sixteen wolves with it. David Scott of Appanoose County trapped a wolf cub that he wanted to tame for his sons. He put a collar around the animal's neck and chained it to a post, but the next day the wolf and chain were both gone. Two years later, the wolf was recaptured and still had the chain attached to it.[12]

About 1850, a large white wolf appeared near Oxford in Johnson County and soon had a reputation as a sheep killer. The wolf escaped from one trap, losing a toe in the process, and seemed immune to poison. Two men finally caught it in two traps that were chained to a heavy weight. The wolf was strong and dragged the trap and the attached weight three miles before the men caught up with it. Their dogs attacked the wolf so they could not get a clear shot at it. The wolf eventually got free from the trap, but one of the men killed it with his pocket knife before it could escape.[13]

As in the western states, poison was sometimes used to kill wolves. However, little has been recorded on this practice in Iowa. In Story County, a man put poison in an ox carcass and killed two wolves in one night in the mid-1850s. A trapper in Ida County added strychnine to pieces of deermeat and left it out for the scavengers. He killed several kinds of predators, including lots of wolves.[14]

Decline of Wolves and Coyotes in Iowa

To most settlers, all wolves were considered varmints and were shot, trapped, or poisoned whenever possible. Thus, the gray wolf disappeared rapidly from Iowa, and few details are available on its demise. Gray wolves were gone from Madison County by 1862, and one killed in Sac County in 1868 seems to have been the last one there. By 1867, J. A. Allen noted that they were less common in settled areas than they had been twenty years previously. A gray wolf shot along Lizard Creek in November 1876 was the last one in Pocahontas County. The last record for Iowa that seems to be valid is the report of a gray wolf in Butler County, probably in the winter of 1884–85. A farmer armed with a pitchfork and accompanied by his dogs managed to drive it away, thus ending the era of gray wolves in Iowa.[15]

There are a number of post-1900 reports of gray wolves in Iowa, none of which have good supporting details. Although Herbert Osborn thought there might be a few still around in 1905, Van Hyning and Pellett considered them extinct in Iowa by 1910. There were reports of packs of gray wolves in Lee and Henry counties in spring 1914, one killed in Iowa in 1925, and two passing through Emmet County in the winter of 1935–36.

There are numerous reports of bounties paid for "wolves" even up until recent years, but all of these animals must have been coyotes. In general, gray wolves seem to have disappeared rapidly from Iowa and probably were extirpated from most of the state by the 1860s.[16]

Like the wolf, the coyote was familiar to most early arrivals in Iowa and was greatly persecuted. The combination of hunting, trapping, and poisoning led to a rapid decline in their numbers. However, coyotes were able to coexist with humans and thus never were completely extirpated. By about 1890, they were considered uncommon in Iowa. Reports from several counties suggest that their numbers may have been lowest about 1910–20. They were common in Sac County in the 1850s but were very rare there by 1917, and only five were trapped in the county in the winter of 1913–14. In Floyd County, they were still common in 1897, but by 1917 they were rare. In Clay and Palo Alto counties, they were practically extinct by 1912. By 1937, coyotes were considered occasional and irregular throughout Iowa, especially in the less-settled areas, indicating at least a partial recovery in their numbers.[17]

Wolf and Coyote Bounties

An important aspect of the attempts to eliminate wolves from Iowa was the bounty system. Wolves were the main animal that the bounty system was established to try to control. The first bounty in Iowa was established in 1817 and called for a two-dollar payment for adult wolves. This payment must have been too high, for the law was repealed the next year. In 1834, Iowa became part of the Territory of Michigan, which had a five-dollar bounty on wolves. Two years later, Iowa became part of Wisconsin Territory, which had no bounties. The first session of Iowa's territorial legislature in 1840 gave counties the choice of whether to offer bounties, and many counties decided it was too expensive. In 1844, the territory required bounties and distinguished between coyotes and wolves, offering two dollars for adult and one dollar for young gray wolves, and one dollar for adult and fifty cents for young coyotes. Even though required, some counties apparently did not pay bounties. In 1858, the state passed its first bounty law, setting payment at three dollars for timber wolves and $1.50 for coyotes. Two years later, the payment was lowered to one dollar, and both species were

animals. Say's lists of the birds and mammals were the first for Iowa. In 1823, Say accompanied Long on a second trip, this time to northern Minnesota. Say's book, American Entomology, *established him as one of the founders of the science of entomology in the United States. In 1827, he moved to a commune in New Harmony, Indiana, where he died in 1834.*

Source: Weiss, H. B., and G. M. Ziegler. 1931. Thomas Say: early American naturalist. *Charles C. Thomas, Springfield, Illinois.*

lumped together under the term "wolf," a category that persisted in all later bounty laws. In 1892, the bounty was raised to five dollars for adults and two dollars for whelps, with stiff fines for individuals who presented false claims. Predictably, some people thought that the bounties were too low, so in 1913 the bounty was raised again to twenty dollars for adults and four dollars for whelps, the highest ever. After several more changes, bounties were set at ten dollars and four dollars in 1945.[18]

With bounties on wolves in effect in Iowa continuously since 1840, it is pertinent to ask what effect they have had on wolf numbers. Through the years, the bounty system has been open to abuse and fraud. Although bounties were supposed to be paid only for animals taken locally, there was no way to prevent people from bringing animals in from another county or state and asking for payment. The temptation was greatest if the amount paid differed between counties, or if a county did not pay bounties. Animals that died of other causes (e.g., road kills or disease) could also be claimed. Because counties typically asked for just the animal's scalp, fraud was possible. Clever people could manufacture several "scalps" from a single skin and make multiple claims. Also, if counties required different body parts (e.g, scalps, lips, or ears), multiple claims could be made on a single skin. One county auditor recalled seeing the same pelt presented for payment three times. Undoubtedly, many scalps of dogs or other mammals were presented as wolves for bounty payment. Another type of deception involved wolf farming. People who trapped or hunted wolves for their bounties would intentionally avoid killing all the wolves in their area, effectively farming the animals. One way they did this was by trapping just the young wolves and leaving the adults so they could continue to breed. This, of course, completely defeated the purpose of the bounty system, namely, to eliminate the wolves.[19]

The cost of bounties to the counties has been high. From 1909 to 1970, with one year of records missing, about $867,000 was paid for wolf bounties, an average of almost $14,000 per year. Annual payments were as high as $29,700 in 1915, when bounties were $20, but still were $18,000 in 1924, when the amount paid per animal was much lower. In general, bounty payments have been higher in counties along the Missouri River and in southwestern Iowa and relatively low in eastern Iowa.[20]

As far as eliminating "wolves" is concerned, the effects of the bounty system are mixed. The gray wolf has been eliminated from Iowa, at least in part due to the bounties paid for killing them. The loss of habitat certainly has also been a factor. In contrast, the coyote has at least held its own in the state. For a time, its numbers were much reduced, but it seems to have adapted to humans and now is doing quite well in Iowa.[21]

Epilogue

The status of both species of wolves has received considerable attention in recent years. Despite vigorous control programs, the coyote has expanded its range in this century so that now it occupies virtually all of the United States and most of Canada south of the arctic regions. Much of its range in the eastern United States is new for the species, but it seems to have adapted well to this area. Despite our best efforts to eliminate the species, it has thrived.[22]

In Iowa, coyote numbers began to increase in the late 1950s. This increase coincided with the continued clearing of timber. Presently, coyotes occur statewide, with the greatest numbers in southern and western Iowa and the fewest in the intensively farmed north-central region.[23]

Along with the increase in their numbers, there has been renewed interest in hunting coyotes. In recent years, the value of coyote pelts has increased greatly, and hunting coyotes for their pelts has somewhat replaced hunting them for bounty payments. In the early 1960s coyote pelts were worth only about one dollar each, but by the late 1960s they were worth about five dollars each, and in 1975–76 the price was fifteen dollars. Although not all coyote pelts are sold to fur buyers, there clearly was a dramatic increase in the harvest, going from fewer than one hundred in the early 1960s to more than 12,000 in 1974–75. In recent years, about 7,000–10,000 coyotes have been taken yearly by hunters and trappers in Iowa. Coyote pelt prices dropped in the 1980s, and the number taken has decreased.[24]

In contrast, the gray wolf's numbers declined and their range contracted in North America until about 1930. Intensive predator-control programs were an important factor contributing to their decline. The control programs have been curtailed in many areas, wolf numbers have increased, and the species has reoccupied parts of its former range. Currently, gray wolves are found in Alaska, Canada, and limited parts of northern United States, although they have not reoccupied much of their former range in the United States. Conservatively, about 30,000–40,000 wolves live in North America, mostly in Canada and Alaska. They are still the subject of intense controversy, and their future survival probably depends on how well humans will tolerate them and let them coexist with us.[25]

8. Foxes

The foxes are members of the canid family, a wide-ranging group of doglike predators. Two or perhaps three species of fox occurred in Iowa when pioneers first arrived in the state. These were the familiar red fox, the woodland-dwelling gray fox, and perhaps the swift fox of the Great Plains. Although all foxes were valued for their fur, they also were considered a threat to settlers' livestock and poultry. In Iowa, as in many other states, local governments often paid a bounty for each fox a person killed, thereby providing an additional incentive for settlers to kill foxes. Foxes seem to be very adaptable animals; despite the thousands that have been shot or trapped over the years, both the red fox and gray fox are still common in Iowa.

The red fox is the most abundant and widespread of the foxes in Iowa, and presumably it was also the most abundant when Europeans reached Iowa. However, little is recorded in the early literature beyond saying that it was present in an area. Although red foxes are adaptable and will inhabit a variety of habitats, they typically live on prairies or the edge of wooded regions, placing their dens on hillsides or along creek bottoms and hunting on nearby open areas.

The overall picture of red fox populations in the Midwest is one of change. Before Europeans arrived, red foxes were largely confined to the Great Lakes states but occurred as far south as northern Iowa. As the region was settled in the 1800s, red foxes expanded their range south and east. At the same time, their populations declined some in the North. This gradual shift in numbers continued until about 1930. Since then, red fox numbers have generally increased throughout the Midwest.[1]

Several factors probably account for this population shift. One is the habitat change that occurred as the region was settled. Settlers cleared forests and planted a variety of crops, creating a diverse landscape that seems to have favored red foxes. A second factor is competition among the various foxlike mammals. Gray wolves, once found throughout the region, were hunted relentlessly and soon disappeared from much of the Midwest. As wolves were eliminated, coyotes increased and replaced wolves in a number of areas, especially in the western parts of the region. In the areas where coyote numbers increased, red foxes tended to disappear in turn. Apparently, competition between red foxes and coyotes accounted for the decline of red foxes in the northern Great Plains, and it may have also affected fox numbers in Iowa, too. Finally, trappers and settlers reduced red fox numbers by killing many for their pelts or because they were considered pests. The combination of these factors seems to have led to major shifts in red fox numbers and distribution in the Midwest over the past century.[2]

The few specific early records of red foxes in Iowa suggest that they were rare or did not occur in central and southern Iowa in the early 1800s and that they invaded those areas after settlement. J. A. Allen said that they were not numerous in 1867 in the nine counties in west-central Iowa with which he was most familiar but were common to the north. Foxes (presumably red foxes) were considered numerous in Dickinson County until about 1875, but by 1922 they were found there only occasionally. In Sac County, they were common from 1880 to 1885, but then heavy trapping and the use of dogs to aid in hunting reduced their numbers. They were also poisoned there with strychnine, a means of control that was more common in states to the west. By 1917, only about one a year was caught in Sac County, indicating a considerable reduction in their numbers. Deermeat laced with strychnine was also used to poison many foxes in Ida County. Foxes were formerly common in the Charles City area but were largely gone by 1898 and were gone from the Algona area by 1910.[3]

In the late 1800s red foxes began to occur in southern Iowa. They first appeared in Washington County about 1866 and in Madison County about 1880. One killed in Johnson County in November 1894 was called the first local record. In the late 1800s and early 1900s their numbers increased in southern Iowa, and by 1910 they occurred statewide. A long-time trapper in Cedar County said that in the early 1900s the red fox was much more abundant there than the gray fox. Since originally that area probably was mainly gray fox country, this suggests that the switch to red fox predominance had already occurred there.[4]

In the 1930s, red foxes were still found statewide despite heavy hunting and a year-round open season. Data on pelts sold and estimates of the actual number of red foxes in Iowa provide some indication of population changes over the years. The number of red fox pelts taken in Iowa increased steadily from the early 1930s to the mid-1940s, reaching a peak of about 12,000 in 1946–47. In the 1950s only 2,000–3,000 were taken yearly, but by the late 1970s the take had increased again to 20,000–25,000 a year. Since then the harvest has declined steadily, and only 13,000 red foxes were taken in 1989–90. This harvest pattern mirrors the changes in pelt prices, showing the importance of the marketplace in determining the red fox harvest. Estimates of red fox numbers suggest that they peaked in southern Iowa in the 1950s, when there was at least one fox litter per square mile. During the 1950s, mange (a condition caused by a heavy infestation of mites on the fox's body) severely reduced their numbers in southern Iowa, but populations in northern Iowa increased, peaking about 1968. Since then, demand for fox pelts has been high. The increased intensity of agriculture in northern Iowa has resulted in a decline in good fox habitat, and their numbers have decreased in that part of the state, too. Currently, red foxes are found statewide but are most abundant in the northeastern half of Iowa.[5]

As in Iowa, the number of red foxes taken in North America has fluctuated greatly. More than 500,000 were taken annually in the mid-1940s, but that number dropped to fewer than 200,000 yearly in the 1950s, when pelts were almost worthless. The harvest increased again in the 1970s and peaked at more than 500,000 yearly in the early 1980s. Pelt prices peaked at more than $50 each and then dropped in value. Currently, the red fox still ranks as one of the most important North American furbearers.[6]

Economic Value of Red Foxes

Humans have long had mixed feelings toward foxes. Despite the mistrust humans generally have for foxes, they have also viewed foxes as an important economic commodity. Red foxes have long been one of the most valuable North American furbearers. However, few data are available on fur prices in Iowa. In pioneer days, red fox furs brought $1–$3 each in Marion County. Red foxes have several color phases, and pelts from the rare phases are the most valuable. While red fox skins sold for $1–$1.50 each in Sac County in 1864, the cross fox, a yellow-gray or reddish brown form, so-named for the dark cross-shaped pattern on its back, was worth $5. Silver foxes, which are black with silver tips to their fur, were worth $15. In recent years, red fox pelt prices have declined from a high of $64 in 1978–79 to less than $10 in 1989–90. In 1978–79, when both prices and harvest were high, the value of red fox pelts taken in Iowa exceeded $1.5 million. In most recent years, red foxes have ranked third or fourth in value among wild furbearers taken in Iowa.[7]

Another way that foxes were valued was for the bounties that were paid by the counties to anyone who killed a fox. For many settlers and hunters, the payments were viewed as an easy way to supplement their income. The state legislature first added red and gray foxes to the bounty list in 1860, setting the bounty at one dollar for each fox scalp presented to the county. Fox bounties were halted in 1897 and then reestablished in 1951, with the bounty set at two dollars. Through the 1950s all ninety-nine counties paid fox bounties, but in the 1960s many counties stopped payments, and by 1977 only one county still paid a bounty on foxes. From 1937 to 1980, more than two million dollars was paid in fox bounties, and yet Iowa fox populations reached an all-time high in the late 1960s. Clearly, the notion that the number of foxes could be reduced by putting a price on their head was not working.[8]

Until 1969, Iowa had a continuous open season on foxes. However, in the 1960s the number of foxes taken in Iowa increased greatly. There was concern that this heavy harvest would eventually reduce the fox population. Thus, in 1969 the state law was changed so that the season could be closed. By varying the timing and the length of the open season, wildlife managers now had a way to try to control the number of foxes that were taken each year and also to allow both hunters and trappers to take a share of the kill. Fur prices continued to climb during the 1970s, leading to an even higher kill and increased competition between fox trappers and fox hunters for a limited number of animals. There were some heated arguments between the two groups and concern that the arguments might lead to someone's getting hurt. Steps were taken to alleviate this management problem. To try to reduce the kill somewhat, the length of the open season was gradually shortened to about two months. A variety of opening and closing dates for hunting and trapping seasons were also tried. Unfortunately, when the two groups had different seasons, each group often thought that the other group was getting the better season. Finally, wildlife managers realized that having different seasons for the two groups was not feasible, and a single season was set for both hunters and trappers. This compromise seems to be working fairly well, although separate seasons for hunters and trappers might be better for the resource. Winter weather greatly affects the relative kill by the two groups. In winters with good snow cover, hunters usually take more foxes, while in mild winters the trappers have a larger harvest. Although red fox populations in Iowa are not in any danger, they need continual attention to insure that they are not overharvested. Somewhat lost in the controversy over seasons was concern for fox habitat in Iowa. Although foxes are very adaptable, they still depend on woods, fencerows, stream banks, and other similar "waste" land for their den sites and food. The continued loss of such habitat from Iowa threatens to reduce their numbers in the future.[9]

Various methods have been used to hunt foxes. Surprisingly, a few Iowa groups dress up in formal hunting attire and hunt foxes from horseback, using hounds to locate and drive the fox, much in the "genteel" eastern tradition. More commonly, Iowa hunters use dogs to chase the fox, while they follow on foot until the animal is cornered and they can make the kill. Another type of group hunt is the circle hunt, where a number of hunters surround a block of land and then gradually move toward the center of the block, hoping to kill the fox when it is cornered or when it tries to escape. In northern Iowa, when the ground is well covered with snow, some Iowa hunters drive the backroads and try to locate a fox resting on a hillside. Once a fox is located, they try to sneak up within rifle range and shoot the animal. Other hunters track foxes after a fresh snowfall and try to get within shooting range. In recent years, some hunters have used so-called predator calls to try to lure a fox close to them. These calls produce a high-pitched sound that supposedly imitates a dying rabbit. The fox is supposed to hear the call, get "curious," and approach close enough for the hunter to shoot it. Despite the variety of hunting methods available, the fox is a smart animal and provides a challenge to hunters who seek it.[10]

Likewise, foxes are a challenge to trap. Trappers depend on putting their traps in places where the animal normally travels or where they can attract the fox to the traps. Bait and scent are often used to attract foxes to the traps. This battle of wits often leads to frustration when a fox simply cannot be attracted to a trap.[11]

Gray Foxes in Iowa

The gray fox is a somewhat smaller animal than the red fox. Its favored habitats are woodlands and brushy areas rather than the open lands that the red fox favors. The gray fox's original range covered much of eastern United States. It also was found across the Southwest to California and Oregon.[12]

The gray fox, which had a more limited distribution in Iowa than the red fox, was found mainly in the wooded eastern and southern portions of the state. Few people were familiar with gray foxes, and they received less attention than red foxes from most early writers. Gray foxes were very common near Muscatine in the 1850s, but they were not especially numerous in west-central Iowa in 1867. They were found in Sac County but probably were not as common there as the red fox (only one man mentions seeing them). A large gray fox killed in Buchanan County in 1880 was considered a strange animal in that part of Iowa. By 1900, they had disappeared from northwestern and north-central Iowa. Originally common in Floyd County, they were seen there only occasionally by 1916. Thomas Stephens made no mention of them from the Spirit Lake region in 1922, and in 1937 Thomas Scott said they were found only in north-eastern Iowa. Hunting, trapping, habitat loss, and perhaps the poisoning program for wolves and coyotes are all possible reasons for their decline and disappearance from much of Iowa. Emmett Polder has suggested that beaver dams may have been important as den sites for gray foxes and that gray foxes disappeared with the loss of beaver from northwestern Iowa.[13]

Gray foxes seem to have recovered and expanded their Iowa range in the late 1930s or 1940s. From 1940 to 1950, there were numerous records of gray foxes from western Iowa, where they had not been noted in previous years, indicating that they were reoccupying that part of the state. Currently, gray foxes are found statewide, but they are uncommon in northwestern Iowa. They are also hunted and trapped but not nearly to the extent that red foxes are. Their fur is less valuable, and the wooded areas that they inhabit are harder to hunt. They are less abundant than the red fox but are not in any danger of disappearing from Iowa. In recent years, fewer than 1,000 gray foxes have been taken yearly in the state, a drop from the 1,000–2,000 gray foxes that were taken yearly from the mid-1970s to the late 1980s.[14]

The number of gray foxes taken in North America has been quite high recently, peaking at about 400,000 in 1979–80. The harvest has dropped some since then, but with their high pelt prices, they rank about sixth in value among North American furbearers. Based on their continued importance in the furbearer harvest, their population seems secure for at least the near future.[15]

Did the Swift Fox Occur in Iowa?

The third fox reported from Iowa is the swift fox. This Great Plains species formerly was found from southern Canada south to Texas and New Mexico. The swift fox, much smaller than either the red or the gray fox, is about the size of a large housecat. Its most distinctive characteristic is its large ears.[16]

Whether the swift fox ever occurred in Iowa may never be known. Some people called both red and gray foxes "swifts," so it is not always possible to know if writers were talking about those two species or the rarer swift fox. J. A. Allen, in his list of western Iowa mammals, includes this species based on an animal described to him that he thought undoubtedly was this species. Although he notes that it normally did not occur east of the Missouri River, western Iowa seemed to him similar in habitat to eastern Nebraska, where it did occur. Van Hyning and Pellett make no mention of the species in Iowa, and John Bowles lists it as unverified from Iowa. Two somewhat specific Iowa reports are the description of a swift fox that was smaller and not so cunning as other foxes in Calhoun County and the statement that the swift or kit fox was present in Shelby County. In the latter report, the writer makes no mention of other foxes, suggesting that his "swifts" might really be red or gray foxes. The most convincing reports are from Sac County. There, John Spurrell lists both the red and gray fox as present as well as a third smaller fox that lived on the prairie. It was about half the size of a red fox, with tracks the size of a domestic cat. This fox was variously described as lighter in color than a red fox or like a coyote but gray. Spurrell sent a description of one he saw to E. W. Nelson of the U.S. Biological Survey. Nelson's reply indicates that he thought the animal was a gray phase of the swift fox. Among the trappers that Spurrell interviewed, one said he trapped his last swift fox in 1857, another took six in 1858 and then no more, and the third took one in 1862. Because Sac County was settled in the mid-1850s, swift foxes, if they did occur there, must have disappeared soon after settlement. Their skins sold for twenty-five to thirty cents each. In 1867, six small foxes, with dark heads and faster movements and called swift foxes, were turned in for a bounty of one dollar each in Pocahontas County. The last mention of a swift fox in Iowa was by A. A. Mosher, who said a fox that trappers called the "swift" was still found in the Spirit Lake area in 1882. It was about half to two-thirds the size of the common (red) fox and lighter in color.[17]

Since then, there have been no additional reports of swift foxes in Iowa, and it is unlikely that they will inhabit Iowa in the future. Swift foxes were easy to trap, and they also were often killed by poison baits set out for coyotes and other predators. They once were very rare throughout their range but seem to have recovered some in recent years and are still found close to Iowa in parts of Nebraska and South Dakota.[18]

9. Furbearers

One of the major economic attractions that stimulated the exploration and settlement of large areas of central North America was the wealth that could be earned by trading for and selling the furs of various mammals. Several countries actively sought this trade. The first major traders to move into the Midwest were the French. From the French settlements in eastern Canada, they followed the natural water route of the St. Lawrence River and the Great Lakes but rarely traveled as far as Iowa. After the French turned over their North American colonies to England in 1763, British and Spanish traders actively sought furs in Iowa. In the 1760s and 1770s, Spanish traders from St. Louis traveled upstream along both the Mississippi and Missouri rivers. Along the Mississippi, they went as far north as the Des Moines River valley, while on the Missouri River they reached the area where Council

Bluffs is now located. There are few records of this fur trade, but certainly some traders moved up the Des Moines and other rivers that penetrated central Iowa. Late in the century, Spanish land grants led to the establishment of more permanent trading posts near Montrose in Lee County, McGregor in Clayton County, and Dubuque, which was the first permanent European settlement in Iowa. In 1800, Spain sold its holdings west of the Mississippi River to France.[1]

British traders were also active in the region. From major trading posts along the Great Lakes, they traveled as far south as the Des Moines River valley to carry on their trade. France's sale of the Louisiana Territory to the fledgling United States in 1803 added a new player in the fur trade in the upper Mississippi region. The United States moved quickly to consolidate its claim to the region. The Lewis and Clark expedition in 1804–06 helped open the Missouri River valley to fur trading, and soon trading posts were established near Council Bluffs and Sioux City. To protect its new territory, the United States began to establish posts along the Mississippi, including one at Fort Madison in 1808. Fort Crawford at Prairie du Chien, Wisconsin, across the Mississippi River from present-day McGregor, was established in 1816 on the site of earlier trading posts. For a number of years it served as a center for fur trade from much of eastern Iowa. In this early trade, much of the actual trapping was often done by Indians, who then brought the pelts to the post and traded them for various goods. At first deerskins and beaver pelts were the most important items, but as fashions changed, other species also became important. As a result of this early trade, certainly the populations of some furbearer species were reduced by the time more permanent settlers entered Iowa in the 1830s.[2]

When permanent settlers entered Iowa, furbearers continued to be an important commercial commodity. In fall 1844, Asa Blood and six others traveled from Buchanan County to Clear Lake in Cerro Gordo County and trapped there for about a month. They caught nineteen beaver, sixteen otter, thirty to forty raccoon, and assorted other furbearers and sold their catch for $350. One writer claims that in the first few years after settlement in northwestern Iowa, settlers earned more money from fur trapping than from farming. In Emmet County, trapping was the principal business of some settlers, and for some it provided the cash they used to purchase land. Several accounts give an indication of the economic potential of trapping. Three men trapped $7,000 worth of furs in Palo Alto County in 1858, and one man made $75 in one day. In the late 1860s through the mid-1870s, when hordes of grasshoppers consumed the grain crops for several years, trapping was a major source of income for many settlers.[3]

The techniques used by most trappers were simple and labor-intensive. Some men trapped full-time in the winter, living in a primitive shelter on the trapping grounds and staying there all winter or until supplies ran out. Perhaps typical were five men from Pocahontas County who spent six weeks trapping in Osceola County in the winter of 1870–71. At that time, Osceola County was largely unsettled prairie land. The men lived in a dugout along the Ocheyedan River, the frozen earth forming the roof to their shelter. Heat came from a fire in one corner of the single room. Apparently, trapping was poor, and they did not get much return for their efforts. At least they survived; other trappers were not so fortunate, and some died when they ran out of food or were caught away from shelter in bad weather. Full-time trapping was not an easy way to earn a living.[4]

Several species of furbearers, including bear, fox, wolf, mink, muskrat, raccoon, otter, and weasel, were abundant in Iowa at the time of settlement. Fur returns from the Western Outfit of the American Fur Company, the major United States firm, provide some evidence of the trading activity and relative importance of various species. The territory of that section of the company included trading posts at Prairie du Chien, Wisconsin, and Fort Mendota, Minnesota. From 1835 to 1838, they handled more than 700,000 muskrat and only 1,241 beaver, indicating the importance of muskrat even in those early days. Other important species included deer (29,906), raccoon (20,868), and mink (15,669). Although these were not all taken in Iowa, it is reasonable to assume that many Iowa-caught pelts passed through the outfit. Several of these species are discussed in other chapters and will not be mentioned here. For others, the record is sketchy and little can be said other than that they were found in Iowa and were trapped. The emphasis in this chapter is on three of the most important furbearing species, the muskrat, otter, and beaver. These three, besides being important furbearers, also illustrate the population changes that some furbearing mammals underwent during the settlement of Iowa.[5]

As was typical for wildlife in general, furbearers were considered a resource to be exploited, and at first there was no concern to regulate the harvest. The first state restriction on furbearer trapping in Iowa seems to have been passed in 1872, when the season for beaver, mink, otter, and muskrat was closed between 1 April and 1 November. There is little evidence that this closure was actively enforced, and beaver and otter populations continued to decline despite the nominal protection.[6]

Muskrat

The muskrat was probably the most abundant furbearer found in Iowa at the time of settlement. Muskrat, which inhabit ponds, lakes, marshes, streams, and rivers, were especially abundant on the prairie marshes of north-central and northwestern Iowa, where they were the most important furbearer that settlers trapped. In Greene County, early settlers considered muskrat hides one of their most profitable crops. Somewhat surprisingly, one writer says that muskrat did not appear in the Webster City area until the early 1850s, several years after settlement. They soon became abundant in the area and were a mainstay of the trapping industry.[7]

One of the first records of muskrat trapping in Iowa is the report of 1,353 pelts valued at twenty-five cents each ($338.25 total) in the inventory at the trading post at Fort Madison in 1809. The price for muskrat pelts varied over the years but generally was in the range of fifteen to twenty-five cents apiece, although it was as low as three to eight cents each in Des Moines in 1866. Two trappers in Pocahontas County trapped 1,835 muskrat in six weeks in 1870 and sold them for $300, about sixteen cents per skin. In Sac County, muskrat skins sold for eight to ten cents each in 1857 and ten to fifteen cents each in 1870. Spurrell says that at that time, a trapper could make good wages at ten cents a skin. Other prices recorded include five cents each in the Webster City area around 1850, twenty cents each for prime skins in Buchanan County in 1863, and ten cents per pelt in Harrison County in the 1870s. As late as 1865, Indians still trapped muskrat near Perry and received three cents for each pelt. Flickinger's claim that muskrat skins were worth twenty to thirty-five cents each in Pocahontas County in the late 1850s and 1860s is higher than other accounts.[8]

Besides their ordinary cash value, muskrat skins were at times treated like money in a barter economy. A person buying a small item at a store might pay for it with a raccoon skin and receive a rabbit or muskrat as change. Flickinger says that during the bank crisis of 1857, the muskrat hide was a more reliable form of currency than paper money. In early years, trapping, especially for muskrat, was the only way that some settlers could get cash to pay their taxes.[9]

Few records of the trapping take of individuals exist. The two Pocahontas County trappers mentioned previously received $300 for six weeks' work in 1870. Herkimer Norton of Fonda was paid $105 for one month's catch and $500 for the winter; besides muskrat, his take included a few otter and mink. Three men trapped 6,250 muskrat in the winter of 1870–71 in Sac County. That year, muskrat skins sold for twelve to fifteen cents each, so the men probably grossed $750–$937 for their catch.[10]

Besides the trappers, dealers who acted as brokers also profited from muskrat. Theodore Dunn of Fonda took in 2,000 hides from one group of trappers on just one day in 1878, a year when prices were high. In the winter of 1878–79, 57,000 muskrat skins were shipped from Pomeroy alone.[11]

Prime marshes with many muskrat were valuable property, and sometimes squabbles arose over who had trapping rights to a marsh. In December 1878, four trappers from Sioux Rapids moved into an area of Pocahontas County that local trappers already had claimed for the season. When the locals asked them to leave, the intruders said that they would not and that they would defend "their area" with guns if necessary. The next day, eight local people went to the trappers' cabin and ordered them to leave at once. There were probably some heated words exchanged, but eventually the intruders left and no blood was shed.[12]

One of the more interesting anecdotes about muskrat in Iowa involves two of the most famous criminals of the 1800s, Jesse and Frank James. In the late 1860s, after establishing their notoriety, this pair disappeared for some time before resurfacing in June 1871, when they robbed a bank in Corydon, Iowa. Not surprisingly, one story claims that the James brothers spent part of that time in Iowa. A Palo Alto County man claimed that two men who bought 1,800 muskrat pelts at thirteen cents each from him were the James brothers. He said he recognized them from wanted posters that came out after the Corydon robbery, and he recalled that they had used a hundred-dollar bill as part of their payment. It will probably never be possible to substantiate this story, but it adds an interesting footnote to the history of trapping in Iowa.[13]

Muskrat generally were caught with steel traps set near or at their lodges. Because they were easy to catch and did not take the skill that some other furbearers required, muskrat were trapped by many settlers. If the ice was clear, it was also possible to spear them through the ice. One man speared seventy-five in one day in Pocahontas County. Orin Sabin recalled spearing muskrat through the ice at Spirit Lake in 1892 and selling them for five cents each.[14]

Another use of the muskrat was for its meat. Muskrat flesh is edible, and settlers often used the hindquarters for food. This was a source of jokes on individuals who did not understand what the expression "eating a rat" meant. One story relates how a new settler in Pocahontas County ate breakfast at his neighbor's house. The newcomer thought he was eating chicken and was taken aback when his hosts told him he had been eating muskrat meat.[15]

Muskrat reproduce rapidly, and even when large numbers are taken, they are almost impossible to eliminate through overtrapping. Thus, although huge numbers were trapped in Iowa, muskrat were not extirpated from the state as some other furbearers were. Apparently, there was some concern about muskrat numbers in the 1920s, and they were given full protection in Iowa from 1925 to 1928.[16]

Although there certainly are fewer muskrat in Iowa now than at the time of settlement, that is mostly because there is much less habitat now. Muskrat are still an important part of the trapping industry in Iowa. Most years they are the most numerous furbearer taken in Iowa, with more than 700,000 taken in some years. The ease of capturing them has encouraged many neophyte trappers to develop their skills by trapping muskrats. Fur prices vary from year to year but generally are in the range of a dollar or two per pelt, much more than early trappers received but, considering inflation, not really an increase at all.[17]

Muskrat are also one of the most valuable furbearers in North America. In 1982–83, about 7.4 million muskrat were taken in North America. The value of their pelts was about $28 million, making it the second most-valuable furbearer on the continent.[18]

River otter (hereafter called otter) were once found throughout most of the United States and southern Canada. Otter are almost always found near water, where they feed on fish, crayfish, and other aquatic animals. They are one of the largest and most valuable of the furbearers. The numerous records of otter in Iowa at the time of settlement suggest that they were fairly common then, but few specifics are given. In general, it appears that otter were largely gone from Iowa by about 1890. Since then, there have been a number of reports, most of them along the Mississippi or Missouri River.

One of the first notices of otter in Iowa is the listing of 176 skins valued at two dollars each at Fort Madison in Lee County in 1809. In Sac County, they were numerous in the mid-1850s. One man took five there in one day in 1856, for which he received \$2.50–\$3 per pelt, and one was sold in Des Moines in 1866 for \$10, a high price for those days. Otter pelts sold for \$5–\$15 each in Pocahontas County in the 1850s and \$8 each in Buchanan County. A forty-pound individual was taken in Emmet County in 1886, when pelts sold for \$5–\$7 each. At Webster City in the 1850s, otter skins sold for seventy-five cents to a dollar per foot, a pricing system that encouraged trappers to stretch the skins a bit. Some of the range in prices is probably due to the variation in the size of the animal involved.[19]

By the late 1800s, otter began to disappear from much of Iowa. Several taken in Pocahontas County in 1881 may have been the last for that county, and by 1882 A. A. Mosher said they were no longer present in Dickinson County. Herbert Osborn indicated that they disappeared from Linn County about 1880, and one taken near Cambridge in spring 1881 was one of the last for central Iowa.[20]

The last otter reported from southwestern Iowa was killed in Shelby County near Kirkman in 1895. An otter caught on the Wapsipinicon River in Buchanan County in 1898 was one of the last for that part of the state. Clement Webster said a few were left on the Little Cedar River in Floyd County in 1900, and John Smith thought only about half a dozen were left on the Des Moines River in Kossuth County in 1910. In 1912 and 1913, individuals were caught in Floyd, Sac, Marion, and Monroe counties. Otter commonly wander, and some of the later records probably represent such individuals. Except for the northeastern corner of the state, where they may never have been wiped out, otter were certainly gone from most of Iowa by 1900.[21]

The loss of otter from Iowa occurred with little notice or comment. Habitat loss may account for some of the decline, but unregulated trapping was probably more important. Otter fur was valuable, and certainly heavy trapping pressure was a factor in their decline. Otter are fairly easy to catch with steel traps set along their runways, near dens, or on their slides. Because they and beaver commonly live in the same areas, otter are often caught in traps set for beaver. It is probably not coincidental that both species declined and disappeared from Iowa at about the same time.[22]

From about 1915 to 1955, little was written about otter in Iowa, and presumably they were absent from most of the state. Two, however, were trapped near Smithland in Woodbury County in 1929, and a small population persisted along the backwaters of the Mississippi River and its tributaries in northeastern Iowa. By 1958, they were established in northeastern Iowa from the Minnesota border south along the Mississippi River through Jackson County. By 1970, that range had extended further south along the Mississippi River to the Davenport area, and a few were also present along the Missouri River. However, most of the interior of Iowa had no otter.[23]

Currently, the river otter is considered a threatened species in Iowa. In 1985, the Iowa Department of Natural Resources began a program to try to reestablish otter in parts of Iowa where they had been absent for many years. Otter obtained from Louisiana were released in several areas of Iowa (fig. 4). The first release of sixteen otter was made in March 1985 at Red Rock Reservoir near Runnells. The animals survived well, so more were obtained. From 1986 to 1990, an additional 206 otter were released at ten other sites throughout Iowa (map 8). It is too early to tell, but perhaps these releases will provide the nucleus for a population that will spread and reoccupy much of Iowa.[24]

On a continental basis, the harvest of otter has increased to about 40,000 annually in the early 1980s. Although this is small compared to the harvest of some other furbearers, it is not clear whether the rate can be sustained. The continued loss and alteration of the wetland habitats that otter inhabit are factors that will require constant attention if this species is to survive.[25]

Fig. 4. River otter release at Peterson, Iowa, in May 1987. Courtesy Lowell Washburn.

Beaver

When Europeans arrived in North America, the beaver was one of the most abundant furbearers they found. From an estimated population of sixty million in 1500, beaver were trapped and hunted relentlessly until perhaps only 100,000 survived by 1900. During the 1700s and 1800s, the beaver was the most widely sought furbearer in North America and was the backbone of the North American fur industry. Beaver pelts were used both for coats and for felt for hats. In the 1830s, fashions changed and silk hats began to replace felt hats. This quickly led to a drop in prices and a decline in the demand for beaver pelts.[26]

The beaver, like the muskrat and otter, was abundant throughout Iowa at the time of settlement. It, too, was found almost strictly near water, living along rivers and streams where it built its familiar dams and lodges. More than the otter or muskrat, the beaver was actively trapped well before Iowa was officially opened for settlement. By the late 1700s, there were a few trading posts scattered along the major rivers of Iowa, and certainly the beaver was a major trading item at these posts. The inventory

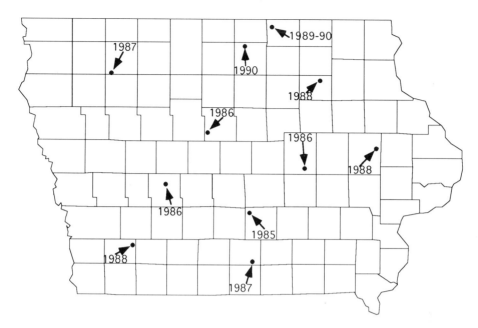

1987

1989-90

1990

1988

1986

1986

1988

1986

1985

1988

1987

at Fort Madison in Lee County in 1809 listed 710 pounds of beaver skins valued at two dollars per pound. Native Americans were an important part of this early trade. An Indian chief was said to have trapped sixty beaver at the headwaters of the Boyer River in the winter of 1819- 20. One of the early surveyors in northwestern Iowa said that Indians caught beaver by probing into their dens with a pole with a hook on the end and snagging the animal.[27]

When Iowa was opened for settlement in 1833, beaver were still common to abundant throughout the state, and many observers made note of them. As with other wildlife, settlers often named geographic features after the beaver. The numerous Beaver Creeks and a town in Boone County remind us of this furbearer. Like the other furbearers, they were seen as a ready source of cash and were actively sought by trappers. They soon disappeared from much of the state. Beaver were numerous in Kossuth County in the early 1850s, so much so that in 1854 their noise kept a survey party on the Des Moines River awake all night. However, they were much less common in Kossuth County after the severe winter of 1856–57. There were many dams on the Des Moines River in Kossuth County in the 1860s, indicating at least a temporary recovery, but by 1910 the animals were gone. By 1867, J. A. Allen thought they were largely gone from eastern and southern Iowa. Despite the establishment in 1872 of a closed season for beaver between 1 April and 1 November, their numbers continued to decline. They were once plentiful in Allamakee County, but the last one there was trapped in the early 1880s, about the same time that they disappeared from Johnson County. There were still a few in Dickinson County in 1882, but by the 1920s those, too, were gone. Seven trapped in 1886 were the last reported in Sac County. One was taken in Cherokee County in February 1887, and a few were still present in Linn, Tama, and Harrison counties in 1890 or 1891. About fifteen beaver, including a fifty-five-pound individual, were trapped near Irwin in Shelby County in 1888. Although several experts said beaver became extinct in Iowa in the 1890s, a few were still present in Ida and Pocahontas counties in 1904.[28]

Despite the value of beaver fur, little has been recorded on specifics of trade for their pelts. In the early days, they sold by the pound, as evidenced by a value of two dollars per pound for those on hand at Fort Madison in 1809. In western Iowa in 1819–20, beaver skins were exchanged evenly, by weight, for brass kettles. The skins were bundled into packs of one hundred pounds, each of which contained seventy to eighty skins. At the time, a pound of beaver skin was worth about three dollars in St. Louis, so individual skins were worth about $3.75–$4.25 each. The price was about two dollars per pound in the mid-1800s; because an average-sized beaver pelt weighed about a pound, or slightly more, the typical price for each animal had dropped somewhat since earlier in the century. William Ingham bought $700 worth from one trapper in Kossuth County, probably in the mid-1850s, but he does not give an individual pelt price. Pelts sold for $3.50–$5 each in Emmet County and $5–$15 in Pocahontas County in the 1850s. The rapid disappearance of beaver from Iowa certainly suggests that they were easy to trap. One man caught six beaver in seven nights in Sac County. Presumably he could have caught more, but he used only one trap. One trapping technique often used was to cut holes in the beaver's dam and then set traps in the damaged areas. When the beaver attempted to repair the damage, it was easily caught.[29]

After their disappearance around 1900, beaver soon reinvaded the state from the northwest. Beaver were found in Iowa in 1930, and by 1936 they had occupied most of the Missouri River valley and many of its tributaries. Between 1937 and 1943, the

Iowa Conservation Commission live-trapped beaver from western Iowa and stocked them in central and eastern Iowa. Beaver were released in Jackson (1940), Muscatine (1940 and 1941), and Lee (1941) counties. A population peak was reached about 1946–48, after which their food supply became limited and their spread through Iowa slowed. In the fall of 1949, the trapping season for beaver was reopened for the first time in many years, and about 2,500 were taken. Trapping results showed that by 1952 beaver were found in almost every Iowa county, a remarkable recovery. Since then, beaver have continued to maintain their populations throughout Iowa. In recent years, the number of beaver taken annually in Iowa has fluctuated, reaching a peak of 18,500 in 1988–89.[30]

In North America, from a population low in the early 1900s, beaver numbers and harvests have increased fairly steadily. In the early 1980s, 500,000–1,000,000 pelts were sold annually. However, beaver pelts no longer bring the prices they once did and have dropped to less than ten dollars each in recent years. Thus, the beaver has fallen behind the raccoon, muskrat, red fox, and coyote in the overall value in the North American fur trade.[31]

Besides their pelts, beaver have long been valuable in other ways. They were used for food, and the extract from their scent glands was used in early medicines. The wetlands that form behind their dams provide habitat for a variety of wildlife and also prevent valuable topsoil from eroding downstream. In the wrong places, though, beaver can be a pest, and conservation agencies frequently get complaints from landowners. The water that accumulates behind their dams may flood croplands, parks, roads, and other human developments. The trees they use for their dams and food may have been planted for some special purpose; when beavers cut down those trees, it does not endear them to humans. Beaver also may feed in croplands, and, given their size, they can eat a lot of corn or other plants in a short time. In the 1980s, this damage was estimated to total $75–$100 million annually in the United States, far exceeding the value of their pelts. Still, beaver are a fascinating wildlife species, and most humans have welcomed their return to Iowa.[32]

Other Furbearers

Besides the three species already considered, a number of other mammals, including several members of the weasel family, were trapped for their furs. One of the most important was the mink. One writer claimed that in Ida County mink traps were baited with live prairie-chickens, an indication of the abundance of the prairie-chicken at that time. Ellison Orr recalled trapping six to twelve mink per winter near Postville in the mid-1870s. Mink pelt prices were quite variable and ranged from $1.50 in Van Buren County in 1854, $5 or more in Pocahontas County in the 1850s, and $3 in Floyd County in the 1850s, to as low as fifty cents in Des Moines County in the 1850s and seventy-five cents in Van Buren County in 1859 and 1861. In northwestern Iowa, mink were very plentiful in the late 1850s, and their fur commanded a high price. At times, mink skins, like muskrat hides, were used as legal tender. According to Fred Phippin, in the 1870s or 1880s John Gilbert of Spirit Lake once bought 750 mink skins, not paying more than seven dollars apiece for them. When the price went up to thirteen dollars, he still sold them for seven dollars because he was an agent and did not want to harm the buyer he worked for. Herbert Osborn said mink were sought out by early trappers, and he thought that their numbers were much reduced by 1905. As late as 1915, eleven mink skins sold for thirty-seven dollars in Shelby County, indicating little increase in price from the pioneer days.[33]

Mink are still trapped in Iowa and elsewhere, and their fur is valuable. In most recent years, 20,000–30,000 mink have been taken in Iowa, but in 1989–90 the harvest dropped to only 8,300. The total North American harvest of wild mink rose from a low of fewer than 50,000 annually in the early 1900s to almost 800,000 annually in the 1940s. It has since dropped to about 500,000 in the 1980s. However, the farm-mink industry has grown and reduced the demand for wild mink, so that wild mink pelts no longer command the high prices they once did. In the early 1960s, wild mink accounted for twenty-five percent of the value of the wild fur industry in the United States, but by 1970–76 the figure had dropped to only three percent. Several factors, including a change in fashion away from short-haired furs, a greater reliance on farm-raised mink, and the movement of mink ranches from the United States into foreign countries, account for this dramatic change.[34]

Raccoon were also trapped, although they receive surprisingly little mention in historical records. At the trading post at Fort Madison, 3,585 raccoon skins were listed as worth $896.25, only twenty-five cents apiece, in 1809. Bonebright-Closz, who settled near Webster City in 1848, said they trapped hundreds of raccoon and sold the pelts for less than fifty cents each in Des Moines. Four were worth eighty cents each in Shelby County in 1915. During the 1970s and 1980s, raccoon were the most valuable furbearers in Iowa. Their long fur was fashionable, and prices were relatively high, with a peak price of about thirty dollars per pelt in the late 1970s. In the late 1980s, prices dropped rapidly to less than five dollars per pelt. Raccoon have adapted well to humans, so that sizeable populations live within most towns and cities as well as in the countryside. Raccoon are not only trapped but also actively hunted. Even with this heavy exploitation, their numbers seem to be doing well. During the late 1970s and 1980s, about 300,000 raccoon were sold yearly to fur dealers in Iowa, with a peak of 390,000 in 1986–87. About equal numbers are taken by trappers and hunters.[35]

The success of the raccoon is not confined to Iowa. Raccoon seem to be highly adaptive and currently thrive in a variety of habitats, including some that place them in close contact with humans. Their range has expanded and the number harvested in North America has increased greatly since the 1930s. Raccoon currently are the most important furbearer in North America. In the early 1980s, about 4.2 million raccoon pelts were taken annually. Their value in 1982–83 was $94 million, more than three times the value of the next most-important species, the muskrat. To date, they show every indication of being a species that can coexist well with humans.[36]

10. Passenger Pigeons

One of the most distressing stories in the history of North American wildlife is that of the demise of the passenger pigeon. Although similar in appearance to our familiar mourning dove, the passenger pigeon was larger, about thirteen to sixteen inches in length. Its body was slender with a long pointed tail and a small head. The head of the male was slate blue, the back of the neck had shiny iridescent feathers, and the throat and chest were a rich russet. The rest of the bird was largely brown or gray. Females were somewhat smaller than males and similar but duller in color.[1]

Most observers of birdlife in the early 1800s agree that the passenger pigeon was the most abundant land bird on the entire North American continent. Even if Alexander Wilson's estimate that a flock that flew over him near Shelbyville, Kentucky, in about 1806 numbered two and a quarter billion birds is exaggerated, their numbers must have been stupendous. Each spring, huge flocks of passenger pigeons left their wintering grounds in the southern United States and flew north to feed and nest in the extensive oak, beech, and chestnut forests in the Great Lakes states and southern Canada. At the nesting colonies, single trees might contain dozens of nests, and the colonies themselves often covered several square miles. One incredible colony in central Wisconsin in 1871 covered an area of 6–8 miles by 125 miles. Since the pigeons nested in such enormous colonies, they had to find areas where huge food supplies were available during the nesting season. The trees that provided their food—mainly oak, beech, and chestnut—typically produced large crops of nuts once every several years. Thus, the nesting colonies usually moved from year to year, and the pigeons themselves were somewhat nomadic. The pigeons and their young were easy to catch or shoot, and tremendous numbers were taken and shipped to markets. The persecution of the birds was relentless, especially in the 1870s and 1880s, and the pigeons simply could not produce enough offspring to offset the mortality rate. Their numbers decreased rapidly, so that only scattered flocks remained by the 1890s. The last passenger pigeon died in the Cincinnati Zoo in 1914. The species deserved better than that.[2]

Migration

Iowa was at the western edge of the major migratory pathways of passenger pigeons and at the southern edge of the main breeding range. Most records of passenger pigeons in Iowa are from the eastern half of the state, especially along the Mississippi River. In most years, migrating flocks appeared in mid-March, but in some years they appeared as early as mid-February. In the 1860s or early 1870s, W. J. McGee saw an estimated 600,000,000 near Dubuque in one day. Apparently, some years pigeon flocks migrated through central Iowa. John Smith noted that a person could see a hundred flocks in a day along the Des Moines River near Algona but said that there never was a great migration flight up the Des Moines River.[3]

The flocks were described as being wider than they were long, so that waves of birds, stretching from horizon to horizon, would sweep by in succession. In spring, flights might last two or three days, although most birds passed by in a single day. The flocks flew at a height of 100–150 feet and often cast a shadow on the ground as they passed. In late afternoon, the migrating pigeons landed in a clump of trees to roost for the night. The birds rapidly filled up every inch of space on the branches, and late arrivals often attempted to land on the backs of the earlier arrivals, causing a constant uproar in the roost. Sometimes the birds were packed so tightly that their weight was enough to break off branches five or six inches in diameter.[4]

After the nesting season, the pigeons dispersed and fed on a variety of berries and other food. The individual flocks in fall generally were smaller than those in spring. In Iowa, there are few records of the southward flights. The fall flocks that McGee saw in western Dubuque County were much smaller and more scattered than those in spring. The southbound birds passed through Iowa from mid-September to as late as mid-October.[5]

Nesting

Although passenger pigeons must have nested regularly in the woodlands of north-central and especially northeastern Iowa (map 9), few accounts of nesting were recorded. The best is that of Ellison Orr, a Waukon naturalist and archaeologist who grew up near Postville in Allamakee County. Orr's account describes a nesting area extending along the Yellow River from Moneek in Winneshiek County through Allamakee County to the Mississippi River and encompassing an area about twenty miles long and two miles wide. Nearly every tree in the area had at least one nest, and larger trees might have one or two dozen nests or more. The nest itself was a simple thin platform of sticks and weeds, through which the single white egg was visible from the ground. Orr does not give a year but says he was very young when he saw this large colony. Orr was born in 1857, so this probably occurred sometime in the mid-1860s. He says the old nests remained in the trees for at least six years after the nesting, and scattered pairs of nesting birds were still common in the area in the 1870s. Orr provides the last record of a nest in northeastern Iowa (and the last reported for Iowa), one he found in the late 1880s or early 1890s north of Postville in Allamakee County. Sadly, he took the egg for his egg collection.[6]

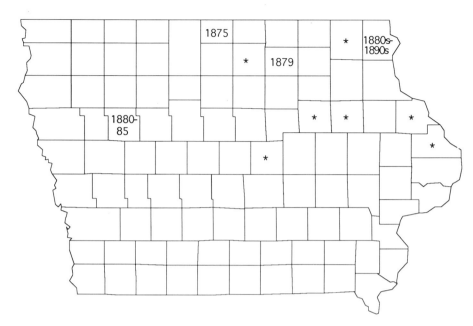

Map 9. Nesting records of passenger pigeons in Iowa. Date indicates year of last nesting in each county. An asterisk indicates a county where passenger pigeons nested but with no specific date for the record.

Orr suggests that large numbers of pigeons nested in that area only once, at least according to his memory. This is not unexpected, for many of the nesting colonies were used once or for a few years and then the birds moved on. Their transience was at least partly due to persecution by hunters who killed the adults and knocked the young out of the nest. Such an easy source of meat must have attracted settlers from miles around.

Another large nesting concentration is hinted at by the presence of many passenger pigeons near Independence in June 1858. Large numbers of pigeons at that time of the year almost certainly meant that they were nesting nearby, probably in the woodlands along the Wapsipinicon River. Other than that, most nesting records in Iowa are of just a single nest or a few nests. The westernmost nesting report in Iowa is from Sac County, where about twenty pigeons were said to have nested in a grove of trees north of Wall Lake sometime between 1880 and 1885. The open prairies of that part of Iowa are different from the usual nesting habitat of this species, but the observer, John Spurrell, generally was accurate on other wildlife he reported from that era.[7]

McGee said that considerable numbers of pigeons nested in

western Dubuque County. However, his claim that the nests had two eggs rather than the usual single egg and the scattered pattern of the nests strongly suggest that he was referring to the similar but smaller mourning dove rather than the passenger pigeon.[8]

Exploitation of Passenger Pigeons

Passenger pigeons were commonly used for food, for the fat that the young birds contained, as targets for pigeon shoots, and on some occasions as food for pigs. Schorger, using a variety of sources, gave mixed reviews for how good pigeon meat tasted. Judging from the millions that were shipped to markets and the high market demand for the birds, they must not have tasted too bad. Homer Seerley, who grew up in Keokuk County in the 1850s, wrote that he had eaten so much pigeon and prairie-chicken that he longed to eat a domestic chicken.[9]

Passenger pigeons were taken by humans in several ways. The simplest way was to use long poles to knock the flightless young birds out of the nest. Adults were also knocked down from roost trees at night and swiftly dispatched.

Birds often were shot, although it seems likely that for the average person shooting was used only when birds could not be taken by other, cheaper means. Orin Sabin recalled that his father never shot at pigeons; there was too great a chance of missing the rapidly flying pigeons, and why take the risk when he could count on shooting six to ten mallards or five or six prairie-chickens with one shot. The cost of shells or bullets made it expensive to shoot such a small bird unless the person could afford to do so just for sport. Sport hunters used shotguns to shoot birds in pass shooting, gathering at places where many birds flew by during migration or on their way to roosting or feeding areas (fig. 5). A more common method was to shoot the birds in their roost trees at night. One could hardly miss, given the way they concentrated then. Orr claimed that his father once killed nine roosting pigeons with one shot from a squirrel rifle when the birds were lined up on a sloping limb. The story sounds good anyway.[10]

Commonly, flying birds were killed by knocking them from the air with long sticks. Passenger pigeons were swift flyers but

Fig. 5. Shooting wild pigeons in Iowa. From Leslie's Illustrated Newspaper, *21 September 1867.*

often flew low, just clearing trees, hills, or other obstacles in their path. Orr describes how, when the birds were flying into a headwind along the Mississippi River in northeastern Iowa, they would turn and fly up lateral stream systems and then barely clear the bluffs that rimmed the valleys. Boys and men hid in the brush near the tops of these bluffs and knocked the birds from the air with long cane poles as the flocks swept by. Sabin offers an account of a similar experience near Spirit Lake. Hiding behind a low willow hedge, farmers knocked the birds down with willow sticks. Local farmers had even cut off the tops of some of the willows, creating a notch in the hedge so the pigeons would fly lower and be easier to kill. His account is notable because the big flight he recalls occurred in 1891, one of the last records from Iowa, and because the birds generally were not found so far west in Iowa.[11]

Nets were also a popular way to catch pigeons. Several different types of net were used, all with great effectiveness at different times. Roosting birds often were caught in a long net attached to two long poles. Several men at each pole held the net aloft and positioned it near a tree full of roosting pigeons. Torches were

Ellison Orr,
1857–1951

Born in a log
house near
McGregor, Ellison
Orr attended
school in nearby
Postville, taught
school there, and
later farmed. In
1904, he moved to
Waukon, where he
worked for a bank
and a telephone
company. He
spent most of
the rest of his life
in Waukon. After
he retired,
Orr worked for
the Iowa
Archaeological
Survey and made
extensive
collections of
artifacts left by
Native Americans
of the area. Orr
also was a keen
observer of the
wildlife and
recorded a
number of his
observations on
birds of the region.
In particular, his
recollections of the
passenger pigeons
he saw as a child
in northeastern

held on the side of the tree opposite the net, and then sticks or stones were thrown into the tree to disturb the pigeons. In the uproar, the pigeons would fly away from the torches and into the net. When the weight of the birds in the net indicated it was full, the net was lowered and the birds removed. A variation of this method involved using a funnel-shaped net with a collecting bag at the narrow end and wing nets extending out from the sides to lead the birds toward the funnel.[12]

Orr gives a detailed account of the netting methods used by professional pigeon catchers. Such men followed the pigeons throughout the year, keeping track of pigeon movements by telegraph. At each place they found pigeons, they hired local farmers to haul the birds to the nearest railroad and then shipped the birds to markets in larger cities like Chicago and Milwaukee. The netters used a twelve-by-twenty-foot net of one-inch mesh to catch pigeons. Wherever they found pigeons nesting or gathering, the netters sought out a likely nearby feeding area, often a field near a grove of trees. Grain was bought and spread over the ground for a few days to lure the pigeons to the field. Once pigeons were using the site to feed, a net was set up with its ends tied by rope to two springy poles. The net was then loosely piled on the ground alongside the bait site, and the ropes to the spring poles were held in place by a trigger device at each end of the net. The trapper hid nearby and waited for the pigeons to land at the bait site. He held a string which, when pulled, released both triggers, causing the spring poles to pull the net up and then drop over any pigeons feeding on the bait. The netter then killed the pigeons, piled them out of sight, and reset the net for another catch. This net is very similar in principle to the rocket nets that modern-day wildlife biologists use to catch a variety of animals.[13]

As a further attraction for the pigeons, stool pigeons were often used. Such birds were attached by a line to the trapper and were left sitting on a hinged perch near the bait site. When the trapper saw a pigeon flock nearby, he would release the hinge on the perch and the bird, suddenly losing its perch, would flutter to the ground. Presumably, the flock of wild birds would think that the stool was dropping down to feed and would land to feed with it. Other netters used flyers as lures—pigeons that had their eyelids sewn shut. Again, when a flock of pigeons approached, a flyer with a line attached to it was thrown into the air. The flyer would flutter to the ground, looking like a bird landing to feed. Judging by the size of the catches, stool pigeons must have been very effective in attracting birds to the bait sites.[14]

Birds taken in Iowa were either consumed locally or shipped to out-of-state markets. Ed Volkert of Dubuque used a net that was thirty by sixty feet. He took as many as 1,500 birds in one morning and sold the live birds for ten cents each to be used as targets for trapshooting. The crippled birds were killed and sold by the barrel, which went for a dollar on the market in Chicago. In the 1860s, farmers trapped the birds with nets set in their wheat fields and sold them by the wagonload in McGregor. One observer saw three large wagons, with sideboards attached to increase their capacity, filled with pigeons caught in one night's work in a roost.[15]

Birds that were killed for the market were not cleaned but were packed whole in a barrel and covered with ice for shipment. The waste from such methods must have been incredible, for a delay in shipping commonly meant that the shipment would spoil and have to be thrown out. Although no figures are available to judge the size of the market kill in Iowa, it certainly was not as great as the kill in Wisconsin or Michigan, where hundreds of thousands of pigeons were shipped to market. Nevertheless, thousands of birds must have been taken in Iowa and shipped, mainly to markets in Milwaukee or Chicago. Prices varied considerably from year to year and even seasonally. From 1871 to 1875, pigeons sold for forty cents to $1.50 per dozen in Milwaukee. In 1880 they sold for $1.25 to $1.75 per dozen in Chicago, while in 1882 prices in Milwaukee ranged from forty cents to $1.25 per dozen.[16]

Iowa are the most detailed record of the species in early Iowa.

Sources: Field, H. P. 1951. Ellison Orr— 1857–1951. Journal of the Iowa Archaeological Society 1:11–13. Keyes, C. R. 1945 Ellison Orr: naturalist, archaeologist, citizen. Iowa Bird Life 15:26–28.

Passenger Pigeons as Pests

Pigeon flocks often were a nuisance to farmers in spring and summer. At those times, the birds commonly fed on wheat and oat seed in fields. Since this was before the time of much farm machinery, crops were planted by hand; a person would walk across the field, scattering the seed. Then a harrow, consisting of a wooden frame with steel teeth projecting from it, was dragged across the field to cover the seed with dirt. Flocks of pigeons would gather on the fields and feed on the grain seed before it was covered. Orr noted that as the flocks moved across the field, the birds at the trailing edge of the flock would find all the grain gone and would fly over the other pigeons to get to the leading edge of the flock where grain was plentiful. Other pigeons would follow suit, and soon the flock would look like a whirlwind, moving rapidly across the field as the pigeons ate all the seed the farmer had sown. As a child, Orr said he often was chosen to watch the field and scare off the pigeon flocks until the seed could be covered by the drag.[17]

Epilogue

The impact of the heavy exploitation of passenger pigeons in Iowa and elsewhere gradually became apparent. One writer says the last major flights in Iowa, in which thousands of birds flew by continuously for several days, occurred in 1859. Although they did not occur every year, major flights passed by in 1855, 1857, and 1859. Another flight in 1854 lasted three days and also was very large. Flocks that were several miles long were seen at Montpelier in Muscatine County until at least 1857. Passenger pigeons disappeared from Delaware County about 1867; another observer says the last great flights in Iowa were in 1868 or 1869, when huge clouds of pigeons swept across the sky, the lines of birds extending as far as one could see. Another flight, somewhat smaller, passed by a year or two later, and after that pigeons were seen much less frequently.[18]

By the 1870s, there were strong signs that the number of passenger pigeons passing through or nesting in Iowa was declining. According to Moran, there were lots of pigeons in Clinton County until 1871. Large flocks went north that year but did not return; in 1876 he saw his last birds in the county. Frank Bond saw several large flights in eastern Iowa from 1872 to 1875 but noted that they were not nearly as large as those described earlier in the century. W. J. McGee said he saw only occasional flocks in Dubuque County in the early 1870s, and by 1876 even those no longer appeared. Passenger pigeons were still common enough in 1875 that George Poyneer, an enthusiastic hunter from Clinton, killed thirty in one day on an island in the Mississippi River. Nauman said flocks in southeastern Iowa in the years just after the Civil War obscured the sun, but by 1880 these were gone.

After 1880, the numbers reported in Iowa dwindled rapidly, and at most only small flocks were seen by the 1890s.[19]

The last passenger pigeons reported in Iowa were two in Linn County in 1901 and three in Kossuth County in 1903. These birds may have been misidentified, but Clement Webster, a long-time observer of Iowa's wildlife, claimed he saw one in Charles City in 1898. The last verified record for Iowa, a young male shot near Keokuk in September 1896, is now at the University of Michigan. Similar stories can be told for the rest of the passenger pigeon's range. Market hunting for pigeons hit its heyday in the 1870s, and the species' numbers declined rapidly in that decade. Large nesting concentrations were reported in Wisconsin in 1885 and 1887 and in Pennsylvania in 1886. However, their colonial nesting habits meant that hunters could concentrate their efforts in a small area, and few young survived. Flocks and nesting colonies continued to be reported into the mid-1890s, but the numbers mentioned were usually dozens or a few hundred birds rather than the thousands described only a few years earlier. They were persecuted even as laws giving them some protection were passed, and the end of the 1800s brought with it the demise of the passenger pigeon. The last verified record of a wild bird is one killed in Pike County, Ohio, in March 1900. There are numerous questionable records from after that time, including a few from Iowa, but the fate of the pigeon had been sealed. With the wild pigeons gone, the only ones that remained were a few captive birds at several zoos. Most of them were old, and their breeding record was poor. These birds gradually died off until only a single old female named Martha remained at the Cincinnati Zoological Gardens. She died on 1 September 1914 at age twenty-nine years, and the species was gone.[20]

Although numerous theories have been raised to try to explain the extinction of the passenger pigeon, the continued exploitation, including the harassment of nesting colonies (some years the pigeons produced no young), played a major role. The logging of the forests in which they nested probably hurt them as well. A recently proposed idea is that the loss of mast-producing trees triggered the species' decline. As the remaining habitat became increasingly fragmented into smaller and more isolated woodlands, the pigeons were less able to locate adequate food supplies for raising their young. Human exploitation may have

Fig. 6. Plaque at Wyalusing State Park in southwestern Wisconsin commemorating the demise of the passenger pigeon. Courtesy Mike Meetz.

DEDICATED
TO THE LAST WISCONSIN
PASSENGER PIGEON
SHOT AT BABCOCK, SEPT. 1899.
THIS SPECIES BECAME EXTINCT
THROUGH THE AVARICE AND
THOUGHTLESSNESS OF MAN.

hastened their decline, but habitat loss alone may have been enough to cause the species' extinction.[21]

A memorial plaque for the passenger pigeon was erected in Wisconsin's Wyalusing State Park, just across the Mississippi River from Iowa's Pikes Peak State Park near McGregor (fig. 6). It reads in part, "This species became extinct through the avarice and thoughtlessness of man." Probably little more needs to be said.

11. Prairie-Chickens

Two closely related species of grouse inhabit the grasslands of North America. The lesser prairie-chicken inhabits the drier prairies from Kansas and Colorado south into Texas and New Mexico. The greater prairie-chicken, the species that occurred in Iowa, was once found from southern Canada south to Texas and from Colorado east to the Atlantic Coast. Two subspecies of the greater prairie-chicken inhabited coastal prairies: the heath hen lived along the Atlantic Coast from New Hampshire to Virginia, while the Attwater's prairie-chicken occupied the Gulf Coast of Texas and Louisiana. By 1870, the heath hen's range was limited to Martha's Vineyard, an island off Cape Cod, Massachusetts; the last individual had disappeared from there by 1932. Attwater's prairie-chicken numbers have diminished as the coastal plains of Texas have been settled, and in spring 1990 the popu-

*Besides the greater
prairie-chicken,
another prairie-
inhabiting grouse
was once found in
Iowa. The sharp-
tailed grouse, a
bird of the brushy
grasslands typical
of the drier regions
of the Great
Plains, was found
by the early settlers
in northwestern
Iowa. Most early
writers called both
species "prairie
chickens," and
thus it is not
possible to know
which species the
writer means. As
Iowa's prairies
were converted to
agriculture,
sharp-tail
numbers declined,
and the species
soon disappeared
except for a few
birds that
migrated into
Iowa to spend the
winter. The last
definite record of
a sharp-tail in
Iowa was in the
1930s. In 1990,
the Iowa*

lation was estimated to number only 470 birds, most on or near a refuge near Houston.[1]

The greater prairie-chickens that lived on grasslands in interior North America fared somewhat better. As Europeans settled the Midwest, they created ideal habitat conditions for greater prairie-chickens. Thus, as settlers moved west, prairie-chickens expanded their range north and west and occupied areas that originally were inhabited by the closely related sharp-tailed grouse. Within a few decades, though, habitat conditions changed again, and prairie-chicken numbers began a long-term decline that has continued to the present time. Currently, prairie-chickens are most abundant in eastern Kansas, and only remnant populations survive in Illinois, Wisconsin, Minnesota, North Dakota, and Colorado.[2]

The Prairie-Chicken in Iowa

In Iowa, prairie-chickens were once found statewide wherever there was suitable grassland habitat. Although they were common at the time of settlement, there is evidence that prairie-chicken numbers increased over much of the state after settlement, especially in the nonwooded sections. The early settlement pattern created a landscape checkered by numerous small fields of various grain crops, hayfields, pastures, and remnant stands of native prairies. This landscape probably provided ideal prairie-chicken habitat, including food, winter and nesting cover, and exposed areas where males gather to display to females (called booming grounds). Under these conditions, the birds flourished, and their numbers peaked in the 1870s or early 1880s.[3]

Unlike most grouse, some prairie-chicken populations are migratory. In the 1800s, several observers noted regular migrations of thousands of prairie-chickens to and from Iowa. In fall, these flocks tended to fly to the southeast, and in spring they flew back to the northwest, indicating that Minnesota and the Dakotas were their source. The birds usually flew low, 20–50 feet above the ground, so that they were just skimming over treetops. Hunters often took advantage of this and shot many as they flew by. The flights were most obvious at dawn and dusk, suggesting that the birds rested part of the day and that the migration was rather leisurely.[4]

In winter, the local nesting birds along with migrants from the north often gathered in flocks of 200–300 or more birds in old grain fields and stubble cornfields. Williams, writing in 1884, describes a winter flock near Charles City that in flight was half a mile long, fifty yards wide, and three to four birds deep. If each bird occupied an area of two by two yards and the birds were three deep, the flock contained 33,000 birds, a number unimaginable today.[5]

Hunting Prairie-Chickens

Because of their abundance and the ease with which they could be killed, prairie-chickens quickly became one of the major game species hunted by early settlers in Iowa. During the peak prairie-chicken years in the 1870s and 1880s, tens of thousands were killed. Local hunters shot or trapped many, both for their own use and for sale on the market. Professional market hunters came to Iowa and killed chickens to ship to markets in the East. The birds also attracted hunters and sportsmen from Iowa cities as well as from Chicago and other out-of-state cities, who generally traveled by train and stayed in a small town or on a farm, hunting in the nearby countryside. Based on the number of birds killed on some of these hunts, prairie-chicken numbers must have been stupendous.

Various methods were used to hunt prairie-chickens. At times, the birds were so plentiful that they could be shot right in a farmyard or even from a window. Sitting birds were occasionally shot with a rifle, but usually a shotgun was used. Some knowledge of the bird's habits and movements generally increased hunting success. In fall, one of the favorite methods of sport and market hunters was to hunt fields after the grain had been harvested. The stubble fields (wheat, rye, and barley were said to be the best) often held many prairie-chickens feeding on the waste grain. The birds tended to gather near the edges of the fields, especially from dawn to midmorning. In midmorning, they moved to thicker cover, such as prairies, standing corn, or hayfields. Late in the afternoon, they returned to the stubble to feed again. Some hunters simply waited at a point where they could intercept birds moving from field to field and shot the birds as they flew by.[6]

A more popular method, especially for sportsmen, was to hire a team of horses and a wagon for a day (fig. 7). With a team and dogs, one or two hunters would strike out at dawn and begin a day of hunting in the stubble fields. Prairie-chickens formed cov-

Department of Natural Resources released thirty-seven sharp-tailed grouse in Monona County, but it is not clear whether this restocking attempt has been successful.

Source: Johnsgard, P. A., and R. E. Wood. 1968. Distributional changes and interactions between prairie chickens and sharp-tailed grouse in the Midwest. Wilson Bulletin 80: 173–188.

Fig. 7. Group of
hunters with horse-
drawn wagon
ready for a day of
hunting near
Granger, Iowa, c.
1880. Courtesy
State Historical So-
ciety of Iowa, Des
Moines.

eys of about five to sixteen birds, so the hunters depended on the dogs to find the covey and point them. It was claimed by some that dogs used to hunt in forests in the East were useless in Iowa and that the best dogs were those that had been trained to hunt in large fields. Some hunters let the dogs do all the running and got out of the wagon only when the dogs had pointed a covey, while others walked the edge of each new stubble field.[7]

In general, prairie-chickens were tame and could be approached closely before they flushed, so shooting them was fairly easy (fig. 8). Birds missed on the first flush did not fly far and could be flushed again. The birds that were shot were put in the wagon and cleaned later. In northwestern Iowa, market hunters would take a cask of ice in the wagon. By putting their kill on ice immediately, the hunters could preserve the birds until they returned to the nearest train station, where the prairie-chickens were packed in barrels and later shipped east. Other hunters gutted them and stuffed them with a wad of hay. If hung in a cool place, the birds would stay fresh for a week if the weather was not too warm.[8]

Although some of the land was open prairie and readily accessible, by the 1880s much of Iowa had been settled, and hunters might encounter a farm that was posted no trespassing. Wilson Sawyer, who market-hunted near Spirit Lake in 1887, said he usually considered this an indication that hunting would be excellent on that land and hunted there anyway. He wrote a colorful account of how the landowner was handled. Whenever a

farmer, sometimes even with a pitchfork in hand, was seen approaching, Sawyer's group of hunters would hastily take out a bottle of whiskey they kept especially for this occasion and pretend to be taking a short break from their hunt. They would greet the farmer with sweet talk and offer a drink from the bottle. Sawyer said this technique usually subdued the farmer's hostility and kept the hunters from being jailed for trespassing.[9]

The number of prairie-chickens killed on some of these hunts boggles the mind. Hunting contests were held yearly in Delaware County from 1864 to 1866. One man shot 103 birds in 1864; in August 1866 two teams, each with twenty-two men, killed a total of 916 prairie-chickens. Two hunts in Marshall County, probably in the early 1860s, had a similar kill. One party killed 708 prairie-chickens south of Marshalltown, while another group of six killed 311 in one day. A hunter in Buchanan County claimed he shot 157 chickens in one day with 150 shots. In 1869, four hunters took 337 near Independence in a day and a half. Although these are extremes, clearly thousands of prairie-chickens were killed yearly in Iowa.[10]

Prairie-chicken hunting could also have tragic endings. In August 1872, two teams of Boone County hunters had a competitive three-day hunt to see who could shoot the most prairie-chickens. The losing team was to treat the winners to dinner at the best hotel in town. As hunters were reporting in at the end of the hunt, one of the top hunters reported his kill (fifty-five birds) and slapped his hand against his thigh to emphasize the total. Unfortunately, his dog took the sound as a signal to come to its master, jumped from the wagon where it had been sleeping, and knocked over a loaded gun. The gun discharged and killed the man. A total of about 1,500 prairie-chickens was taken in the three days, but there was no banquet that night.[11]

Trapping Prairie-Chickens

Despite all the prairie-chickens that were shot in Iowa, some observers suggest that even more were caught in a variety of traps. In 1894, a writer in western Iowa complained that dozens of traps could be seen along the roads near Onawa and that more prairie-chickens were trapped than were shot by sportsmen and market hunters. Many people had spare time during the winter, and prairie-chickens provided a supplement to their diet and an extra cash crop from their land. Trapping would have been cheaper and easier, and, given the market for the birds, it probably would have been more profitable than hunting with a gun. The birds were abundant and were easy to catch. Also, prairie-chickens tended to get wilder and harder to hunt later in fall, and their winter flocks were difficult to approach. Thus, trapping was the most feasible way to take them at this time of the year. At least two different types of traps were used, drop-door traps and figure-four traps.[12]

The drop-door trap consisted of a box with a door at the top (fig. 9). Traps often were made of laths and might measure four by four by eight feet. The door, usually just a shingle, was hinged and counterbalanced with an arm that held several ears of corn. Brush, sticks, or other materials piled around the trap forced birds to stand on the door to get at the corn. Once the bird was on the door, its weight pushed the door down, dropping the startled bird into the trap. The counterbalance then pulled the door back up and automatically reset the trap for the next bird. Up to a dozen birds could be caught in one baiting of the trap, and one man said he once caught twenty-three in a single set. If the birds were not eaten immediately, they were salted and hung to dry like beef or frozen whole for later use.[13]

The other type of trap was a figure-four trap, a drop trap in which a box or cage was placed over a bait station. One side of the trap was supported by three sticks, notched in such a way that they would hold up one side of the trap until an attached string was pulled or a bird bumped into the sticks. The configuration of the sticks when the trap was propped open looks like the num-

ber four, hence the name. The trap was baited, and then the operator waited for birds to visit it or else checked the trap periodically to see if birds were using it. Four or five birds often could be caught in one set.[14]

Several writers indicate that prairie-chickens were a problem in crops, especially buckwheat, which they seemed to be very fond of. They also took corn and would feed on both standing corn and corn in shocks. One young boy in Muscatine recalled being paid ten cents per day in the 1850s to keep them out of wheat fields. In the 1860s, prairie-chickens were considered a pest near Panora because they fed on wheat and corn. This reputation as a pest provided another inducement for settlers to catch prairie-chickens.[15]

Markets for Prairie-Chickens

Although many prairie-chickens ended up as dinner for whomever caught or shot them and others undoubtedly were left to rot, there also was a good business in selling the birds. In the days before refrigeration, fresh (or nearly fresh) meat was in demand, and prairie-chickens were an important part of that market. Most of the time the birds were frozen whole and then shipped to market. There is one report of a merchant who stewed and canned the meat before shipping it east, but that was un-usual. For the private table, often the breast meat was dried and salted before being stored for later use. Although most writers indicated a fondness for prairie-chicken meat, predictably at least one said he ate so much of it that he longed for domestic chicken.[16]

Market hunting for prairie-chickens dates back to territorial days in Iowa. One of the earliest records of market hunting is the report of one hundred taken from Maquoketa to Dubuque in December 1842. Few figures remain to tell us how great this market was, but it is reasonable to assume that some years fairly large numbers were sold. Prairie-chickens could be bought for twenty-five cents a dozen in Burlington around 1840 and $1.50 per dozen in Muscatine in 1854. In 1858, quail and prairie-chickens worth $1,300 were shipped from Iowa City to New York City. One dealer alone shipped thirty dozen prairie-chickens that year. S. H. Greene recalled selling prairie-chickens in Dallas County for fifty cents a dozen in the winter of 1859–60. In De-cember 1863, one man in Buchanan County (evidently a dealer) sold $350 worth of prairie-chickens in one day, and sales of $50 to $100 were frequent. In 1864, three carloads of prairie-chickens were shipped from Marshalltown to Chicago at a price of two dollars per dozen. At about the same time, birds shot or trapped in Harrison County were said to get two to four dollars per dozen. In the 1870s, whole frozen birds sold for twenty-five cents apiece in Buchanan County. About 1870, Abraham West, who lived near North English, trapped and sold more than $400 worth of prairie-chickens in one winter for fifty cents apiece, a price that seems a bit high compared with other prices given for the period. In the winter of 1871–72, a firm in Waterloo shipped 3,600 prairie-chickens to the East Coast.[17]

H. Clay Merritt, a market hunter from Illinois, wrote the most comprehensive description of market hunting in Iowa. He first hunted in Iowa in 1861, when he bought prairie-chickens for one dollar per dozen and then shipped them to Chicago. From 1870 to 1872, he hunted near Cresco and shipped his birds from Prairie du Chien, Wisconsin, to New York City. He packed them in wooden boxes, separating layers of birds with layers of ice, straw, and sawdust. In 1871, he shipped 400 dozen prairie-chickens and claimed he lost only seven birds due to spoilage. He made a profit of $500 in a month. In 1872, he built a freezer in Cresco in which he froze and stored his birds before shipping them. However, he attempted to economize on ice, and some of the birds spoiled. The poor quality of the birds and the large number of birds flooding the market caused him to lose money that year.[18]

Merritt also noted that market prices fluctuated from year to year. In 1856, prairie-chickens sold for a dollar a pair, a price that dropped to 75–85 cents a pair by 1860. During the early part of the Civil War, prices dropped to only 25–65 cents per pair, but by 1864 they reached $1.25, and in 1865 they were up to $1.50 per pair. During the rest of the 1860s, prices remained around $1.12 to $1.25 per pair. In the 1870s, they dropped a bit but generally remained around a dollar per pair. Prices also varied seasonally, tending to be lowest in December when supplies were greatest and then gradually rising after Christmas.[19]

Population Decline

Prairie-chickens probably could have survived the high mortality they suffered from hunting and trapping if habitat conditions had remained favorable for them. However, during the late 1800s, Iowa continued to be settled and the human population increased rapidly. As a result, more land was farmed, and the landscape continued to change. Prairie-chickens breed fairly early in spring and usually use the thick, rank vegetation standing from the previous fall as cover for their nests. As the human population grew, the small stands of prairie grasses, pastures, weed fields, and other "waste" land that provided nesting cover were planted with crops, and nesting habitat disappeared.

Most writers suggest that prairie-chicken numbers peaked in Iowa in the 1870s or early 1880s and then began a long downward slide. The combination of the change in habitat and continued hunting, both legal and illegal, was too much for the chickens, and by the 1880s their numbers started to decline. They declined first in eastern Iowa, but by the 1890s the decline was also noticeable even in their traditional strongholds in north-central and northwestern Iowa. As early as 1887, John Smith, a hunter and conservationist, said: "I do not see any help for them [prairie-chickens] in the state of Iowa." There simply was not enough "waste" land for them to survive. By 1898, Clement Webster lamented that daily bags had dropped from 30 to 150 to only 7 or fewer birds per hunter. Locally, prairie-chicken numbers had their ups and downs. An observer in the Waterloo area

Herbert Quick,
1861–1925

One of Iowa's
most notable
authors, Herbert
Quick was born in
Grundy County
and spent his
childhood in the
Steamboat Rock
area. He became
a teacher, working
in several small
towns in Iowa,
and then became
a lawyer. He
practiced law in
Sioux City, where
he also served a
term as mayor.
Eventually, he
settled on a career
as a writer. His
best-known books
are The Hawkeye
and Vandemark's
Folly. *His*
autobiographical
One Man's Life
describes his
experiences
growing up on the
prairies of Iowa.
In this work, he
frequently
describes the
wildlife that he
encountered
during the early
days of settlement

noted that they were scarce there in the early 1870s, abundant in the early 1880s, scarce in the late 1880s, common in the late 1890s, and scarce again by 1909. In general, by 1900 prairie-chickens were uncommon over most of Iowa, although favorable weather during the breeding season probably boosted populations locally in some years. From then the pattern was largely one of steady decline, even after hunting was banned in 1917.[20]

A variety of factors probably had an effect on their numbers. Prairie-chickens, like other grouselike birds, seldom live more than two or three years. They have the potential to produce many young in one year, so their populations can rebuild rapidly from high mortality that might occur during a harsh winter. Still, several bad years in a row can have a great effect on their numbers. Certainly, the heavy hunting and trapping mortality they experienced from about 1860 to 1900 and especially from 1880 to 1900 had a severe impact on their numbers. A common complaint was that many birds were shot before the hunting season officially opened (15 August before 1878 and 1 September starting in 1878). This meant that young birds that could barely fly often got shot.[21]

Up until about 1880, the habitat in Iowa was probably better for prairie-chickens than it was before settlement. The planting of various small-grain crops provided a ready food supply, and as long as pastures and hayfields provided good nesting cover, their numbers increased or at least held their own. Toward the end of the century, though, habitat change probably became a factor in their decline. More land was cultivated, and the marshes that had provided good winter and nesting cover were drained. Gradually, prairie-chicken numbers began to decline. Fred Pierce of Winthrop noted that although domestic hay provided good nesting cover, many prairie-chickens were killed and their nests were destroyed when the hay was mowed, ironically the same problem that the introduced ring-necked pheasant now faces.[22]

Another threat was fire. Farmers commonly burned the grasslands and prairies each spring to remove the standing dead plants and to try to control grasshoppers. If left undisturbed, this residual cover provided excellent nesting habitat for prairie-chickens. When grasslands were burned, many prairie-chicken nests were destroyed in the fire. It was common practice for people to gather eggs from the nests after the fire had passed. The cooked eggs were eaten at once, while fresh eggs could be stored for later use. The number of eggs (prairie-chickens usually lay about ten to fourteen eggs per nest) that could be gathered gives an idea of the abundance of the species. Herbert Quick recalled gathering as many as 200 eggs after a single fire in Grundy County in the late 1860s or early 1870s, and a farmer near Spirit Lake found thirteen dozen eggs after one fire in 1885.[23]

Yet another threat to prairie-chickens was mortality from collisions with barbed wire and utility lines. Prairie-chickens fly low, and many birds flew into these wires and were killed. The result of this overall high mortality and loss of habitat was the decline and eventual disappearance of prairie-chickens from Iowa.[24]

in Grundy County.

Source: Andrews, C. 1970. Prose poet of the prairie. Iowan 19:23–27, 53.

Laws Affecting Prairie-Chickens

In spite of their abundance, prairie-chickens were one of the first wildlife species to receive protective legislation in Iowa. The first bill to provide protection for prairie-chickens in Iowa was passed in the 1856–57 legislative session. The bill closed the hunting season from 1 February to 15 July. For the next several years, seasons were changed slightly, and in 1862 the closed season was set to last from 1 February to 1 August. An attempt to provide more protective laws in 1866 was postponed indefinitely when the committee chairman spoke out against the birds. He claimed that because of damage caused by prairie-chickens, settlers were unable to raise their crops. In 1868, the closed season was extended to include January. All these laws pertained only to shooting; trapping was supposedly allowed only in December. Also, the laws did not limit trapping or shooting on one's own property as long as the game was for private use, an obvious loophole.[25]

An 1874 bill prohibited market hunting except from 15 August to 1 December but left the rest of the year open to hunting. Market hunting was prohibited outright in 1876, and in 1878 the season was closed except from 1 September to 1 December, a season length that was left intact for most of the remaining years that prairie-chickens were hunted in Iowa. That same year, a landmark law setting a bag limit of twenty-five prairie-chickens per day was passed. By current standards, this does not seem to be much of a limit, but it was a significant reduction for those days. Still, one wonders what effect it really had when a five-to-six-day fall hunt in western Iowa by four men in 1881 averaged fifteen to thirty birds per gun per day. Game-law enforcement was still largely a dream for the future. The final law change for prairie-chickens was a reduction in the bag limit to eight in 1915, only two years before the season was closed for good.[26]

Even with protective legislation on the books, the laws were seldom enforced, and the prairie-chicken population declined. Some complaints were registered about the lack of enforcement, but most seem to have been one group's complaining that another group got birds before they could. Although sportsmen complained that local farmers killed all the birds before the season opened, they then saw nothing wrong with taking more birds than they could use when the season was open. In 1884, three Decorah men were each fined $38 or thirty days for shooting prairie-chickens before the opening of the season, the first time the law was enforced in Winneshiek County. Still, hunters in Charles City felt it necessary to hire their own game warden in 1896 to ensure that the laws were obeyed. That same year, writers in Sioux City and Nevada complained of seeing prairie-chickens sold in the market and served in restaurants in their towns.[27]

In northwestern Iowa in 1891, it was said that the young birds were openly hunted in July and August, well before the season began. Birds were shot and frozen by the barrel at the nearest icehouse before being shipped east. Clearly, legislation had little effect on halting the decline of prairie-chickens in Iowa.[28]

Epilogue

After 1900, the prairie-chicken population continued to decline. Even when hunting was stopped in 1917, the decline continued. By the 1930s, the only nesting prairie-chickens in Iowa were about one hundred pairs in Wayne and Appanoose counties on the Missouri border, a few near Spirit Lake, and perhaps a few other isolated birds elsewhere. Flocks continued to show up in fall and winter, such as the 500 found near Livermore in Humboldt County from 1935 to 1940, but clearly the golden days were over. Many of the reports after about 1925 probably record vagrants from other states rather than birds that were nesting in Iowa. The migrants may have augmented local breeding populations and helped the species persist in the state after its population was no longer self-supporting.[29]

Soon, the only remaining nesting chickens in Iowa were those

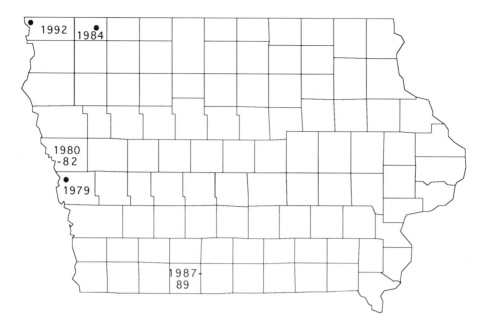

Map 10. Recent records of greater prairie-chickens (circles) in Iowa and sites of the two recent releases of greater prairie-chickens.

in Wayne and Appanoose counties, the northernmost birds of a population that persisted in Missouri. Even there, drainage and cultivation of grasslands led to further declines in their numbers. The estimated fifty in Appanoose County in 1952 dwindled to ten in 1954, only one in 1955, and then none. A few other stragglers and migrants were reported elsewhere, but in reality the species was gone from Iowa. Periodically since then, individuals have been seen in Iowa, such as one in Harrison County in 1979, another in Osceola County in 1984, and one in Lyon County in 1992.[30]

In 1900, ring-necked pheasants, a species native to China, were introduced into Iowa. Pheasants now are found statewide, and they are easily the most numerous upland game bird in the state. Pheasants seem to be more aggressive than prairie-chickens and sometimes lay their eggs in prairie-chicken nests. They also may disrupt them on their display grounds. Throughout the Midwest, the prairie-chicken seems to have been unable to survive in areas with good pheasant populations. Thus, competition with pheasants may have been the final straw in the disappearance of prairie-chickens from Iowa.[31]

In recent years, there have been several attempts to restore at least token populations of prairie-chickens in the state (map 10).

In February 1980, the Iowa Conservation Commission released fifty-three prairie-chickens on a hillside prairie in the loess hills east of Onawa. These were wild birds that had been caught in Kansas and traded to Iowa. After the release, there were some scattered sightings and then the birds disappeared. A similar release of forty-nine birds in 1982, this time with some of the birds equipped with radio transmitters so their movements could be followed, had similar results. The transmitters showed that many birds quickly left the steep prairie ridges where they were released and moved to the nearby flatlands of the Missouri River floodplain. Since these lands are almost entirely covered with crops, it is doubtful that they could find suitable nesting cover. A few birds persisted for several years and then they also disappeared.[32]

The most recent stocking attempt was made in south-central Iowa. From 1987 to 1989, 254 prairie-chickens were released in Ringgold County, where there are numerous grasslands and pastures on both private and state-owned land. These birds have established four display grounds and have produced several broods, indicating some initial success for this release.[33]

Despite this cause for optimism, the potential competition with pheasants is a problem that needs to be addressed. In order to reduce such competition, it may be necessary to control pheasant populations in areas where prairie-chickens are released. The state of Illinois already is trying to control pheasant numbers near the sanctuaries it has established for its remnant prairie-chicken populations. In the meantime, the bird is gone from Iowa, and there is little likelihood that a population will get established in the state by natural means. Thus, Iowa, which once had some of the finest prairie habitat in North America and was at the very center of the greater prairie-chicken's Midwest range, no longer supports a native population of the bird most symbolic of prairie habitat.[34]

12. Wild Turkeys

Wild turkeys figure prominently in the hunting lore of North America. Native Americans made extensive use of turkeys for food and used turkey feathers for clothing and ceremonial purposes. European settlers soon found that turkeys were good-tasting. Thus, turkeys were one of the most important game birds for settlers as they moved west. Turkeys occurred over most of the eastern United States west to Arizona, Colorado, and South Dakota. One expert conservatively estimated the pre-Columbian turkey population in the United States at ten million birds. Turkeys are versatile in their habitat requirements, living on grasslands as well as in woodlands. The presence of acorn-producing oak trees was often a major factor in determining where they were found. Although turkeys are wary birds, they are easy to kill, especially at night, and thus they were rapidly

Althea Sherman,
1853–1943

One of the most
interesting of
the pioneer
ornithologists in
Iowa, Althea
Sherman was
born in Clayton
County. In 1865,
she moved with her
parents to the tiny
settlement of
National, also in
Clayton County.
Sherman
attended Upper
Iowa University
and later
graduated from
Oberlin College,
where she received
both an A.B. and
a master's degree
in art. She
taught at
Carleton College
in Minnesota
and in public
schools in Tacoma,
Washington. In
1895, she
returned to
National to care
for her parents
and stayed there
the rest of her life.
A meticulous
observer of
wildlife, she
published

killed off over large parts of their original range. Because of heavy hunting pressure and habitat loss, their numbers declined drastically. By the 1930s, it was estimated that fewer than 30,000 turkeys were left; by 1949, in the eastern United States, wild turkeys were found on only about twelve percent of their original range.[1]

Turkeys in Iowa

When settlers first arrived in Iowa, they found the wild turkey common to abundant in the forested regions of the state. There are numerous records of turkeys from southern and eastern Iowa. An early trader, Thomas Anderson, said turkeys were abundant in isolated woodlots in southern Iowa in the winter of 1801–02. The report of flocks of hundreds of turkeys near Muscatine in 1843 and records in William Savage's diary noting that he killed fifty-seven turkeys near Salem in Van Buren County from 1856 to 1863 attest to their original abundance. Turkey River in northeastern Iowa got its name from the numerous gobblers seen near it. There are few records from north-central and northwestern Iowa, although turkeys probably were found in most wooded areas along the major rivers that penetrated those prairie regions. Sixteen were shot in one day near the Boone River in Hamilton County in the mid-1800s. In 1867, turkeys were still abundant in the Little Sioux River valley near Washta in Cherokee County. One settler, A. J. Whisman, claimed he killed eight turkeys on a single hunt in the late 1860s. Wildlife historian Arlie Schorger estimated that at the time of settlement turkey populations in Iowa averaged only about five birds per square mile, about half the density found in other states to the east. Their large size and good-tasting flesh made them a tempting target, and they were eagerly sought by hunters. Turkeys were easy to shoot or trap, and they disappeared rapidly. Starting in 1857, turkeys received statewide protection between 1 February and 15 July, but in the 1800s game laws were poorly enforced and turkey numbers continued to decline.[2]

Although hunting certainly was a major factor in the disappearance of turkeys from Iowa, it was not the only factor involved. Habitat loss was also important in their decline. The eastern wild turkey, the variety found in Iowa, was mainly a bird of woodlands. At the time of settlement, about nineteen percent of Iowa was covered by forests, much of it in eastern and southern

Iowa. Trees were valuable for building material, railroad ties, fence posts, and fuel. Though there is little record of the clearing of forests, the rapid settlement of the state in the mid-1800s must have led to much cutting of timber. Additional thousands of acres were cleared to provide more farmland. This loss of woodland cover must have contributed to the decline in turkey numbers.[3]

Few records exist to document the turkey's disappearance from Iowa. Althea Sherman said the last birds in Clayton County were taken in 1853 or 1854, and they disappeared from Shelby County in the early 1860s, where one of the last was a thirty-two-pound bird. In Madison County, many died in the cold winters of 1847–48 and 1855–56, and the last roost was gone by 1862. Charles Babbitt said they were abundant near Council Bluffs in the mid-1850s, but many died in the severe winter of 1856–57. William Savage killed five in one day in August 1863 in Van Buren County, suggesting that they were still common there. None were left in Linn and Iowa counties by 1870, and after two were shot in Montgomery County in 1872–73, only a few remained there. Bohumil Shimek saw three in Johnson County in 1882 and said only a few were still present there. The last one killed in Jefferson County, a twenty-six-pound bird, was taken about 1890. One killed in Cherokee County in 1897 was probably the last wild turkey taken in northwestern Iowa.[4]

By 1900, wild turkeys persisted in Iowa only in the southeastern and south-central parts of the state. Single birds were seen in Appanoose County in 1902 and Davis County in 1905, two were seen near Donnellson in Lee County in 1903, and one was taken in Monroe County about 1906. Three found in Lucas County in 1910 apparently were the last wild turkeys reported in Iowa. Strangely, the hunting season for turkeys was not closed until 1924, some fifteen years after wild birds had disappeared from Iowa.[5]

extensively in various national journals and in 1912 was elected to membership in the American Ornithologists' Union, only the fourth woman to have that honor. She was probably best known for the special wooden tower she had built so she could observe the nest life of chimney swifts. This tower was moved in 1992 from northeastern Iowa to Iowa City for restoration.

Source: Taylor, Mrs. H. J. 1943. Iowa's woman ornithologist Althea Rosina Sherman 1853–1943. Iowa Bird Life 13:18–35.

Hunting and Trapping Turkeys

Turkeys could be hunted in several ways. Shooting methods included still hunting, where the hunter waited for a turkey to pass by, and turkey calling, where the hunter tried to lure a turkey close by imitating its call. Another favorite shooting method was night hunting. Flocks of turkeys usually roosted together in trees at night, and if there was any moonlight, their bulky silhouettes were easy targets. Records of night hunting in Iowa date back at least to 1843, when the artist John James Audubon planned to shoot turkeys at a roost on the Big Sioux River near present-day Sioux City; a heavy rainstorm forced him to cancel the hunt.[6]

Besides shooting turkeys, settlers also trapped them. A trap used in the 1850s in Hamilton County was made by digging a narrow trench about ten feet long, with the bottom gradually sloping down until it was about one-and-a-half feet deep. A wooden pen, consisting of a latticework of sticks or boards, was constructed over the deep end of the trench. The trap was then baited with a trail of corn leading down the trench to its end. The turkey would walk into the trench, and, with its head pointed down, follow the bait to the end of the trap. When it finished the bait, or if it was alarmed, the turkey would finally raise its head and poke it through an opening in the latticework forming the top of the trap. However, once the turkey had pushed its head through an opening, it had difficulty freeing itself, and thus it was held captive in the trap. A Clinton County couple using a trap like this said that they once caught twenty-four turkeys in one set. A similar trap, but somewhat larger and covered with hay, was used to trap turkeys in Ida County. Even steel traps normally used to catch furbearers were sometimes used for turkeys. In 1861, William Savage loaned two traps to a Van Buren County neighbor so he could catch a turkey.[7]

Not surprisingly, turkeys sometimes fed on settlers' crops and were considered a pest. A story from Jasper County relates that in 1845, settlers had problems with turkeys' feeding on their corn. One woman supposedly hid in a corn shock and waited for the turkeys to arrive to feed. When a large gobbler climbed onto the shock, she reached out and grabbed the turkey's legs, only to be cut by its spur. If true, it certainly was an exciting way to catch a turkey.[8]

Probably most turkeys taken in Iowa were for home consumption, though if someone got more turkeys than he or she could eat, there was a ready market of people willing to buy the extras. Turkeys sold for twenty-five to fifty cents each in Scott County in 1837, and they brought fifty cents apiece on the market at Muscatine in 1854. In early days in Black Hawk County, dressed turkeys sold for seven cents a pound. However, Savage got as little as thirty cents for a turkey he shot near Salem in Van Buren County in 1856. Market hunting undoubtedly was a factor in the decline of turkeys in Iowa. As late as 1893, an entire flock of thirteen turkeys in Des Moines County was killed by a Burlington game dealer.[9]

Epilogue

Starting in 1920, only a few years after the original wild turkeys had been wiped out, Iowans began efforts to reintroduce turkeys into Iowa. The early efforts failed because they depended on game-farm birds, which were simply not hardy enough to survive in the wild. The birds either disappeared soon after their release or else settled into a semi-domestic life, hanging around farmyards much like large chickens. After these failures, the state finally turned to birds captured from the wild. In 1960–61, the Iowa Conservation Commission obtained thirty-nine wild turkeys from Texas and released them in the Yellow River Forest in northeastern Iowa, the largest block of forest remaining in Iowa. Although these turkeys survived, they never really thrived there. Wild birds obtained from Nebraska were released into Stephens State Forest in Lucas County and in the loess hills in Monona County in 1966. Ten wild birds from North Dakota were released along the Upper Iowa River in 1969. None of the releases was successful in establishing wild turkeys in Iowa. Even though these were wild birds, they were varieties of turkey that did not adapt well to Iowa.[10]

There were two key elements in the eventual success of turkey releases in Iowa. The first was using birds captured in the wild; the second, stocking turkeys that came from habitats similar to those they would encounter in Iowa. The turkeys from Texas, Nebraska, and North Dakota, although wild birds, were adapted to habitat conditions different from those they encountered in Iowa. Finally, in 1965 and 1966, eleven wild turkeys trapped in Missouri were released into Shimek State Forest in Lee County in extreme southeastern Iowa. These birds were acclimated to deciduous forests similar to those found in eastern Iowa. The turkeys thrived, and by 1973 the flock had increased to 400–500 birds and had spread onto surrounding private land. A similar release of twenty Missouri birds into Stephens State Forest in Lucas County in 1968 was also successful, and by 1974 that population numbered 400–500. Soon the Iowa Conservation Commission began trapping turkeys from these populations and releasing them elsewhere in the state. In 1974, there were enough turkeys to support a limited hunting season. The population continued to increase and expand its range, both naturally and by releases of turkeys at other places in Iowa. Since 1965, more than 2,900 turkeys have been released at more than 200 sites over most of the state. Iowa's turkey population is estimated to number 75,000–100,000 birds, with densities of forty to fifty birds per square mile of timber in the best areas. About ninety-five percent of the suitable habitat has turkey populations, and the species has reoccupied virtually all of its historic range in Iowa, one of the greatest game-management success stories for a wildlife species in the state. The area open to turkey hunting has gradually been expanded, and in 1989 the entire state was open to turkey hunting. Turkeys are hunted in both spring and fall, and in 1990 more than 12,700 turkeys were taken by hunters. Such success was certainly not imagined possible when eleven birds were released in Lee County in 1965–66.[11]

The successful restocking of turkeys into much of Iowa has run against conditions that many biologists thought would limit their success. Twenty years ago, it was generally thought that turkeys needed forests covering at least 10,000 acres, including many mast-producing trees (such as oak), to survive. Iowa has no forests of such magnitude, and yet turkeys have thrived here. In fact, by 1974 only about four percent of the state was covered by forests, much of it fragmented into small blocks. An important key to success seems to be food. Although acorns are an important food for turkeys, in Iowa turkeys also often feed on corn, especially in winter. With this abundant food supply, turkeys did not need huge forests and in fact often thrived in narrow bands of trees along rivers and streams. The turkey densities found in some parts of Iowa are among the highest densities reported anywhere and probably much higher than in presettlement days.[12]

The comeback of the wild turkey is not limited to Iowa. Nationally, through restocking and better management of their populations, turkey numbers have increased to an estimated 3.5 million birds and wild turkeys now occupy a range larger than their original distribution. The success biologists have had in reestablishing wild turkeys in North America could not have been even imagined fifty years ago.[13]

13. Quail

The quail (or bobwhite, as many people know it) is a small upland game bird that was found throughout the Midwest at the time of settlement. A bird of brushy areas, hedgerows, weedy fields, small-grain fields, and other edge habitat with fairly thick cover, the bobwhite was found over most of the eastern United States west to the Great Plains.[1]

Quail are very sensitive to both habitat change and severe weather, and over the years their numbers in the Midwest have fluctuated greatly. In presettlement days, they were largely confined to the edge of prairies and woodlands or other areas where such natural disturbances as fires and windstorms led to growth of the shrubby cover that they prefer. With settlement, their numbers increased and their range expanded because the early settlers in the Midwest farmed in a manner that often created good quail habitat. Their farms tended to be small, with a mixture of cropland that provided food for quail and pastures or hayfields that provided nesting cover. Farmers also cut down the trees on their land and established fencerows along the edges of their fields. Both practices provided more of the edge habitat that quail prefer. However, by the early 1900s farming was becoming more intensive; "waste" land was put into crops, pastures were converted to grain fields, the remaining woodlots were grazed or cut, and hedges were removed. People also began to have more leisure time and increased the hunting pressure on quail. All of this led to a decline in quail numbers. In the 1930s, there was a brief break in the cycle when the depressed economy led to the abandonment of many farms and marginal agricultural land. The brush and weeds that often sprouted up on these lands provided good quail habitat, and quail numbers increased for several years. Since then, however, the overall trend has been continuing loss of quail habitat and a continuing decrease in their numbers.[2]

Quail in the 1800s

At the time of settlement, Iowa was near the northwestern edge of the quail's range. Quail were once found throughout Iowa, although the best quail habitat was in southern and especially southeastern and south-central Iowa. In western Iowa, brushy cover along river valleys provided them with some suitable habitat, while the prairies of north-central and northwestern Iowa were probably marginal quail habitat. Thus, quail in Iowa have been especially susceptible to environmental change, and their numbers have fluctuated greatly. Probably the two major factors affecting quail numbers have been habitat change and weather. The former tends to affect numbers on a long-term, more permanent basis, while the latter leads to year-to-year changes in numbers.

There is evidence that the general population changes for quail in the Midwest have also occurred in Iowa. Most of the very early accounts say little more than that quail were present. One writer said that in the 1850s quail were very common near Muscatine, a region of the state where they should have been common. As Iowa was settled, several early farming practices created some habitat that was favorable to quail. Trees and shrubs were often planted around homesteads on the otherwise treeless prairies, and shrubs and hedges were established around fields, especially in southern Iowa. Both practices provided good quail habitat. Herbert Quick recalled that there were few quail on the prairies in Iowa until humans provided shelter and grain for them. In northwestern Iowa, quail were scarce in Sac County in 1854 but had increased there by 1866. Likewise, quail were not found on the prairies of northwestern Iowa in the 1870s, but by the mid-1890s they were common there. As an indication of their abundance in 1880, two men flushed nineteen quail coveys and a group of hunters shot 250 quail near Glenwood in southwestern Iowa, both in one day. Rudolph Anderson said that by 1907 quail were more common than in the early days of settlement. Overall, quail probably reached their peak abundance in Iowa in the late 1800s.[3]

A Sand County Almanac, and especially for the essay "The Land Ethic" in that collection. In the late 1920s, Leopold made a survey of game populations in several midwestern states including Iowa. His inventories were the start of modern game management in Iowa and several other states.

Source: Errington, P. L. 1948. In appreciation of Aldo Leopold. Journal of Wildlife Management 12:341–350.

Quail and Weather

Quail numbers in Iowa are greatly affected by the severity of winter weather. Deep snow and extended cold often lead to the loss of many or all the quail from an area. Iowa typically experiences especially severe winter conditions every five to ten years or so. Aldo Leopold lists sixteen severe winters between 1863 and 1931, some of which affected quail in nearby states as well. In the intervening years, quail numbers usually increase rapidly as long as other mortality is not high. Thus, quail numbers tend to fluctuate from year to year, and it is difficult to determine the long-term trend in their numbers.[4]

Historically, there are numerous records of the adverse effect of severe winters on quail. According to one of the earliest references to such mortality in Iowa, quail were annihilated in the Council Bluffs area by the deep, thickly crusted snow that covered the ground in the winter of 1856–57, a winter that greatly affected other wildlife species as well. Many quail died in the bad winters of 1882–83, 1883–84, and 1884–85, leading noted outdoor writer Emerson Hough to say that it was not until 1900 that they regained the abundance noted in the early 1880s. Another writer said that he saw only two quail in the Winterset area in 1883, an indication of their scarcity at that time. However, in 1890 two men killed fifty and forty-four quail on two hunts in the same area. A writer from Fort Dodge thought that the heavy snow in December 1892 would greatly reduce the number of quail in that area. A blizzard in January 1909 killed many quail in Shelby County, and they were still rare there in 1915. The winter of 1912 was a severe one in general for quail in Iowa. Cold weather and heavy snow in February nearly wiped out quail near Waterloo, and there was much mortality statewide. Deep snow and extended cold weather in early 1936 led to some loss of quail, but their numbers had recovered by 1938. Another severe winter in 1959–60, with extended heavy snow cover in south-eastern Iowa, led to the loss of quail over much of the state. Most recently, many quail died during the severe winters of 1974–75 and 1978–79, when deep snow covered much of Iowa. Other severe weather may also be harmful to quail. Sleet storms nearly wiped them out in Sac County every four or five years in the late 1800s and early 1900s.[5]

Hunting and Trapping Quail

Like other game birds, quail were shot for home consumption and to sell on the market. Quail were hunted from the time the earliest settlers arrived, but over the years hunting pressure gradually increased. Quail meat was considered very tender and good-tasting, and thus, despite their small size, they were one of the most desired market birds. They sold for twenty-five to thirty-seven cents per dozen in 1842 in Muscatine and still sold for thirty cents per dozen there in 1854. In 1858, $1,300 worth of quail and prairie-chickens was shipped from Iowa City to New York City. In 1861, H. C. Merritt, who spent most of his time hunting shorebirds and prairie-chickens, bought quail from hunters in Iowa for a dollar per dozen. He planned to sell them in New York City for two dollars per dozen, but freight costs were too high and he made no profit. Quail were still for sale at Iowa markets in Nevada and Sioux City in 1896.[6]

Sport hunting became very popular in the late 1880s, when people began to have more leisure time (fig. 10). Undoubtedly, many quail were shot by sportsmen who were mainly interested in prairie-chickens. Ellison Orr recalled that quail were easy to trap or shoot and said that his father once killed nine with one shot. Newell noted that it was possible to kill ten to twelve birds with a single shot into a covey, a tactic showing less-than-sporting ethics. Iowa first set a bag limit for quail, twenty-five birds per day, in 1878; in 1915 it was lowered to fifteen birds per day. The quail-hunting season in Iowa was closed in 1917; a limited season was reopened in 1933 and further expanded in 1940.[7]

Fig. 10. Quail Shooting. *From* The Art of Wing Shooting, *1895, by William B. Leffingwell.*

Early Iowans also used a variety of traps to capture quail. One trapper used wooden laths to make a trap thirty-six inches long by twenty-four inches wide. He dug a trench under one of the narrow ends, starting about a foot from the trap and extending about a foot into the trap. Grain was spread inside the trap and along the trench. Quail would follow the trail of grain into the trap, but once they were inside it, rather than escaping back through the trench, they would try to fly and thus could not escape. The calls of the quail inside attracted more birds into the trap. Another man recalled using a figure-four trap (described in chapter 11), baited with corn, to catch quail near Woodbine in Harrison County in the 1870s. Quail were probably also caught in the same drop-door traps used for prairie-chickens. William Savage used nets to trap quail near Salem in Van Buren County, catching as many as seven in a single set. In December 1860, he sold twenty-one quail for fifty-two and a half cents or two and a half cents each. In 1868, Iowa forbade trapping quail except on one's own land, but it is doubtful if this law was enforced to any extent.[8]

Quail in the 1900s

Starting around 1900, quail numbers in Iowa began gradually to decrease, a decline that has continued up to the present. Clement Webster, who noted that quail were rapidly disappearing from the Charles City area, was one of the first to call attention to the population decline. Habitat loss was probably the main factor, although severe weather could cause a temporary decrease.[9]

The land-use pattern in Iowa has steadily changed since 1900. During this time, farming has become much more intensive, and much marginal land has been put into cropland. Many woodlots have been grazed or logged, and hedges, fencerows, weed fields, and brush piles that once provided good quail habitat have now been planted with row crops. The landscape of Iowa has gradually changed, with fewer and larger farms growing only a few kinds of crops. This has reduced the habitat available for quail, and quail numbers have declined. A particular example of habitat loss can be found in the removal of the osage orange trees that many early Iowa farmers planted as a cheap substitute for fencing. The thousands of miles of those hedges in Iowa provided ideal habitat for quail. By 1931, osage orange and other hedges had been mostly removed from Iowa. According to Tjernagel, when the hedges and willow rows were removed from central Iowa, the quail disappeared.[10]

Since about 1950, federal agricultural programs often have affected quail habitat. Undoubtedly, the Soil Bank Program of the late 1950s and 1960s provided much good habitat for quail and boosted their numbers temporarily. In contrast, from 1965 to 1968, with federal cost-sharing money, brush was removed from 6,334 acres on 490 farms in just three counties in the heart of the quail's southern Iowa range. The brush removal greatly lowered the value of the land for quail. Similar habitat loss has occurred over much of their Iowa range, contributing to a decline in quail numbers.[11]

Short-term weather patterns have probably had less impact than long-term habitat changes on quail numbers in Iowa. Quail have always had to face periodic severe weather, but with the large broods they produce, their numbers can recover rapidly. Eldon Stempel noted that other than the bad winter of 1912, they did fairly well during the early part of this century. They declined after the severe winter of 1936 but then generally increased in numbers until the winter of 1959–60 caused another decline.[12]

Epilogue

Currently, quail numbers in Iowa are much reduced from what they were in the past. They have recovered from the severe

1978–79 winter, especially in southern Iowa, but even there quail numbers are not as great as they once were. In central and northern Iowa, quail are seen and heard less often than they once were. The number taken by hunters in Iowa has declined from more than a million birds in the early 1970s to a few hundred thousand birds in recent years. Despite this decline, quail still continue to rank as the number two gamebird in the state (behind the pheasant). The Conservation Reserve Program of the 1985 federal farm bill calls for a ten-year set-aside of some farm land. With about two million acres enrolled in Iowa, this program may help provide, at least temporarily, some habitat suitable for quail. There is no threat that quail will be extirpated from the state, but they certainly are less a part of Iowa's fauna than they once were.[13]

Nationally, quail numbers have shown a similar population cycle. Their numbers grew rapidly with the diverse agriculture typical of early settlement days and then declined as the more intensive agriculture of recent years brought the loss of much of the habitat they depend on. Data from the federal Breeding Bird Survey and the annual Christmas Bird Count indicate a decline in quail numbers both in Iowa and in North America during the last several decades. However, quail are still common over much of southeastern and south-central United States, the core of their range.[14]

14. Ruffed Grouse

The ruffed grouse (or partridge or pheasant, as it formerly was called) was once found in wooded and brushy areas and second-growth woodlands over most of eastern North America from southern Canada south as far as northern Georgia and Arkansas. Ruffed grouse also were found in the Rocky Mountains as far south as Utah.[1]

Ruffed Grouse in Iowa

When settlers arrived in Iowa, ruffed grouse were found state-wide wherever there was suitable habitat. They were most common in the eastern half of the state but also lived in wooded areas of western Iowa. Their Iowa range seems to have gradually con-

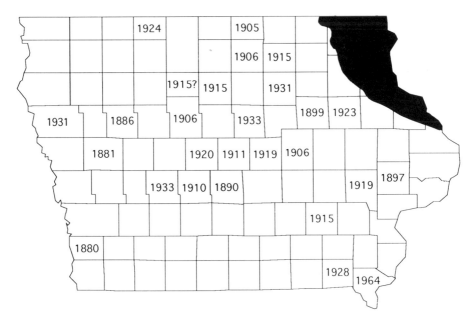

tracted so that now they are found only in the northeastern
corner of the state (map 11). The decline was apparent as early
as 1897, when Clement Webster noted that they were less
abundant in Floyd County than they once had been. By 1907,
Rudolph Anderson commented that where they formerly were
common, now they were rare.[2]

Ruffed grouse were not nearly as abundant in Iowa as some of
the other upland game species, such as prairie-chickens or quail,
and they received much less comment by settlers. Thus, there are
few specifics on their original distribution and decline in Iowa.
Records of grouse in western Iowa include a few birds at Glenwood in Mills County in 1880, at Vail in Crawford County in
1881; the last bird in Sac County was reported in 1886. According to Charles Babbitt, in twenty years of hunting in the
mid-1800s in the Council Bluffs area, he never saw ruffed
grouse. They apparently disappeared from southwestern Iowa in
the early 1900s. An isolated population was still present in 1931
in the loess hills south of Sioux City in Woodbury County, but
those birds now are gone.[3]

In central Iowa, grouse were once present along the Des
Moines, Skunk, and Iowa rivers and their tributaries, but almost

William Savage,
1833–1908

Born in England,
William Savage
lived for a time in
New York, and
from 1855 on
lived on a farm
near Salem in
northeastern Van
Buren County.
His education was
simple, but he
developed an
interest in birds
that was expressed
through his
paintings, many
of which are now
in the State
Historical
Museum in Des
Moines. Savage
was also a diarist
and for many
years kept simple
notes on his daily
activities. The
diaries are also in
the State
Historical
Museum and
provide a record of
the simple,
everyday activities
of a farmer in
Iowa in the late
1850s and early
1860s. Some of the
notes are comical.
Savage seems to be

nothing has been reported about them. Between 1900 and 1920, they disappeared from Boone, Cerro Gordo, Dallas, Humboldt, Marshall, Story, Webster, Worth, and Wright counties. The last birds seen along the Des Moines River apparently were some found in Emmet County in 1924. The last grouse in central Iowa were birds still present in Guthrie and Hardin counties in 1933, but none inhabit those counties now.[4]

Eastern Iowa was the heart of the ruffed grouse's range in Iowa. From 1856 to 1863, William Savage shot about twenty-five grouse near Salem in Van Buren County, indicating that they were fairly plentiful. In southeastern Iowa, grouse were present in Keokuk County in 1915 and in Van Buren County in 1928, and a few birds were reported in nearby Lee County in 1964, suggesting that grouse may have persisted there until recent times. In east-central Iowa, they were gone from Johnson and Tama counties by 1920, and a small population in Buchanan and Delaware counties disappeared about 1923. Thus, although a few may have remained in southeastern Iowa, by about 1940 grouse seem to have been restricted to the northeastern part of the state. Even there their range has contracted; they were last reported in Floyd County in 1915, and a population still present in Butler County in 1931 has now disappeared. Grouse are currently confined to about eight counties in northeastern Iowa, from Jackson and Dubuque counties north to Winneshiek and Allamakee counties, although occasionally a few have been seen outside of that area. The loss of woodlands and the practice by many landowners of allowing their livestock to graze in their woodlots, thereby damaging or removing the underbrush, probably were the two major causes of the decline and eventual disappearance of the ruffed grouse from most of its Iowa range.[5]

Hunting Ruffed Grouse

Little has been recorded on grouse hunting in Iowa. Three hunters killed four or five dozen grouse along the Wapsipinicon River, probably in Bremer County, on a hunting trip in the late fall of 1864. Hamlin Garland recalled shooting a few grouse near Osage in the 1870s. In 1903, one man took more than twenty in one day along the Cedar River in Linn County, suggesting that they were easy to kill. Ellison Orr recalled hunting them in late fall by walking the roads in northeastern Iowa and looking for birds in the adjacent brush or timber (fig. 11). As long as he stayed on the road, the birds were not alarmed and were easy to shoot. Another hunter in the 1850s in Dubuque County said he usually got four or five braces (pairs) of grouse in a day. He found them good sport to shoot because of the dense cover they lived in. The birds flew too rapidly to allow time for him to bring the gun all the way up to his shoulder, so he usually shot his gun from chest height. He said the meat was whiter than prairie-chicken and, when roasted, made a dinner fit for a king. Presently, grouse are best hunted in northeastern Iowa, by walking through brushy areas on ridges or along the sides of ridges. Dogs help flush more birds and increase hunting success.[6]

State legislation gradually provided protection for the ruffed grouse, although much of the attention was probably a by-product of concern for other species. Hunters, conservationists, and legislators were much more interested in more important game species, such as prairie-chickens, quail, and turkeys. A daily bag limit of twenty-five was established for grouse in 1878, but with the lack of enforcement such a limit probably had little meaning. In the late 1880s, closed seasons were established for grouse. In 1896, the grouse season was reduced to only two months, October and November. Two years later, the open months were shifted to November and December, a change that made it too easy, according to the state fish and game warden, for hunters to track the birds in the snow. In 1904, the open season was moved to 1 October to 15 December. Finally, in 1923, the legislature closed the grouse hunting season for nine years, but that closure continued for forty-five years. In 1968, parts of northeastern Iowa were reopened to hunting, and grouse have been hunted there yearly since then. In the late 1960s, the fall population was estimated to number about 12,000 birds, probably a conservative estimate. Population surveys from 1961 to 1978 indicate that the population is stable and does not show the large fluctuations typical of grouse in more northern areas. However, the estimated number taken by hunters varies considerably, ranging from as few as 5,000 in some years to as many as 24,000 in others.[7]

Epilogue

In the past thirty years there have been several attempts to reestablish grouse in parts of their former Iowa range, starting with

always losing a cow and having to spend part of the day locating it. Amongst such entries are many notes on the wildlife he hunted, the mammals he trapped, and the prices he received or paid for the animals. Savage's diary provides valuable insight into life in early Iowa.

Source: Savage, W. 1933. William Savage. Iowa pioneer, diarist, and painter of birds. Annals of Iowa, 3rd series, 19: 83–90.

the release of grouse at Shimek State Forest in southeastern Iowa in 1962 (seven birds) and 1965 (twelve birds). Although the first two stockings apparently were unsuccessful, since then almost 1,300 grouse have been released at thirty-eight sites in fourteen different counties in eastern and central Iowa (map 12). The birds have come from northeastern Iowa, Indiana, Michigan, and Wisconsin. Male grouse drumming as part of their courtship and broods have been reported from a number of sites, but the success of the releases has not been evaluated at all the sites, and some probably will fail. Thus, it is too soon to tell if ruffed grouse can be reestablished on portions of their former range in the state.[8]

However, in northeastern Iowa, grouse seem to be holding their own. Ruffed grouse are forest birds but specially favor dense, shrubby stands typical of areas in the first ten to thirty years after timber is harvested. The continued decline of forest land in Iowa is a long-term concern for this species, but for the time being there is no need to fear that grouse will disappear from the state.[9]

In the Midwest, ruffed grouse numbers have begun to recover from the lows of earlier this century. The return of second-growth forests and aggressive restocking programs in several states have allowed ruffed grouse to reclaim much of their historical range. In general, their future appears good in this region.[10]

Over all of North America, ruffed grouse seem to be doing fairly well. In total, perhaps five million ruffed grouse are taken

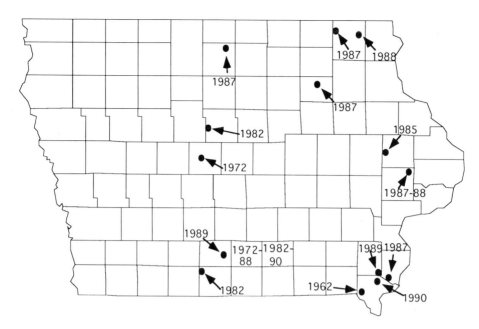

Map 12. Sites where ruffed grouse were released in Iowa, 1962–90. Numerous releases were made in Lucas and Monroe counties in south-central Iowa over the range of years indicated.

yearly by hunters, ranking it among the top game species on the continent. In the northern parts of its range, the populations go through regular cycles, reaching a peak about every ten years, but overall they seem to be maintaining their numbers. In much of the grouse's range, soon after a timber plot is logged, a variety of shrubs and small trees quickly grow up on the once-denuded land. Such cover often provides top-quality grouse habitat. If timber harvests are planned to ensure that such habitat is continuously available, grouse numbers can be sustained indefinitely in an area. Thus, cooperation between wildlife managers and timber companies is important to the long-term welfare of this species.[11]

15. Shorebirds

In addition to such traditional game birds as turkey, quail, and grouse, shorebirds were exploited for food during pioneer days. The rapid growth of cities in the eastern United States created a demand for meat from both domestic and wild animals. Originally, passenger pigeons were one of the most important market birds, but as the pigeon's numbers began to diminish about 1880, market hunters gave increasing attention to shorebirds as a replacement. The arrival of railroads in Iowa and the development of better refrigeration techniques made it possible for Iowans to ship game to markets in midwestern cities and eventually the East Coast, further encouraging market hunting. Thus, for several decades in the late 1800s, shorebirds were extensively hunted in Iowa and elsewhere.

More than thirty species of shorebirds, ranging from several sparrow-sized sandpipers up to the almost crow-sized long-billed curlews, regularly pass through Iowa during migration. A few of these species also nest in the state. During both the spring and fall migrations, and also on the breeding grounds, virtually all the shorebirds were hunted at least occasionally in Iowa. The seven species discussed in this chapter are the ones that are mentioned most often in the literature, and they probably were the most important market species in Iowa. Even for these seven, the record is sketchy. Although shorebird hunting in Iowa did not reach the levels attained along the Atlantic Coast, many birds were killed in some years, and presumably that mortality had a serious effect on shorebird populations.[1]

Nesting Species

The most important market species that nested in Iowa were the American woodcock, which lived in damp parts of woodlands and along the edges of wetlands, and three species that nested on grasslands. One of these three, the upland sandpiper (or upland plover or grass plover, as it was formerly called) is almost strictly a grassland species and is seldom found near water. The other two, the marbled godwit and long-billed curlew, commonly feed in wetlands, although they may nest far from water. These two are the largest shorebirds that occurred in Iowa, and they probably were hunted both during the nesting season and during migration. The three grassland species were harmed as much by the loss of their prairie nesting habitat as they were by hunting. Soon after the settlement of Iowa, two disappeared as nesters, and numbers of the third decreased greatly.

American Woodcock

Of the four nesting species, only the woodcock still is common in Iowa, although its secretive habits make it seem less common than it probably is. Woodcock nest over most of the state wherever there is suitable habitat, but they are more abundant in eastern than in western Iowa. They still are hunted in the fall, when migrants from the north pass through the state. Most of the hunting occurs in northeastern Iowa, where woodcock often are encountered by people hunting ruffed grouse.[2]

At one time woodcock must have been very abundant in Iowa. John Smith wrote that in the late 1800s a person could easily shoot twenty-five to thirty in a day along the Des Moines River in Kossuth County. A more vivid account of their abundance is given by H. Clay Merritt, a market hunter who hunted in eastern Iowa in the 1860s and 1870s. In the summer of 1863, Merritt and a partner hunted the Mississippi River bottomlands near Sabula. They hunted with a dog, and each man commonly shot twenty to twenty-five birds in a day. Merritt said he seldom walked more than half a mile from his starting point to get that many birds. Over twenty days, the two averaged a combined forty woodcock a day. To protect the dead birds from spoiling, they buried them in the moist ground during the day, cooled them in the evening air, and then stored them in an icehouse. Most were shipped by rail to New York City, where, that year, they sold for sixty-five to seventy-five cents a pair. The next year, with another partner, Merritt had shot 1,600 birds by mid-August. In five days, he alone shot 159 birds. Prices that year were as high as $1.12 per pair, although later they dropped to only four dollars per dozen. Two years later, Merritt bought woodcock from local hunters for twenty-five cents each and made a profit of more than $1,000 on birds he shipped east from Sabula. In 1868, he hunted the Mississippi bottomlands near Lansing, although not always in Iowa. That year, he killed and shipped 3,000 woodcock. In 1871, Merritt moved away from the river to near Cresco, where he concentrated on prairie-chickens but also managed to ship 2,000–2,500 woodcock, selling them for at least a dollar a pair. His last big woodcock hunt was in 1873, when he and a partner killed 171 woodcock in one day near the mouth of the Upper Iowa River, the biggest one-day kill he ever had. In six or seven days, the two killed 800 woodcock, which they sold for $1.25 a pair. Merritt was a businessman, and woodcock hunting was an important part of his livelihood.[3]

Long-billed Curlew

The long-billed curlew is a large shorebird with a long, downward-curving bill. There are few specifics on the long-billed curlew in Iowa, and it disappeared soon after settlement. They were noted as nesting in Ida County, in Sioux County, and in the Algona area about 1870, and in Buena Vista County in the 1880s. Herbert Quick was familiar with them in the Steamboat Rock area in the late 1860s or 1870s, and they were still reported from the Humboldt region in 1881. In the early years, they were considered abundant in Cherokee County. Originally common in

Sac County, curlews were rare after 1876 and last nested there about 1885. Bohumil Shimek said that long-billed curlews still were found everywhere on the prairies of northwestern Iowa in 1882. Long-billed curlew nests and eggs were seen in Kossuth County, probably in 1883. By 1889, long-bills were considered almost extinct in the Manson area, and virtually no other mention is made of them in Iowa. They apparently disappeared as a nesting species by about 1890. There are only a few records of this species in the state in recent years, all vagrants seen during migration. Currently, their nearest nesting area is in the sandhills of north-central Nebraska.[4]

There are several reports of hunters taking curlews. Curlews were shot for food in Sioux County, while a Cherokee County historian said their meat had a delicate flavor. Dick Harker gave the name "curlew" to two kinds of birds that he hunted near Spirit Lake in the 1880s. One he said had a bill eight inches long with a curl on the end, and the other had a straight bill about five inches long. The former was almost certainly the long-billed curlew; the latter, probably a marbled godwit.[5]

Marbled Godwit

The marbled godwit, a large shorebird with an upward-curving bill, disappeared almost as rapidly and with even less notice than the curlew. Many of the godwits in the early reports were probably migrants, such as the dozens that were seen in the Algona area every May and October until about 1870. Godwits nested in Sac County but were rare there after 1875. J. W. Preston saw a marbled godwit nest in Kossuth County, probably in 1883. One of the birds that Harker hunted near Spirit Lake in the 1880s and called curlew was probably the marbled godwit. Godwits were probably gone as a nesting species from the state by about 1890. Marbled godwits are still uncommon migrants in Iowa and pass through the state every year, mainly in western Iowa. Currently, their closest nesting area is in northeastern South Dakota.[6]

Upland Sandpiper

The upland sandpiper was the most widespread of the three prairie shorebirds and was common on grasslands all the way to the East Coast. Many early writers mentioned upland sandpipers, probably largely because their melodious whistle drew attention to them and because they nested in pastures where settlers often saw them. Outdoor writer Emerson Hough recalled hearing many of them passing over Iowa City one night in 1878; the flight lasted more than an hour.[7]

Their numbers declined with settlement, however. John Crone noted that upland sandpipers formerly were abundant in Buena Vista County, but in the late 1880s many were killed for the eastern markets. They had become less abundant near Manson by 1889, and Clement Webster said they had practically vanished from Floyd County by 1910. There is little mention of market hunting for them in Iowa. They sold for ten cents each at Manson in the summer of 1889. Upland sandpipers shot by Harker in the Spirit Lake area in the late 1800s sold for $1.25 per dozen. Merritt indicates that this species was hunted most heavily in the Midwest from the late 1870s to about 1890, with 50,000–60,000 birds shipped annually from Nebraska alone. Over that time, the price dropped from four dollars per dozen to about sixty cents per dozen, a price that hardly covered the cost of hunting them. The decline of upland sandpipers has continued up to the present time. They still occur throughout the state, but there are few areas where they could be considered common. Today, they are most often encountered in the pastureland of south-central Iowa. They require relatively thick grasslands for nesting habitat, and the current emphasis on row crops limits the amount of suitable habitat available for them in Iowa.[8]

Migrant Shorebirds

Most of the shorebirds found in Iowa occur as migrants, passing through the state for brief periods in the spring and fall. Several of these species were among the most important market birds in the 1800s. The three that are mentioned most often in Iowa are the American golden-plover, eskimo curlew, and common snipe.

American Golden-Plover

Golden-plover winter in southern South America and breed on the arctic tundra of Canada and Alaska. Most of them fly north through central North America, passing through Iowa each spring, whereas in fall most migrate along the coastlines or over water. Thus, in Iowa they usually were hunted in the spring. Edward Forbush called them the most numerous of the North American shorebirds and noted that large numbers of golden-plover passed through Massachusetts each fall. Numerous observers mentioned the huge flocks of golden-plover that they saw in the early days in Iowa, especially on the prairies of north-central and northwestern Iowa. Herbert Quick reported seeing thousands in the Steamboat Rock area in the late 1860s or 1870s, and immense flocks were seen near Pomeroy in 1877. John Smith said he saw hundreds in the Algona region in the 1870s, and Bohumil Shimek saw great clouds of golden-plover in northwestern Iowa in 1882. Thousands were seen on burned prairies in Sac County in spring 1876, and a bushel of plover could be shot in an hour. In 1875, Merritt (the woodcock hunter) hunted golden-plover in southwestern Minnesota and northwestern Iowa near West Bend. That year birds sold for two to three dollars a dozen. By about 1880, so many market hunters flooded the market with birds that the prices dropped to only $1.25–$1.50 a dozen, and few were taken after that year. Dick Harker, who hunted in the Spirit Lake area from 1881 to 1895, said he killed thousands of golden-plover, more than any other species. One spring, he took 2,000 shorebirds in a month, including golden-plover, upland sandpiper, godwit, snipe, and yellowlegs. He said golden-plover sold for $1.50 per dozen. They were still abundant near Manson in 1889, when thousands were killed and stored in icehouses at Laurens until the following fall or winter. That summer, the going price for plover, curlew, and snipe was ten cents a bird, and one man said he shot 50–125 birds per day.[9]

Golden-plover commonly gathered on burned prairie land, feeding on grasshoppers and other insects. Merritt said they were easy to approach with a team and wagon, and they could be herded together so that a single shot might kill twenty to forty plover. The wounded birds would act as decoys and draw the flock back for continued shooting at the flock's remnants.[10]

Emerson Hough described two methods used to hunt golden-plover on the open prairies of the Midwest. Most often, one or more hunters rode in a horse-drawn wagon, searching for golden-plover. When the birds were sighted, the wagon was steered toward the edge of the flock. The birds often allowed a horse and wagon to approach them closely, especially if it did not approach the birds head-on. Once the hunters were within shooting range, they got out on the side of the wagon away from the birds, made a quick run toward the flock, and shot at their prey. A second method required more skill but often led to greater harvests. The hunters first located a feeding area that was used repeatedly by the birds and took note of the flight paths they used to approach the feeding ground. Then they built a small blind near one of the flyways and put out decoys near the blind. The most skillful hunters also learned to imitate the whistle note given by the plover. By waiting in the blind and skillfully calling the birds in closer, the hunters could kill 200 golden-plover in a day or 1,000 in a week. Market hunters in particular used this method successfully.[11]

By the 1890s, plover numbers were much diminished, and few people continued to hunt them. Edward Forbush said that many were marketed in Massachusetts until about 1890 or 1891, but by 1904 they were almost gone from that state. Golden-plover still migrate through Iowa each spring, and sometimes flocks numbering in the hundreds are encountered. Still, it is obvious that the numbers are much reduced from what they once were.[12]

Eskimo Curlew

The story of the eskimo curlew, a small relative of the long-billed curlew, is similar to that of the golden-plover, a species with which it commonly associated. Each spring, great flocks of eskimo curlews (often called doe birds or dough birds because they were so fat) migrated north through central North America toward their arctic nesting grounds. In fall, they flew to the Labrador coast and then south over the Atlantic Ocean to South America. The main spring passageway was west of Iowa in Nebraska and Kansas, but certainly large flocks were also found in Iowa. Smith noted that large flocks of eskimo curlews were found in the Algona region in the 1870s. He also saw thousands in northwestern Iowa in May 1866. He said that they were seen there only in spring, but they were not fat enough then to be good eating. Dick Harker, a market hunter in the Spirit Lake area, recalled that the eskimo curlew had delicious meat. He arrived in Spirit Lake in 1881 and said he killed only twelve to fifteen dough birds in his lifetime, which suggests that he arrived after they had greatly declined in numbers in Iowa. By 1889, they were considered almost gone from the Manson region. One of the early sportsman's guides listed Lake Mills in north-central Iowa as a curlew-hunting area. The last eskimo curlew recorded in the state was one taken at Davenport in May 1901. The last big spring flights in the Midwest were from about 1875 to 1880, while the last big fall flights on the East Coast were from about 1885 to 1890. By 1900, the species was almost extinct.[13]

There has been considerable speculation on what caused the decline of the eskimo curlew. Since thousands were killed on the Great Plains in spring, many people have considered hunting a leading cause of the species' decline. Some years, when strong winds forced them ashore, many were also shot on the East Coast in the fall. Like the golden-plover, they were easy to hunt. The calls of a wounded bird would attract other members of the flock, so a hunter could easily decimate a flock. Other possible causes for their decline include loss of some critical habitat for either nesting or migration, a catastrophic weather-related loss of birds while they were migrating across the Atlantic, or perhaps some long-term climate change. In any case, the curlew is one of the rarest of North American birds. Several sightings in recent years indicate that a few still survive, but at most the total population must be very small. This species, once an abundant migrant on the prairies, has been at the brink of extinction for more than fifty years and could easily topple over the edge.[14]

Common Snipe

The other migrant shorebird that was often hunted in Iowa is the common snipe. Snipe occasionally nest in Iowa, but most found in the state are migrants. Snipe are birds of flooded fields and, to some extent, mudflats. Contrary to popular folklore, snipe are hunted with a gun rather than a gunny sack. They are secretive but are easy to flush and thus have been commonly hunted, even up to the present day (figs. 12 and 13). There are

Fig. 12. Snipe Shooting. *From* The Art of Wing Shooting, *1895, by William B. Leffingwell.*

Fig. 13. Folding tin snipe decoys made by the Kurtz Company. The decoys, manufactured about 1900, were found for sale for $12 per dozen in 1945. Courtesy State Historical Society of Iowa, Des Moines. Photograph by Chuck Greiner.

numerous accounts of hunters' shooting snipe, although some may have used the term "snipe" to describe any of a number of species of shorebirds. Orin Sabin market-hunted in the Spirit Lake area from 1892 to 1899. He and others used horses to pull a harrow over mudflats to keep the plants from growing too tall and then baited the flats with grain. Although the grain was probably mainly used to attract ducks, the open mudflats attracted shorebirds. Sabin recalled being paid to pick up snipe (and probably other kinds of shorebirds) after the hunters had shot them. There are several accounts of Iowa hunters' taking many snipe, although none of them approach reports from Louisiana and New Brunswick, where some hunters averaged a kill of fifty to one hundred or more snipe a day. A hunter near State Center killed forty-two snipe and 209 prairie-chickens on a hunting trip in October 1875. The most prolific hunter's report was that of George Poyneer, who hunted near Clinton. He claimed that he shot 182 snipe in 1874 and 230 the next year; in April 1875, he and two others shot 127 in one day at Goose Lake in Clinton County.[15]

Epilogue

The first protective measure for shorebirds in Iowa occurred in 1862, when a six-month closed season (1 February – 1 August) was established for woodcock. In 1878, a closed season was also established for snipe, and a bag limit of twenty-five was set for both snipe and woodcock. As the accounts in earlier chapters have indicated, these laws probably had little effect on shorebird hunting. Iowa's closed seasons were changed slightly several times, but shorebirds received no real protection until the Migratory Bird Treaty Act was implemented in 1918. This treaty between Canada and the United States outlawed market hunting and thus eliminated that source of mortality for shorebirds. Because of population declines, hunting for common snipe was banned in the United States from 1941 to 1953, and Canada reduced its bag limit. The season was reopened in 1954. Because there was no hunting for a number of years, some hunters probably never returned to snipe hunting, and the harvest now is probably lower than it was in the past. Recent estimates are that about 900,000 snipe and 1.6 million woodcock are taken yearly in the United States and Canada.[16]

The hunting season for woodcock was reopened in Iowa in 1972 after being closed for many years. Neither the snipe nor the woodcock is subject to intense hunting pressure, and many are probably shot incidentally by hunters seeking ruffed grouse, rails, or waterfowl. About 5,000 woodcock and 15,000 snipe are taken yearly in the state. Certainly, the loss of adequate breeding, migratory, and wintering habitat represents a greater threat than hunting to the survival of these species. From 1970 to 1988, counts of woodcock during the breeding season indicate that the species' numbers have declined in the eastern United States and Canada, the heart of its range.[17]

A lasting contribution of this group of birds to Iowa is the naming of two towns in northwestern Iowa after shorebirds. When the Des Moines and Fort Dodge Railroad (later the Rock

Fig. 14. Sign announcing the Plover, Iowa, centennial in 1982. Plover is one of several Iowa towns named for birds that were hunted nearby.

Island) was extended north from Fort Dodge toward Spirit Lake, the railroad president, Charles Whitehead had the privilege of naming new towns as they were built. Whitehead was a hunter, and thus he named towns after two of his favorite game birds, the plover (fig. 14) and curlew.[18]

144   *Shorebirds*

16. Cranes

At the time of Iowa's settlement, both species of cranes native to North America, the sandhill crane and the whooping crane, nested on the prairie wetlands of northwestern and north-central Iowa. Both species also stopped in Iowa on their migrations between their wintering grounds in the southern United States and Mexico and their breeding grounds in the northern United States and Canada. Numerous accounts mention the large number of migrant cranes settlers encountered, especially in spring. Most of the migrants were sandhill cranes, although some writers also mention seeing whooping cranes. For instance, members of the Stephen Long expedition saw large numbers of migrating sandhill cranes along the Missouri River near Missouri Valley in mid-April 1820. Clement Webster, a careful observer in the Charles City area, noted that vast numbers of both species could be seen in Floyd County in the early days, and George Monlux saw thousands of sandhill cranes at the headwaters of the Iowa River in Hancock County in May 1871. In the 1860s, thousands of cranes were reported during the fall in northwestern Dallas County, and thousands were seen at Latimer in Franklin County in spring 1884. The noted botanist Bohumil Shimek reported that both whooping and sandhill cranes were present in northwestern Iowa in 1882.[1]

During the spring, cranes perform spectacular courtship displays in which the pairs face each other, bow their heads and necks, and jump stiff-legged into the air. Several writers mention watching these strange antics during the crane's migration stops in Iowa. One of the most amusing encounters with cranes occurred at Irvington in Kossuth County in the spring of 1857. A settler named Luther Bullis put the whole community into an uproar when he reported that a group of Sioux Indians was approaching the town. Since this was only a few months after the Spirit Lake massacre, the concern of the citizens is understandable. Fortunately, it was soon realized that Bullis had just seen some sandhill cranes displaying and had mistaken their movements and jumping for a group of Indians on horseback.[2]

Cranes Nesting in Iowa

The sandhill crane was the more abundant of the two species of cranes, although there are few specific records of its nesting in Iowa. Nesting records for sandhill cranes include Ida County, Shelby County until the late 1870s, Sac County until 1878, Dickinson County in 1882, near Eagle Lake in Hancock County in 1883, and Palo Alto County in 1891. A half-grown young sandhill crane was seen west of Fort Dodge in 1855. The last nest recorded in Iowa was found by Rudolph Anderson near Hayfield in Hancock County in 1894.[3]

Whooping cranes undoubtedly were less common than sandhill cranes in Iowa. However, Robert Allen, an authority on whoopers, thought that the wetlands of north-central Iowa were the heart of the whooping crane nesting range in North America. Allen knew of nesting records from ten Iowa counties from the years 1868 to 1894, mostly from north-central Iowa (map 13). Besides Allen's records, another nest was found (and soon collected) at Pomeroy in Calhoun County in 1877. The last nest from Iowa and one of the last seen anywhere for some sixty years

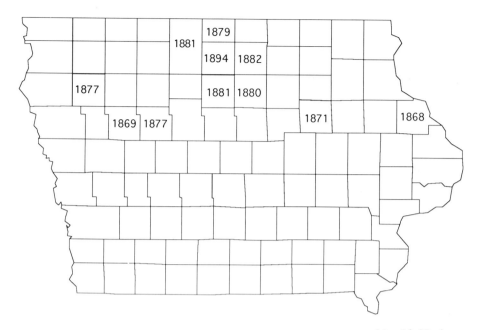

Map 13. Nesting records of whooping cranes in Iowa. Date indicates year of last nesting in each county.

was found, also by Rudolph Anderson, three miles north of Hayfield in Hancock County in 1894. Like many before it, the eggs were removed from the nest and put into an egg collection.[4]

Two factors—loss of their wetland habitat and mortality from humans—probably were responsible for the disappearance of cranes as nesting birds in Iowa. At the time of settlement, several million acres of Iowa were covered with prairie wetlands. The wetlands were rapidly drained and converted to farmland, so that by 1906 fewer than a million acres remained. Cranes depend on wetlands for nesting and feeding habitat, and with the loss of that habitat, the birds disappeared.[5]

Exploitation of Cranes

Cranes are large birds: adult whooping cranes weigh fourteen to seventeen pounds; sandhill cranes, eight to thirteen pounds. At least a few people found them worth hunting, which is not surprising given their size and the fact that their meat usually was considered good-tasting. A hunter in Shelby County shot a large white crane, the meat of which he considered the finest he had ever eaten. A writer in Calhoun County shot two sandhill cranes and one whooping crane in 1877 and commented that they were

Rudolph M.
Anderson,
1876–1961

One of Iowa's
pioneer
ornithologists,
Rudolph
Anderson was
born near
Decorah, the son
of a member of the
Iowa legislature.
Early in his life,
he had an interest
in natural history,
especially birds,
and by 1894 he
had published
articles in
national
magazines. Like
many naturalists
of the time,
Anderson was an
egg collector (or
oologist). In 1894,
he visited the large
marshes near
Hayfield in
Hancock County
and collected eggs
from the last
sandhill crane
nest reported from
Iowa until 1992
and the last
whooping crane
nest ever in Iowa.
Anderson received
a doctorate in
zoology from the

good eating. However, others found their flesh tough and un-palatable. An early settler in Buchanan County tried to cook cranes several times. He first attempted to cook an old bird, and although his wife boiled it (with a turnip) for two or three days, it remained too tough to chew, and finally he threw it away. The next year he shot a young crane, but it also was too tough to eat, and he fed that one to his hogs.[6]

Cranes were wary and hard to hunt, and a hunter needed great patience to be able to get close enough to shoot them. A Kossuth County hunter shot them with a rifle, which was probably the usual way to kill them. Another man in that county claimed that he had killed more than one hundred whooping cranes, an astonishing number considering their rarity even in the 1800s. Another man claimed his father killed two whooping cranes in northwestern Dallas County in November 1862 with a single rifle shot. David Brooks described the novel way he was taught to hunt cranes near State Center in 1875. He and a guide rode in a wagon pulled by a team of horses and scouted the countryside looking for cranes. Once they had found a flock of cranes standing in a field, they drove their wagon as fast as they could downwind toward the cranes. They knew that because the cranes were heavy, when they flushed they would have to fly upwind until they built up some flight speed. This would take the birds directly over the hunters and provide them with easy shots. Brooks shot one sandhill crane and said he would have gotten more if he had used larger shot. In at least one case, a settler set steel traps in grain fields to capture cranes so they could be eaten, while in 1873 another man killed a crippled crane near Emmetsburg with an axe.[7]

Although they were valued as food, cranes were also considered a pest because they fed on grain. In fall, a large flock of cranes could eat a considerable amount of grain in a short time, causing a loss to the farmer. At least one county (Washington) paid a bounty of fifty cents per sandhill crane to try to reduce such losses.[8]

Somewhat surprisingly, a few Iowans tried to keep cranes as pets. An early settler in Ida County, John Moorehead, had a crane that followed his wagon like a dog and took food directly from the cupboard. The writer Hamlin Garland recalled a neighbor's "pet" crane that had the habit of pecking at shiny objects. The owner ended up killing the crane after it almost put out the eye of his daughter.[9]

Another factor in the demise of whooping cranes in Iowa was the gathering of eggs for private and museum collections. In the late 1800s, the eggs of many rare bird species, including whooping cranes, were avidly sought for these collections, and Iowa was a good place to find their nests. At least fifteen sets of whooping crane eggs were collected in Iowa between 1866 and 1894, many of which are still in museums around the country.[10]

By 1900, whooping cranes had disappeared as nesting birds in Iowa. One seen in March 1904 in Sac County, five in April 1911 in Clay County, and one at High Lake in Emmet County in April 1922 were the only records from Iowa for many years. The only recent records from Iowa are several reports of birds that wandered from their normal migration pathway west of Iowa.[11]

North American Cranes in the 1900s

The story of the whooping crane and its fight for survival is well known. The North American population dipped to a low of twenty-one birds in 1944–45 and again in 1952–53. By fall 1992, however, the population had rebounded to about 145 wild birds, with about ninety more in captivity. The nesting area of the last breeding population finally was found in Alberta and the Northwest Territories of Canada in 1954. Those birds migrate to the Gulf Coast of Texas each fall and return north in the spring. Most of the birds pass through central Nebraska, where they often stop to feed and rest. From 1975 to the mid-1980s, whooping cranes were released in Idaho to try to establish a second self-sustaining wild population. Since these birds wintered in New Mexico, they had a much shorter and less hazardous migration than the Canadian population. However, members of this flock did not form nesting pairs, and the experiment was abandoned. With that failure, experts focused their attention on Florida, and in January 1993 fourteen captive-raised whooping cranes were released on the Kissimmee Prairie in south-central Florida. If a population is established there, it would not be exposed to the hazards that the migratory populations experience. The ultimate goal is to establish nesting populations in several different locations, thereby reducing the chance that natural calamities, human-related mortality, or habitat loss might cause disastrous losses to the entire whooping crane population.[12]

In contrast to the whooping crane, sandhill cranes have done fairly well in recent years. A small isolated population in Missis-

University of Iowa in 1903. His dissertation, published in 1907 as the first book on Iowa's birds, is an important summary of birdlife in the state at the turn of the century. Anderson eventually became curator of mammals at the National Museum of Canada.

Source: Anon. 1962. Obituary of Dr. Rudolph M. Anderson. Iowa Bird Life 32: 92–93.

sippi is considered endangered, but other populations generally have held their own or increased in number, especially those birds that nest in Canada, Alaska, and Siberia and winter in Texas, New Mexico, Mexico, and nearby areas. In 1961, a hunting season was reopened for sandhill cranes in several Great Plains states and in the Prairie Provinces of Canada. About 15,000 cranes are taken yearly in the United States, Canada, and Mexico. Even when crippling losses are included, the kill is less than four percent of the estimated population of 550,000 cranes, and hunting currently presents no threat to their survival.[13]

In Iowa, sandhill cranes had disappeared as nesting birds by 1900. One writer noted that by 1910 flocks still passed over the state but seldom stopped. For many years, even migrating sandhills were considered rare in Iowa. However, in the past ten to fifteen years, the number of sandhill cranes reported in Iowa has increased dramatically. West of Iowa, several hundred thousand sandhill cranes spend about a month each spring along the Platte River in central Nebraska before they migrate north to their breeding grounds. Most cranes seen in spring in Iowa are presumably stragglers from the Nebraska flocks, but it is unlikely that these birds will ever stop to nest in Iowa. A more encouraging situation involves the sandhill cranes that nest in Wisconsin and other Great Lakes states. During the past twenty-five years, their numbers and nesting range have increased rapidly, and now they nest over much of Wisconsin.[14]

In June 1992, two pairs of sandhill cranes, one with two young and the other with one, were seen repeatedly at Otter Creek Marsh in Tama County. Cranes had been seen there for several years, so the nesting was not totally unexpected. This is the first report of cranes nesting in the state in ninety-eight years. Other seemingly suitable nesting habitat is available in eastern and northern Iowa, and perhaps sandhill cranes will occupy some of the sites in the near future. The bugling of cranes would be a welcome addition to the sounds of spring in Iowa.[15]

17. Waterfowl

Many explorers and early settlers commented on the abundance of ducks and geese that they encountered in Iowa. This is not surprising, since Iowa once had a tremendous amount of waterfowl habitat. The best area for waterfowl in Iowa was the wedge of land extending from Des Moines north to Mason City on the east and Spirit Lake on the west. The gently rolling topography of this region is dotted with thousands of shallow depressions that fill with water from snow melt and spring rains. At the time of settlement, an estimated six million acres of this region were covered by a mixture of prairie and shallow wetlands, ideal habitat for many waterfowl species.[1]

Besides the thousands of wetlands that dotted the interior of Iowa, there were also thousands of acres of wetlands along the major river valleys. The Mississippi had innumerable shallow

Jack Musgrove,
1914–1980

Born in
Iowa City, Jack
Musgrove
attended the
University of
Iowa. In 1938,
he went to work
for the State
Historical
Department as a
museum assistant.
In 1960, he
became curator of
the State
Historical
Museum and was
its director when
he died. He had a
special interest in
waterfowl and,
with his wife,
Mary, and a
then unknown
artist named
Maynard Reece,
collaborated on
the book
Waterfowl in
Iowa, which first
appeared in 1943.
The book was a big
success, and five
editions were
published, the
most recent in
1977. In the
1940s, Musgrove
did extensive
research on the

backwater areas, the Missouri had many old oxbows and wet-lands in its broad floodplain, and rivers such as the Des Moines, Skunk, and Iowa also had much wetland habitat. All of these provided habitat for both nesting and migrating waterfowl.[2]

Waterfowl were an important resource that settlers used in a variety of ways. They provided a needed source of food for many early settlers and were commonly hunted. Besides their flesh, their eggs were also gathered and eaten, and even their feathers were used for filling pillows and feather beds and for feather dusters.[3]

Waterfowl at the Time of Settlement

Waterfowl were a familiar form of wildlife to early settlers, for millions of waterfowl nested in or migrated through Iowa every year. During the breeding season, about a dozen species of ducks, as well as Canada geese and a few trumpeter swans, nested in Iowa. Every spring and fall, the nesting birds were joined by huge flocks of migrating waterfowl.

One of the first reports of waterfowl in Iowa is found in the journals of Lewis and Clark. In July and August 1804, as they traveled up the Missouri River, they saw ducks and geese (almost certainly Canada geese) and their young a number of times along the western border of Iowa.[4]

Although many writers spoke of seeing large numbers of nesting waterfowl in Iowa in the early days of settlement, few indicated how many were present other than to describe the number of birds that were killed on a particular hunt. One was John G. Smith, a hunter and longtime resident of Kossuth County. In 1904, he wrote lamenting the loss of game. He thought that in the 1860s there were 10,000 Canada goose nests in Kossuth County and ten times that many ducks nesting there. We will never know how accurate his estimates were, but the point is clear: he thought that large numbers of waterfowl nested in the county at the time. Bohumil Shimek recalled that in 1882, in the area north and northwest of Wright County, almost every musk-rat house had a goose nest on it. In the 1930s, noted wildlife biologist Logan Bennett estimated that before most of Iowa's wetlands were drained, perhaps three to four million ducks, mainly blue-winged teal, northern shoveler, mallard, redhead, ruddy duck, and northern pintail, were raised in the state every year.[5]

Migrating waterfowl were also plentiful in Iowa. Although large flocks of waterfowl must have migrated along the Missouri River, little was written about them. In spring 1820, the Stephen Long expedition noted large flocks of ducks and geese migrating north along the Missouri River in western Iowa. Charles Babbitt said that the spring of 1857 had a notably heavy duck migration. The deep snow of the previous winter melted rapidly, flooding many low-lying areas and the corn shocks that had been left there over winter. The huge flocks of ducks feeding on these fields provided easy hunting, and hunters averaged a hundred ducks a day. Babbitt also saw fields that appeared white from the flocks of snow geese resting on them. He saw one flock that he estimated numbered 40,000, small compared to the flocks seen in the 1980s and 1990s. These geese were easy to hunt, but their flesh was poor, and they were not sought by hunters.[6]

With waterfowl so abundant, it is not surprising that settlers exploited them for food. In the early days after settlement, hunting probably consisted mainly of an individual's shooting a few birds for the next meal. With vast numbers of waterfowl available and relatively few people to take them, such hunting probably had little effect on overall waterfowl populations. However, by about 1880 two other types of exploitation, market hunting and sport hunting, became common and undoubtedly had an effect on waterfowl numbers.

Market Hunting

Along with the prairie-chicken, waterfowl were probably the major wildlife group that was market-hunted in Iowa. Fortunately, waterfowl enthusiast Jack Musgrove interviewed some of the hunters and provided a written account of a fascinating part of the history of the state's wildlife. Waterfowl hunting was centered in two areas, along the Mississippi River and in northwestern Iowa, especially around Spirit Lake. The extension of railroads across Iowa in the 1860s and 1870s meant that wild game could be transported rapidly to large-city markets. As a result, market hunting, which previously had been concentrated along the Atlantic Coast and Great Lakes states, now became common in the prairie states. Tens of thousands of ducks and geese were killed in Iowa and shipped to markets elsewhere.

One of the first things the market hunter needed was a way to preserve the game until it could be sold. In early spring and late

market hunters who had worked in Iowa in the late 1800s. His interviews with hunters from the period who were still living preserve a part of Iowa's history that otherwise would have been lost.

Source: Iowa curator Musgrove dies. Des Moines Register, 14 December 1980, p. 9B.

fall, this was no problem because the air was cold enough to freeze the birds. In warmer seasons, especially early fall, refrigeration was a problem because birds might not keep long enough to reach the market in a saleable form. The usual way to solve the problem was to build a freezer. Richard Harker, who hunted in the Spirit Lake area from 1881 to 1895, described one in some detail. His freezer was a building fourteen feet on a side, although other dimensions would work. It was built with tight-fitting lumber, and the inside was lined with open shelves made of laths. This allowed air to circulate and rapidly freeze any animals placed on the shelves. Around this central room he added three more walls for insulation, each built of two-inch lumber and spaced six inches out from the previous wall. The inner six-inch gap was filled with sawdust, the next was left open, and the outer one was filled with sawdust. Galvanized pipes, which opened to the outside so they could be drained, were run through the building. In winter, blocks of ice were cut from a nearby lake or pond and stored in an icehouse for later use. To lower the temperature inside his freezer, Harker would chop ice into fine pieces and fill the galvanized pipes, adding salt to help in the freezing process. On hot days, it took 300–400 pounds of ice to fill the pipes. He said frost formed on the pipes in only a few minutes, and a whole duck could be frozen solid overnight. When the birds were frozen, they were stored in the back of the freezer, and fresh birds were put on the shelves to freeze. There were undoubtedly modifications of this plan, but the basic principles were the same. The result was a place where birds could be frozen and held until they were ready to be shipped to market. It also gave hunters some control over the prices they received. They could hold birds until after the season and then sell them when prices might be higher. Around 1890, there were two freezers in Spirit Lake and another in nearby Arnolds Park.[7]

Probably the most detailed description of market hunting for ducks in Iowa comes from Harker, who hunted in the Spirit Lake area north to Heron Lake, Minnesota. He was part of a seven-man group that hunted from 15 August to freezeup in November. In an average year, the seven shot about 14,000 ducks. Dude Gilbert, a legendary shooter from Spirit Lake, was the top hunter and killed about 3,000 birds in a fall. They shipped their birds from Lakefield, Minnesota, to Chicago and New York. The prices they received for whole frozen birds varied greatly by species: $2–$2.50 per dozen for blue-winged teal, $6–$7 per

dozen for mallards, $8–$10 per dozen for redheads, and up to $12–$15 per dozen for canvasbacks. In the 1890s, canvasbacks sold for as much as $36 per dozen. Small or less desirable ducks like scaup, goldeneye, bufflehead, and merganser went for ten cents each in spring and $1.50 per dozen in the fall. The hunters had to provide their own guns, but their boss paid them $75 per month and provided everything else—food, shells, and shelter. Commonly, the shelter was just a primitive cabin.[8]

Harker's hunting methods were simple but effective. He used a ten- to twelve-foot homemade boat, pointed at both ends to ease passage through the reeds. A push pole was used to move the boat through the shallow waters where he hunted (fig. 15). He did not use a permanent blind, although he often hid behind reeds or made a temporary blind of any materials readily available. Late in the season, he might use ice blocks or snowdrifts as hiding places. He did not use a duck call but called with his voice and was proud of his ability to attract birds. Instead of using a dog to retrieve birds, Harker visually marked where they fell and waded out to get them himself. On large lakes, he let the wind drift the birds to shore and picked them up there. He used a variety of decoys (figs. 16–19), most of which were homemade, to attract birds close enough to shoot. Harker often mixed coot decoys in with his duck sets, believing that ducks were attracted to mixtures of birds. On one spring hunt, he found many redheads landing far out on the lake away from any pass. He stalked them by crawling out on the ice, putting out a long string of

Fig. 16. Pre-1900 drake mallard decoy from Spirit Lake, Iowa, used for market hunting. Courtesy State Historical Society of Iowa, Des Moines. Photograph by Chuck Greiner.

Fig. 17. Drake mallard decoy made by Swiss immigrant F. Scholer of Burlington, Iowa. Courtesy State Historical Society of Iowa, Des Moines. Photograph by Chuck Greiner.

Fig. 18. Drake canvasback decoy probably made by Albert Olson of Heron Lake, Minnesota, c. 1900, used in market hunting. Courtesy State Historical Society of Iowa, Des Moines. Photograph by Chuck Greiner.

Fig. 19. Hen can-vasback decoy made by Mason, c. 1900, used by market hunter Henry Tennant of Arnolds Park, Iowa. Courtesy State Historical Society of Iowa, Des Moines. Photograph by Chuck Greiner.

decoys on a rope, and hiding under some sheets he placed on the ice. In several days of shooting, he shot several hundred birds, which he let drift to shore and picked up later. One day the ice he was sitting on broke free and started drifting across the lake. Luckily, that day he had a boat with him and was able to get back to shore. Although Harker seems to have respected the hunting season's opening and closing dates, he had several altercations with game wardens because he did not believe in buying a hunting license.[9]

Market hunters used a variety of shotguns for hunting (figs. 20–22). Harker recalls that his boss provided his hunters with pump guns in the mid-1880s. Harker also had a double-barreled gun for ducks and prairie-chickens. Gun brands used then included Spencer, Winchester, Parker, Baker, and Smith.[10]

The preferred hunting method for most market hunters seems to have been pass shooting. Hunters stationed themselves at a place where ducks often flew, such as a point of land sticking out into a lake or a narrow bridge of land separating two bodies of water, and then shot them as they passed by. Some passes, such as the one between Spirit Lake and East Okoboji and the narrow pass on East Okoboji east of the town of Spirit Lake, were famous for the number of birds that could be shot there. John Smith, who came to Kossuth County in 1866, said that until 1882 the duck pass on the north end of East Okoboji was the greatest pass for mixed duck shooting in the United States. Another good pass was at Elbow Lake in Palo Alto County (just

south of Ruthven but now drained), where Smith and another hunter shot 240 ducks in a day.[11]

If the birds were not flying, the hunters might resort to jump shooting. Harker recalled using a push pole to move his boat through beds of reeds and shooting the birds that he flushed. He had a cross pole on his boat and leaned his gun, barrel down, against the pole so that he could reach it rapidly when he flushed a bird. A modern hunter might worry that a too-quick trigger finger would result in a hole shot in the boat's bottom. Apparently this was not a concern to Harker. He said he often shot thirty to forty birds in an afternoon of jump shooting.[12]

A third way to hunt was to creep up on a flock of birds resting on the water or in a field. Once the hunters were within shooting distance, they would jump up and shoot as many as possible before the birds flew out of range. This method could be very effective. Elmer Hinshaw recalls a small boy who, in about 1890, crept up to and killed forty-seven mallards with two shots from a gun with a shortened barrel. Harker and his brother made a similar sneak attack on a flock of 3,000–4,000 green-winged teal and killed about forty birds with four shots. Likewise, one fall Harker and his brothers crawled out on the ice of West Okoboji Lake before dawn to surprise some geese. The four of them shot forty-one geese.[13]

In the fall of 1887, fifteen-year-old Wilson Sawyer worked as a wagon driver for three experienced market hunters. They hunted near Spirit Lake and north into southern Minnesota, starting on 15 August and continuing until the middle of November, when the lakes began to freeze. They mostly hunted prairie-chickens in September and early October and then switched to ducks for the rest of the season. The group killed about 5,000 birds, about half of them prairie-chickens and the

rest ducks. Prairie-chickens and mallards sold for three dollars per dozen, while canvasbacks brought five dollars per pair in New York City. The latter were rare, and they shot few of them. Sawyer said the wages were not high because game prices were low. His wages for the last two weeks were six dollars, the end of his career as a market hunter.[14]

Robert Miller of Spirit Lake recalled several big kills while he was a market hunter. Once he and another hunter killed 485 ducks in a day at Spirit Lake. In 1905, he and two others filled a ten-foot wagon with 232 green-winged teal they shot on Christopherson Slough east of Spirit Lake.[15]

Another area that attracted many ducks and hunters was the Des Moines River bottomland south of Emmetsburg near Rodman. One year in the late 1800s, heavy summer rains left much of the area flooded, and huge flocks of waterfowl gathered there. The train to Rodman brought in a steady stream of hunters, fifty to one hundred a day, who hunted the bottomlands from September to November. Three men shot 214 mallards (all drakes of course!) in two hours and quit because they ran out of shells. They filled their boat with the birds and had trouble getting the heavy boat through shallow water on their return. Two brothers, Judd and John Brownlee, said that they averaged about a hundred birds a day for the season. Those two also shipped 75,000 birds from Rodman and estimated that they sold 250,000 shells in a few weeks during the peak of the hunt. In other years, they had good hunting, but none that matched that year.[16]

Not all the good duck hunting was in northwestern Iowa. The river bottoms along the Skunk River in central Iowa were prime waterfowl habitat and attracted many hunters. In the early 1880s, Buck Lufkin of Newton recalled the sky being filled with mallards in November. At that time, a mixed bag of ducks sold

Fig. 22. Marlin 12-gauge pump shotgun made between 1898 and 1905. This gun was used by the James Wilson family on their farm near Barnes, Iowa. Courtesy State Historical Society of Iowa, Des Moines. Photograph by Chuck Greiner.

for $1.50 per dozen, while in later years prices went as high as $12 per dozen. He and others also hunted in spring, when many waterfowl passed through central Iowa. Fred Carlson of Des Moines, who hunted this area from 1897 to 1906, said his best day's kill was ninety-four mallards and a teal. Another Des Moines man, Pete Butler, hunted the area in the 1850s and 1860s. He was mainly a sport hunter, but once when he had a large kill, he shipped them to Chicago. Most sold for twenty-five cents, but canvasbacks brought sixty to seventy-five cents, and geese went for forty to fifty cents each. All these hunters lamented the dredging and straightening of the Skunk River, which led to the loss of its good hunting areas.[17]

One of the few accounts of market hunting on the Mississippi River in Iowa involves Carl Bauer, who started hunting in 1909 at the age of ten. He continued to hunt near Camanche in Clinton County until 1934 and guided hunters until 1979. Bauer froze his birds in a barrel of ice and shipped them to markets in Clinton, Davenport, and Chicago every week. He sold small ducks like teal and scaup for twenty cents each, while big ducks like mallards went for thirty cents each. His best year was 1918, when he and two others took 750 ducks, mostly mallards. In his poorest year, during World War I, he killed only 175 ducks.[18]

Sport Hunting

Besides market hunters, there were also sport hunters, who did not sell their game on the market (fig. 23). However, these hunters also took many birds, although not on a steady day-after-day basis like the market hunters. Even if some of their hunting stories were exaggerated by bragging, they still must have taken a large number of birds (figs. 24, 25). A few examples of their bags

Fig. 23. A Morning among Teal. *From* The Art of Wing Shooting, *1895, by William B. Leffingwell.*

Fig. 24. H. Claude and Frank E. Horack with a string of ducks, c. 1895–97. Courtesy State Historical Society of Iowa, Iowa City.

Fig. 25. J. C. Hartman and L. M. Hummel with thirty-two ducks shot by Hartman two and a half miles above Waterloo, 26 March 1894. Courtesy State Historical Society of Iowa, Iowa City.

William B. include 82 mallards shot in an afternoon at Big Marsh in 1874,
Leffingwell, 267 ducks taken by five hunters at the Spirit Lake pass in Novem-
1850–1909 ber 1878, and 300 ducks and 32 geese taken by four men in a
day in the 1850s in northeastern Iowa. In 1901, four men hunt-
Born in eastern ing near Dickens in Clay County averaged 68 ducks per day for
Iowa, William six days, more than 400 birds in all.[19]
Leffingwell William Leffingwell, a well-known hunter and writer, recalled
studied law at a hunt in spring 1883 on flooded lands along the Missouri River
the University of north of Missouri Valley. He and a partner killed seventy to
Iowa and then eighty redheads with 120 shells in an hour and quit because they
practiced law were out of shells. He called it the "greatest hour of my life
in Chicago. among ducks."[20]
Throughout his In the early 1880s, Robert Miller, then only a boy, worked for
life, Leffingwell Billy Wiggins, an active sportsman at Spirit Lake. Miller recalled
retained a deep one day when Wiggins shot so many ducks at the pass on East
love for his home Okoboji just east of Spirit Lake that Miller had to get a double
state, especially for box wagon to carry them all. He estimated that it took 1,000
hunting in Iowa. ducks to fill the wagon, and they gave ducks to anyone who
He returned wanted them. Wiggins shot all day, sometimes getting four or
regularly to the five per shot. Another time, Miller and Wiggins together shot
Clinton area to fifty-two Canada geese on the east side of Spirit Lake.[21]
hunt ducks and John Smith of Algona praised the duck hunting in Iowa in the
other game. late 1800s. In October 1882, he killed seventy canvasbacks in a
Eventually, he day. In 1910, he said that most of the breeding grounds had
wrote several been drained, and duck hunting was no longer what it once had
books on hunting. been.[22]
The first, Wild The Spirit Lake area was a popular hunting place for sports-
Fowl Shooting, men from large cities. A special train, known as the Duck Special
published in and run by the Des Moines, Northern and Western Railway
1888, was the Company, carried hunters from Des Moines to Spirit Lake (fig.
authoritative 26). The train usually consisted of an engine, a coach, and a bag-
book on the topic; gage car. It passed through prime waterfowl country on the trip,
The Art of and whenever the hunters saw ducks along the track, the con-
Wing Shooting ductor stopped the train and let them off to hunt. One large
appeared in 1894. slough between Rockwell City and Jolley in Calhoun County
Leffingwell also was a regular stop. When the hunters were ready, the engineer
contributed three gave a blast of the train's whistle, putting the ducks in flight.
chapters to Such a practice is frowned on now, but it certainly was popular a
Shooting on century ago. Schedules were not followed closely, and hunting
Upland, Marsh, from the train apparently was almost as popular as the hunting in
and Stream, the Spirit Lake area. In 1880, a round-trip ticket from Chicago
published in 1890, to Spirit Lake cost twenty dollars. The hunter could stay in the

train car free while hunting at Spirit Lake and could stay in hotels there for about one dollar a night.[23]

Harker recalled that sport hunters resented the market hunters and the large kills they made. One night, sport hunters split open his hunting boat with an axe and ruined it. Another time they shot at him, so the bad feelings ran deep.[24]

For all that was written about duck hunting, relatively little was said about goose hunting. Harker recalled several goose hunts, usually involving what he called brant. This name was applied to both the snow goose and white-fronted goose, two smaller species that were generally considered poorer eating and less desirable. He usually shot geese by hiding when he heard a flock approaching and then shooting them as they flew by. One afternoon he shot nine brant and lamented having to carry them all home. Another time he set his decoys out in a field before dawn and waited for a flock of geese to come within shooting range. Hunting was slow, so he shot two prairie-chickens. The sound of his gun scared up a flock of geese that, unbeknownst to him, had been feeding nearby. It was too foggy to see the birds as they passed over him, but Harker shot three times anyway and claimed he dropped three geese.[25]

Hamlin Garland recalled several tricks that hunters used to get close enough to shoot a goose. These included using a cow as a screen to approach the birds and driving a wagon at full speed into a flock of geese and then shooting them before they all could fly out of gun range.[26]

An amusing waterfowl tale comes from Muscatine in the 1850s. A young boy had heard that you could capture ducks by covering your head with a hollow pumpkin and slowly wading up to them with only the pumpkin showing above water. Once you were close to the birds, you grabbed their legs and pulled them under water. He tried this but found that the ducks would not let him approach close enough to be caught. He did end up with his body covered with leeches though.[27]

which contained chapters by a number of experts on various types of hunting. Leffingwell was especially known for his sportsmanlike attitude toward hunting and his emphasis on promoting proper hunting procedures. In 1909, while on a hunting trip, a dog knocked a loaded gun over, causing it to fire. The shot hit Leffingwell and killed him.

Source: Furnish, W. M. 1980. W. B. Leffingwell, Iowa sportsman. Palimpsest 61: 162–169.

Decline of Waterfowl

Until the late 1800s, most waterfowl species probably still thrived in Iowa, but then a combination of factors began to have an effect on their populations. The continued settlement of the prairie regions meant that there were more people to hunt waterfowl. Both market hunting and sport hunting became more

popular and began to take a toll. More important, the wetlands, which the ducks depended on, began to be drained because they interfered with farming. At first only the shallowest were drained, but eventually better equipment meant that even the deepest ponds could be drained and the land converted to cropland. By 1906, fewer than a million acres of wetlands remained in Iowa. This drainage has continued up to the present time. Overall, the state has lost an estimated eighty-nine percent of its wetland acreage and, with it, most of its waterfowl habitat.[28]

Despite their importance as game animals, waterfowl received little attention in Iowa's hunting laws. Like some other wildlife, waterfowl were so abundant that it seemed inconceivable that their numbers could ever be threatened. In 1878, a closed season for ducks and geese between 1 May and 15 August provided nominal protection during the summer. This closed season was lengthened by a month in 1898. In 1904, a bag limit of twenty-five was set for ducks and geese, but waterfowl were exempted from the possession limits imposed on other game species. Thus, a hunter could have more than twenty-five in possession at one time. With such a loophole and the lack of much enforcement, the laws were largely ineffective. As a result, the clouds of ducks that writers spoke of in the 1800s are only a distant memory.[29]

Waterfowl have long been popular game in Iowa, and a variety of seasons have been fashioned for the various species. Only about 100,000 ducks have been taken annually in the state in recent years, a considerable reduction from the 300,000–400,000 taken in the 1970s and early 1980s. In contrast, the number of Canada geese taken has increased greatly, and about 26,000 were killed by hunters in 1990.[30]

Epilogue

Early in the 1900s, the passage of several federal laws helped waterfowl. The Lacey Act (introduced by Representative John Lacey of Oskaloosa) in 1900 effectively stopped much of the market hunting. The signing of the Migratory Bird Treaty between the United States and Canada in 1916 and a 1918 act of Congress to implement the treaty finally provided recognition that migratory birds, including ducks and geese, were a federal responsibility. Thus, the federal government began to take a role in setting waterfowl-hunting regulations. Spring hunting was banned, and there was some coordination among the states on the timing and length of hunting seasons and on bag limits.

The drought of the 1930s had disastrous effects on North American waterfowl and their habitat. In the height of the depression, many people became concerned about the future of waterfowl in the United States. As a result, the national wildlife refuge system was expanded, with waterfowl benefiting greatly. Money from the sale of duck stamps, from an excise tax on hunting equipment, and from such conservation groups as Ducks Unlimited helped protect waterfowl habitat. Iowans such as Aldo Leopold, J. N. "Ding" Darling, and Ira Gabrielson took a leading role in these actions. The ducks came back, and in the 1950s numbers peaked again.

In recent years, however, the general picture has been bad news for ducks and good news for geese. Despite the purchase of increasing amounts of nesting habitat in the northern United States, Canada, and Alaska, the populations of most duck species have continued to decline. Numbers of both the mallard and northern pintail, two of the most numerous species, are at thirty-year lows, while the redhead and canvasback have shown little response to hunting regulations designed to reduce their kill. Most ducks still nest on private land, where drainage of good duck habitat continues. An increasing concern in recent years is evidence that nest predation rates are very high and may limit duck numbers in some areas. Some experts believe that many ducks now must nest in the increasingly smaller remnants of suitable habitat, where predators can locate the nests easily. Toxic chemicals in the environment probably also take a toll. Whatever the reason, the picture for ducks in general is not rosy.[31]

In contrast, snow and Canada geese have thrived in recent years. Canada geese have been reintroduced to numerous states, including Iowa, and have done well in many of those areas. They seem adaptable enough to thrive in close association with humans and in some cases are now a pest on parks, golf courses, and beaches. Snow geese nest in the arctic, where human intervention is not a major problem yet. Modern mechanical farming methods leave much waste grain in the fields, where geese and ducks can feed on it. This new food supply, along with refuges for migrants and wintering birds, has meant that goose populations have done well in recent years.

In Iowa, the general pattern in the 1900s has been continued loss of waterfowl habitat and, with it, a continued decline in the numbers of most species. However, despite the overall gloomy picture for Iowa waterfowl, three striking success stories stand out. The wood duck, a brightly colored bird of bottomland backwaters and flooded timber, was considered very rare in Iowa in the 1920s and 1930s, and protective measures were taken to ensure its survival. A closed hunting season and the woodies' use of artificial nest boxes have helped the species come back. In Iowa, wood ducks have moved away from the river bottomlands of eastern Iowa and now are found statewide, even on prairie marshes. It is currently one of the most abundant waterfowl species nesting in Iowa.

Historically, Canada geese nested over most of the prairie region of Iowa, probably in great numbers. Their large size made them a favorite meal, and they disappeared from many areas soon after settlement. The last nest reported in Iowa was about 1910, and after that they were seen only during migration. The geese that nested in Iowa were the giant subspecies, a form that was long feared extinct. In 1962, giant Canada geese were found wintering at Rochester, Minnesota, and soon it was discovered that some birds held by Midwest game breeders were descended from wild giant Canadas. In 1964, the Iowa Conservation Commission bought sixteen pairs from game breeders and released them in a fenced pen at Ingham Lake near Estherville. Gradually this flock grew, and in 1971 similar flocks were started near Spirit Lake and Ruthven. In 1972 birds were moved to Lake Mills in north-central Iowa, and in 1976 a flock was started near Colyn in south-central Iowa. Additional releases have been made elsewhere, and the captive flocks have increased and spread out into nearby areas. By 1990, Canada geese were nesting in nearly every county in Iowa. In addition, breeding populations to the north of Iowa have also increased, so that flocks migrating through Iowa may even exceed the numbers seen in the 1800s.[32]

Snow geese also have flourished. Although the species never did nest in Iowa, snow geese migrate through the state, especially along the Missouri River valley. Surprisingly, there is little mention of this migration in the historical literature. Perhaps with the greater amount of habitat available then, the birds were more spread out and did not form the great concentrations we see today. In any case, the flocks seem to be increasing so that perhaps more than one million snow geese regularly migrate through Iowa each fall, and upwards of a quarter of a million can be seen together at the DeSoto National Wildlife Refuge near Missouri Valley in late October and November.

Currently, there is still some good nesting habitat in northwestern and north-central Iowa, where a variety of waterfowl species nest. Outside that region, other than the wood duck, the number of waterfowl nesting in the state is quite small and will never approach the numbers of the past unless habitat conditions improve dramatically. Iowa has long been an important migratory stopover for waterfowl in both spring and fall. Although much of the natural habitat is gone, a number of state and federal wildlife areas provide habitat for thousands of ducks and geese every spring and fall. Also, many of Iowa's natural lakes and rivers, recently created reservoirs, and sheet-water areas are important for migrating waterfowl. In recent years, Iowa has taken on added importance for wintering waterfowl. Several species, especially mallard, Canada goose, and snow goose, gradually have extended their wintering range northward in this century. Plentiful food from the waste grain left behind by modern mechanical harvesters and adequate habitat on some of the refuges have benefited those species. In some years, thousands of the three species have wintered in Iowa. Thus, despite the overall decline in waterfowl conditions in Iowa, the state still supports a good variety of waterfowl that can be enjoyed by many Iowans.

18. Introduced Species

Although North America supports a wide variety of native wildlife species, there is a long history of attempts by humans to "improve" on natural conditions by introducing non-native species to areas where they do not naturally occur. Species that have been introduced into North America range from the European starling and house sparrow to camels and wild boars. Most of these attempts have failed. Unfortunately, some of the species that are now well established, such as the starling and house sparrow, are also pest species.[1]

Upland game birds have been one of the most popular groups for such introductions. A wide variety of upland game birds have been introduced into North America. Many are relatively easy to raise in captivity, thereby providing stock for such introductions. Also, many of these species do not migrate, ensuring that whoever releases the birds will probably have birds remaining nearby where they can be hunted. With the disappearance of the prairie-chicken from the state, it is not surprising that in Iowa, as in other states, there have been a number of attempts to establish non-native upland game birds. At least five different species have been released in Iowa. Some of the releases have been officially sanctioned by Iowa game agencies, while others have been made by private individuals without any official approval. Undoubtedly, there have been many unsanctioned releases for which no records exist. Most probably involved only a few birds, which quickly were killed by predators or died for a variety of other reasons. Overall, two of the five species have been successfully established in Iowa, while the other three have failed.[2]

Ring-necked Pheasants

The ring-necked pheasant, a bird native to China, is by far the most successful introduced game species in Iowa. Ring-necks were first brought to North America in the 1700s. One of the first introductions was by Richard Bache, Benjamin Franklin's son-in-law, who released some along the Delaware River in New Jersey about 1790. For the next one hundred years, there were numerous stocking attempts in the eastern United States, generally with limited success. The first really successful release in North America was in 1881, when twenty-eight birds brought from Shanghai, China, were released in the Willamette Valley of Oregon. The birds thrived and within a few years occupied much of the valley. By 1891, they were being hunted there. With that success, ring-necks were soon being raised in many North American game farms, including one run by a William Benton at Cedar Falls. In 1900 or 1901, a windstorm blew down the fences confining the birds, and about 2,000 pheasants escaped. This seems to have been the first introduction of pheasants into Iowa, although it is possible that other birds had been released earlier. Additional private releases were made in Keokuk County in 1904, Kossuth County in 1907, and O'Brien County in 1908. The last two were successful, and pheasants were soon well established in north-central Iowa.[3]

With the pheasant established in north-central Iowa, there was interest in trying to establish populations elsewhere in the state. In 1909, Iowa first began charging hunters a license fee. In 1910, money from this fee was used to purchase pheasant eggs from private game breeders; the eggs were then distributed to farmers throughout Iowa, who released the young that hatched. The program was continued for the next several years, and some adult pheasants were also released. The state set up its own game farm at the state fair grounds in Des Moines in 1913 and used the birds raised there to supply pheasants for releases all over Iowa. As a result of these efforts, pheasants became well established across much of northern Iowa. However, efforts to establish them in southern Iowa were less successful. In the mid-1920s, a different method was used to supply birds for stocking. Wild birds were trapped in northern Iowa and moved to other areas. Also, sportsmen and farmers were paid to gather eggs (one dollar per dozen) from wild pheasant nests. When the eggs hatched, the young were moved and released. In 1925, 60,000 eggs and 7,000 birds were taken from Butler and Winnebago counties, indicating both a tremendous population of pheasants in those counties and the magnitude of the effort to get the species established throughout the state. Stocking efforts continued in southern Iowa into the 1930s, still with poor success. Aldo Leopold estimated that in all, from 1913 to 1932, 100,000–150,000 pheasants were released in the state, most of them in southern or eastern Iowa.[4]

Statewide, the pheasant population declined some in the 1930s, largely because of bad weather. In 1938, a new state game farm was opened near Ledges State Park in Boone County. Farmers and hunters were also encouraged to become involved in improving habitat conditions for pheasants by providing winter and nesting cover. Accordingly, for about the next twenty years, the state supplied young pheasants to landowners and others for release, but only if it appeared that the birds had a reasonable chance of surviving on the land at the release site. By the mid-1950s, despite the thousands of birds that had been released by the state, pheasants were still not plentiful in southern Iowa. In 1961, the old brood stock at the state game farm was replaced with new, wilder birds. Offspring from this new brood stock were then released in southeastern Iowa. These birds formed the nucleus of a population that is now well established. Thus, after some sixty years of effort, pheasants finally occupied the entire state.[5]

With the immediate success of pheasants in northern Iowa, it was soon evident that they could be hunted. A hunting season of three half-days was opened in thirteen counties in north-central

Iowa in 1925. From that beginning, the number of counties open to hunting and the length of the hunting season were gradually expanded (fig. 27). After a closed season in 1936 and 1937, forty-two counties were opened to hunting in 1938. In 1951 ninety-two counties were open to pheasant hunting, and by 1976 all ninety-nine counties had pheasant hunting. Probably the most unusual hunting season was in 1943, when both spring and fall seasons were held. In addition, hunters were allowed to take up to two hens, one of the few years when hens could be legally hunted. A large pheasant population and the fear of crop damage were the reasons for the liberal limits.[6]

Clearly, the ring-neck is well established as a game bird in Iowa. With some help from stocking efforts, pheasants have gradually expanded their range, so that now they occupy virtually the entire state. This expansion has continued despite their being a legal game bird for nearly all those years. In some of the peak years, almost two million pheasants were taken by hunters in Iowa. In recent years, the kill has been around 1.4 million birds. Thus, the pheasant reigns as the top game bird in Iowa, and Iowa in turn ranks as one of the top pheasant-hunting states in the nation.[7]

Despite the popularity and importance of pheasants as a game bird in Iowa, not everyone has welcomed them in the state. Some farmers were concerned that pheasants would damage their crops, a concern that helped lead to the opening of a hunting season for pheasants in 1925. Sometimes landowners tried to reduce the pheasant breeding population by killing the birds in spring. The report from one county of 160 dead pheasants strung up on two miles of fence was the result of such an effort. Hunting pheasants helped reduce such concerns but led to other problems, namely, conflicts between farmers and hunters who trespassed on their land. Despite a variety of laws to control the conflicts, the problem still exists today. Another negative factor is a concern that pheasants may have competed with prairie-chickens and contributed to their disappearance from Iowa. This has been a problem in Illinois and may limit the success of recent attempts to reestablish prairie-chickens in Iowa.[8]

Although pheasants thrive in Iowa, they need better cover than that provided by such row crops as corn and soybeans. Pheasants typically nest in thickly vegetated grasslands and her-baceous cover. Before about 1950, hayfields, pastures, and other similar lands were readily available in Iowa and provided nesting cover for pheasants. In winter they require thicker cover and commonly will gather in woodlots, farm groves, hedgerows, windbreaks, or sloughs to escape severe weather.

Because most of Iowa's pheasant habitat is on privately owned farmland, changes in local and national farm policies have a ma-jor effect on pheasant habitat and their numbers. In the late 1950s and early 1960s, the federal Soil Bank Program allowed large acreages of land to be idled for several consecutive years. This encouraged landowners to plant grasses and legumes, which often provided ideal pheasant cover on their land. Many pheas-ants were produced on these lands, and the pheasant harvest generally was high during the 1960s. The annual set-aside pro-grams that also idled millions of acres of Iowa farmland were less beneficial to pheasants because the cover on them was often an annual plant.[9]

During the 1970s, farming in Iowa became increasingly inten-sive, and, with that shift, many of the hayfields, pastures, fence-rows, and other idle land that had previously provided nesting and winter cover for pheasants were planted with corn or soy-beans. The change was most obvious in northern Iowa. An in-tensively studied area in Winnebago County in north-central Iowa offers evidence. In 1941 farmers raised a wide variety of crops, while in 1976 they mainly raised corn or soybeans. During that period, fall pheasant numbers in the area dropped· from about 500 to about 25 birds. Similar land-use changes were made over a large area of Iowa. The importance of the winter cover that those lands had provided was soon apparent. In January 1975, a severe blizzard in northwestern Iowa killed perhaps seventy to eighty percent of the pheasants in that area of the state.[10]

Although overall pheasant numbers declined in Iowa in the 1970s, their numbers did increase in southern Iowa as populations became well established there. Because of the generally steeper topography in that part of the state, farming has not been so intensive, and winter and nesting cover are more abundant. Gradually, the center of abundance of pheasants shifted to central and southern Iowa. In the 1990s, the center shifted again, with pockets of high abundance scattered throughout Iowa.

Various government agriculture programs still have a major effect on how much pheasant habitat is available and hence are an important factor in regulating pheasant numbers. The 1985 federal farm bill provided for participating landowners to idle land for ten years under the Conservation Reserve Program. If good nesting or winter cover is planted on the idle land, the program could have a major effect on pheasant numbers. The large number of pheasants seen in the late 1980s and early 1990s suggests that just such an effect is already occurring.

Nationally, pheasant numbers have shown a pattern similar to that found in Iowa. In most states, pheasant numbers peaked twenty to forty years after pheasants were established and then the numbers declined. Habitat has been the major factor in determining population levels throughout the species' range. In 1985, the pre–hunting-season populations in North America were estimated at 31 – 33 million birds, a sizable population but greatly reduced from previous numbers. For example, it was estimated that in the 1940s South and North Dakota alone had more than that many pheasants. Ring-necks are an important game bird across the northern half of the United States. They are capable of withstanding heavy hunting pressure and bounce back rapidly from severe weather-related losses. Their future numbers will depend largely on our ability to provide them with suitable habitat.[11]

Gray Partridge

Gray partridge are native to much of Europe and western Asia. Like the pheasant, they first were brought to North America in the late 1700s, when Benjamin Franklin's son-in-law, Richard Bache, released some on his land along the Delaware River in New Jersey. Numerous other releases were made in many states, especially from 1907 to 1914. In general, most of these were unsuccessful, with the birds soon disappearing. Despite many failures, populations were established in the northwestern United States, on the northern Great Plains, around the Great Lakes, and in the Maritime Provinces of Canada. Birds persist in all those areas, with the Great Plains population the most successful.[12]

Gray partridge were first introduced into Iowa in 1902, when about fifty were released near Waterloo; those birds soon disappeared. The first successful release was in 1905, when twenty-four birds were released in Palo Alto County. There were several more releases by 1910 and many more from 1911 to 1915, concentrated in the northern third of the state. By 1920, partridge had also been released in a number of northeastern, southeastern, and south-central counties, but none of these releases were successful in establishing the species. In all, at least several thousand partridge were released in the state by 1932. From these attempts, partridge became established in north-central and northwestern Iowa.[13]

Despite the initial success with gray partridge, most people were more interested in the highly successful ring-necked pheasant, and the gray partridge was largely overlooked. In the late 1930s, a hunting season was opened for partridge in eleven northwestern Iowa counties. Partridge numbers in Iowa remained fairly low from the 1940s through the mid-1960s, although roadside counts showed a gradual increase in numbers from 1954 to 1964. A severe blizzard that decimated pheasant populations in northwestern Iowa in March 1965 had little effect on partridge. With the reduced number of pheasants, many upland game hunters shifted their attention to partridge, and the harvest of partridge increased.[14]

Since the mid-1970s, gray partridge have gradually expanded their range from their northern Iowa stronghold. From 1969 to 1972, about 1,500 partridge were released in southwestern Iowa, and a small population became established there. In October 1979, 300 were released in three southeastern counties in an attempt to establish the species in that corner of the state; in September 1980, 120 were released near Ottumwa. Besides these stocking attempts, the partridge's range has expanded naturally. Its numbers have increased greatly, so that now partridge are found south to the Missouri border in some parts of Iowa. Like pheasants, partridge live largely on farmland. However, they seem to be able to survive better on intensively farmed land than do pheasants. Thus, they gradually have become an important game bird in the state, and their importance will probably continue to grow. A hunting season for gray partridge was established in 1963. About 8,000 birds were taken the first year, and the number taken by hunters in Iowa has increased since then to almost 150,000 birds in 1990.[15]

Overall, the population of gray partridge seems to be stable in North America. A 1988 survey of biologists from states and provinces with gray partridge populations indicated that numbers were increasing on the Great Plains, stable or declining in the Northwest, and declining in the Great Lakes and Maritime regions. During the 1980s, hunter harvests in North America averaged about 700,000 birds per year, indicating that this is still a relatively minor game bird.[16]

Chukars

Besides the two success stories, at least three other upland game species have been stocked but have failed to become established in Iowa. The chukar, a small quaillike bird native to southeastern Europe and southern Asia, has been stocked numerous times in North America. The chukars that eventually survived in North America came from Pakistan. They were first brought to the United States in 1893, when five pairs were released in Illinois. Since then more than 800,000 chukars have been released in forty-three states, including Hawaii, and six Canadian provinces. Many of the birds were captive-reared and probably had little chance of survival in the wild. Still, the species is now well established in the West from British Columbia south to California and east to Colorado and Wyoming. It is also established on several of the Hawaiian Islands. In the West, chukars thrive on arid and semiarid lands in rough terrain covered with scattered brush and clumps of cheatgrass. Many of these areas were overgrazed in the late 1800s, and the native perennials were replaced by annual grasses. As a result, such native game species as the sage grouse have disappeared, and the chukar has replaced them, becoming well established as a game bird.[17]

Chukars have been released in Iowa several times, but none of the releases has succeeded in establishing a population. In spring

1938, the Iowa Conservation Commission purchased 500 chukar eggs, from which it was able to raise 475 birds. These birds formed the nucleus of a captive-breeding population. In the next two years, the state released 930 chukars in twelve southwestern Iowa counties. Additional birds were released in Allamakee and Clayton counties in northeastern Iowa at the same time. However, these birds soon died out. Within a few years, the program was considered unsuccessful and was stopped. Because the chukar is a common game-farm bird, undoubtedly there have been other releases of the species in Iowa. As recently as 1970, one hundred were released near Davenport. These birds must have nested successfully, because some continued to be sighted in the area into the early 1980s. However, that attempt, like earlier ones, was not finally successful in establishing chukars in Iowa.[18]

Reeves' Pheasants

A second unsuccessful attempt at stocking game birds in Iowa involved the Reeves' pheasant, a large pheasant native to open woodlands of northern China. In the early 1960s, the Iowa Conservation Commission decided to try to establish the species in southern Iowa. At the time, there were few ring-necked pheasants in southern Iowa, and the attempt was seen as a way to provide a comparable game bird for hunters in that part of the state. Because of the Reeves' pheasant's habitat requirements, it was thought that the species might thrive in the hilly woodlands of southern Iowa. The commission began by purchasing about 200 pheasant eggs and some females from Ohio in 1961 to start a captive breeding flock. In January 1963, twenty-two Reeves' pheasants were released in Stephens State Forest in Lucas County in south-central Iowa. More releases were made, so that by mid-1964, 263 had been released in Lucas County, as well as a few near Ledges State Park in Boone County. The stocking program continued, and by September 1966 more than 4,600 birds had been released in Lucas and Monroe counties. In the ensuing years, there were numerous sightings of the birds, mostly within a few miles of the release sites. Several broods were seen in 1965, 1966, and 1967, indicating that they had nested successfully. However, in general, the birds did not do well. The birds that were released were descended from stock that had been in captivity for several generations. They were very tame, and many were killed by predators or died in accidents. To try to remedy this problem, in 1968 another 180 pheasants from a different stock were released in Lucas County. These birds also were tame and were not an improvement over the original stock. Despite all these efforts, Reeves' pheasants did not become established in Iowa. Also, in the mid-1960s, ring-necked pheasant numbers began to increase in southern Iowa, and there was no longer a "need" for the Reeves' pheasant. Thus, the program was stopped, and there are no plans to try again.[19]

Coturnix or Common Quail

The coturnix quail is a small quaillike bird that is common in much of southern Europe and Asia. It has been widely introduced into North America but without any lasting success. The only indication that coturnix quail were ever released in Iowa is the report that some captured in Italy were released in Iowa between 1877 and 1881. This stocking was unsuccessful, and I know of no other such releases. However, because this is such a common game-farm bird, there easily could have been unreported unsuccessful releases in Iowa.[20]

19. Humans and Wildlife in Iowa

The preceding chapters have described great changes in the abundance of numerous wildlife species since the time Europeans settled in Iowa. Many factors, most of them in some way related to humans and their intrusions on the environment, have affected the populations of these species. In general, these factors are of three major types: habitat changes, technological changes, and social and political factors. The sections that follow discuss some of the more important of these and provide an overview of how they have affected Iowa's wildlife over the years.

Habitat Changes

The first explorers to reach Iowa found a land that was largely covered by three kinds of habitat: prairies, forests, and wetlands. In the 160 years since settlers began to arrive, humans have had a dramatic effect on the native habitats. The most obvious change has been the replacement of native vegetation with domestic crops, roads, and buildings. As a result, less than ten percent of Iowa still retains habitat similar to what covered it 160 years ago. Even where native vegetation has remained unaltered, often it has been fragmented into small, isolated tracts. In general, these smaller parcels are less useful to wildlife species than were the original large blocks of habitat, and some species seem unable to survive on such small tracts. Habitat changes have had a more profound effect on Iowa's wildlife resources than any other factor.

Prairies

When the first settlers reached Iowa, they found that as they moved west from the Mississippi River or left the woodlands that dominated the landscape along the major river valleys, much of the rest of the state was covered by tall-grass prairie. Just how much of Iowa was once prairie is not known. One expert estimates that about eighty-seven percent of Iowa originally was covered by prairie. However, others estimate that nineteen percent of the state was woodlands, and wetlands covered about another eleven percent of Iowa, so perhaps seventy percent is a better estimate of the extent of the prairies. Whatever the exact figure, the point is still the same; before settlement, prairie was the dominant cover in most of Iowa. Originally covering perhaps twenty-five million acres of Iowa, most of Iowa's native prairie had been removed by about 1950. Although precise figures are not available, the best estimate is that Iowa currently has about 30,000 acres of prairie remaining. This represents only about 0.12 percent of the original extent of prairie in Iowa. In short, native prairie, the ecosystem that typified most of Iowa, is now endangered in the state.[1]

It is no mystery why so much of the original prairie cover was removed. Although the earliest settlers generally stayed close to woodlands or wooded river valleys, they soon discovered that the prairie soils, although harder to work and often needing draining, were much richer than those underlying forested areas. Soon the prairies were sought out, their sod was broken, and various crops were planted on them. The better-drained prairies were usually the first to be claimed, while the lower, wetter prairies were often bypassed. Eventually, as these areas were drained, they, too, were cultivated and planted with various crops.[2]

In about eighty years, some twenty-five million acres of prairie were converted to farmland, a rate of about three million acres per decade. This conversion of prairie to farmland had a greater impact on the landscape of Iowa than any other factor in the last 200 years. Although the prairie lands first were planted with a variety of crops, including wheat, corn, hay, and oats, in recent decades much of the land has been planted with just two crops, corn and soybeans. Whereas by 1860 Iowa had only about 3.8 million acres of improved farmland, in the late 1980s 18 to 20 million acres were planted with just these two crops yearly. As a hint of how vast these prairies once were, one only has to note which lands in Iowa are now planted in corn or soybeans. In the 1830s, most of that land was prairie.[3]

The native prairies disappeared so rapidly that few people were aware of the loss until it was too late. Despite several pleas to establish parks or preserves to save remnants of Iowa's native prairie, by the mid-1900s most were gone. The few prairies that have been preserved generally are small; the largest is only a few hundred acres. In recent years, there has been much interest in reestablishing prairies. Restored prairies provide a hint of the open landscape that once covered the state and also contain some of the dominant prairie plants. However, many of the rarer or less conspicuous prairie plants often are not found on restored prairies.[4]

Not surprisingly, a number of animals native to Iowa were largely prairie species. Some of these, such as the upland sandpiper and dickcissel (a sparrowlike bird), have been able to survive on the prairie remnants or have adapted to managed lands similar to prairies, such as pastures and hayfields. Others have not adjusted and now are missing from Iowa. As has already been described, these include the bison, elk, greater prairie-chicken, long-billed curlew, and marbled godwit. Other than the prairie-chicken, it is unlikely that Iowa will ever again support viable wild populations of any of these species.

Despite the predominance of prairie in Iowa, appreciable portions of the state were once covered with trees. Forests were most extensive in eastern Iowa but were found throughout the state, generally along river valleys even in north-central and northwestern Iowa. Notes from the original land survey of Iowa in 1832–59 suggest that forests covered 6.7 million acres, or about nineteen percent, of Iowa at the time of settlement, although that may not have all been truly forest.[5]

In most of Iowa, the first settlers tended to claim land covered with trees or near forests, because it provided wood for houses, fences, and fuel. Without a supply of wood, it might have cost a settler $340 to fence forty acres, an indication of the value of wooded land. As eastern Iowa was settled in the 1840s and 1850s, large areas of the original forest cover were removed as settlers cleared the land for their crops. With the advent of railroads in the 1850s, timber was needed for railroad ties, placing another demand on Iowa's woodlands.[6]

By 1875, the extent of forests in Iowa had been reduced to an estimated 2.5 million acres, only about seven percent of the state's area. In a few decades, about sixty percent of its forests had already been lost. No other statewide estimates are available until 1954, when Iowa's forest land covered an estimated 2.6 million acres. Although the methods used in the 1875 and 1954 surveys differ, their results suggest little change in the forest lands of Iowa. Probably any increases in forests because of the abandonment of farms, development of some parks, and planting of trees in towns and farm groves were offset by the continued clearing of other wooded areas. The most recent survey (1974) shows a drop to 1.6 million acres, or only four percent, of the state still covered with forests. In only twenty years, one million acres of forest were lost. Continued clearing for agriculture, growth of towns and cities, new roads, and a host of other reasons all contributed to this loss.[7]

Even more alarming is the fact that only eight percent of the forest land in 1974 is publicly owned. There are no national forests and only a few fairly small state forests in Iowa. Like prairie, much of the state's remaining forest cover is in scattered tracts that often have limited value to wildlife. Iowa has few forest tracts of even 1,000 acres, mostly in eastern Iowa, and thus species that require large wooded tracts probably cannot survive here.[8]

As with prairies, the loss of forests has affected a variety of wildlife. Such species as black bear, gray wolf, mountain lion, ruffed grouse, and wild turkey were largely found in wooded areas. The first three species no longer occur in Iowa, while the range of the grouse is much reduced from the past. Wild turkeys were extirpated but have been restocked and currently are doing well. Other wildlife species live where forests come in contact with other habitats; these species also suffered when forests disappeared. Wood duck, American woodcock, beaver, and river otter all live where woods and wetlands meet, whereas white-tailed deer, quail, and bobcat often live at the edge between woodland and prairie. All these species declined in number at one time or another, although several, such as the wood duck, deer, and beaver, have adapted well and now are thriving in Iowa.

Wetlands

The third habitat type that is important to Iowa's wildlife is wetlands. Wetlands are areas that are covered with water for at least part of the year, such as lakes, rivers, ponds, marshes, and streams. The best estimate of how much of the state was covered by wetlands at the time of settlement is about four million acres (eleven percent), but by 1906 less than a million acres remained. In the 1980s, only about 422,000 acres, or eleven percent, of the original coverage remained. Thus, almost ninety percent of Iowa's wetlands have been lost, mainly to drainage.[9]

Several different kinds of wetlands are found in Iowa. From a wildlife perspective, perhaps the most important type originally found in the state was the shallow prairie marsh. Especially numerous in the glaciated pothole region of north-central Iowa, prairie marshes probably accounted for at least seventy-five percent of the four million acres of wetlands in the state, at the time of settlement, but only about 26,000 acres of the marshes remain now. Thus, perhaps ninety-nine percent of these shallow wetlands have been lost.[10]

Once settlers realized how rich the soil on this land was, they began draining it and converting it to farmland, just as they did with the prairies. The federal Swamp Land Act of 1850, which gave almost 1.2 million acres of public land to the state of Iowa, was one of the first inducements to drain Iowa's wetlands. At first, many marshes were drained by simply running a shallow ditch to the nearest stream or river. Later, farmers organized drainage districts with networks of ditches that removed water from a larger region. Eventually, when drainage tile was developed, thousands of miles of tile were laid beneath the fields, providing even more rapid removal of water from the land. Although prairie wetlands were drained as early as the 1890s, the activity continued well into the mid-1900s. Even today, there is still pressure to drain the few remaining wetlands in Iowa.[11]

The two border rivers and their associated backwater areas, which cover about 325,000 acres, are another important type of wetland. Thousands of acres of this wetland habitat have been converted to other uses, especially along the Missouri River, where many of the oxbow lakes and associated wetlands have been lost as the river was converted to a deep, fast-moving ditch. Along the Mississippi River, soil that has eroded off the land is an increasing problem as it settles and gradually fills in backwater areas away from the river's main channel. These backwater areas are some of the most productive for wildlife.[12]

Smaller rivers and streams, which cover about 52,000 acres, are another type of wetland that is important to wildlife. Again, much of this habitat has been lost, especially through channelization. Usually a channelized stream is straightened, reducing the area covered with water. Channelized streams tend to have a faster current and less vegetative cover, which also diminishes their value to many wildlife species. In addition, runoff from drainage tiles and ditches adds sediments and chemicals to the stream, further reducing its ability to provide good wildlife habitat.[13]

As with prairies and woodlands, the loss of wetlands has affected a number of wildlife species. The sandhill and the whooping crane, waterfowl, and furbearers, such as beaver, muskrat, and otter, all depended on wetlands as a breeding habitat, and waterfowl, cranes, and shorebirds used wetlands during their spring and fall migration through Iowa. Populations of all these species are much reduced now compared to their numbers at the time of settlement.

Technological Changes

In the 1800s, the United States entered an era in which it changed from a rural agrarian society to an urban industrial society. This change was accompanied by tremendous technological growth as humans found ways to do many tasks faster, better, and cheaper. Transportation, farming, and trapping and hunting have all been greatly affected, and many of the technological advances have had direct or indirect effects on Iowa's wildlife.

Transportation

Early in the 1800s, a number of people began building steam-driven locomotives, the beginning of our modern railroad system. Improvements came rapidly, and by the early 1850s, shortly after Iowa had achieved statehood, a fairly good railroad network had been established in much of the eastern United States. The first railroad tracks in Iowa were laid in 1855 along a corridor extending west from Davenport. In 1856, the first railroad bridge across the Mississippi carried trains from Rock Island, Illinois, to Davenport, Iowa, and provided a direct railway connection between Iowa and the East. Other railroads also began laying track in Iowa, and by 1867 trains had reached the Missouri River at Council Bluffs.[14]

In a few decades, Iowa had an elaborate network of railroads that reached almost every town in the state. The coming of the railroad was often the reason a town was established, and many towns withered and died if they were missed by the railroad. This complex railroad network was a major factor in encouraging and supporting the dispersed pattern of settlement that typified Iowa in the late 1800s and early 1900s. Railroads were important in transporting settlers across the state as new areas were settled. Railroads also were vital in transporting supplies to settlers and in carrying their crops and livestock to markets in Iowa and elsewhere. Just as the automobile dominates our lives today, the railroad did so in an earlier Iowa. The network of railroad tracks reached its peak in 1914, when the state had about 10,000 miles of track. By 1989, this had declined to about 3,354 miles, only a third of the peak level.[15]

Over the years, the locomotives continued to improve. Faster travel, along with the development of refrigerated railroad cars in the 1860s and 1870s, provided a way for Iowans to ship meat to markets in the East. Market hunters were able to freeze their kill and ship it hundreds of miles, a breakthrough that made market hunting for prairie-chickens, shorebirds, and waterfowl practical in Iowa and had great impact on those species.[16]

Less recognized was the effect railroads had on Iowa's forests and other habitats. Incredible numbers of trees were cut for railroad ties, contributing to the reduction in forest cover in Iowa. It took perhaps six acres of oak woods to provide the railroad ties needed for one mile of railroad. Although Iowa's railroad ties were not all cut locally, many acres of trees were cleared for that purpose alone. Railroads are also an important land use in Iowa. Each mile of railroad right-of-way covers about twelve acres. Therefore, at their peak, railroads covered about 120,000 acres of the state. Railroad right-of-ways provide important strips of wildlife habitat, especially in areas that are dominated by agricultural crops.[17]

Boat travel was also important in Iowa. Just as early explorers used rivers as highways to reach Iowa, many early settlers reached the state by boat. The development of steam-powered boats in the late 1700s and early 1800s meant that travel by boat became faster. Boat travel was important as a way to move both passengers and freight in early Iowa, but other than removing some bankside trees for fuel, it had little effect on wildlife.[18]

Two sets of rapids on the Mississippi River hampered early boat travel. The worst were the Des Moines Rapids just upstream from Keokuk in southeastern Iowa. Attempts to improve navigation began in the 1830s, when Lieutenant Robert E. Lee directed work to widen and deepen the channel. Later a 7.6-mile canal with three locks was built around the rapids; it opened in 1877. The rapids at Rock Island were less serious, and widening and deepening the channel improved navigation.[19]

Boat transportation has had a much greater effect on Iowa's wildlife in this century because both the Mississippi and Missouri rivers have been greatly altered by humans. To facilitate barge traffic and reduce flooding, eleven dams have been built on the Mississippi River along Iowa's eastern border. At each of these dams, sediment that has washed in from farmlands has settled in the pool above the dam. As a result, thousands of acres of backwaters, prime habitat for much wildlife, have been filled in. On the Missouri, the opposite has happened. To provide a channel for barges, the river has been converted into a narrow, rapidly flowing stream that continues to dig a deeper channel. Consequently, backwaters along the river that once were rich wildlife habitat are now left perched high and dry above the river.[20]

The development of travel by automobile has dominated transportation in the twentieth century. Its effects on wildlife are both direct and indirect. Iowa's road system in 1990 totaled some 112,000 miles, covering thousands of square miles with roads and their right-of-ways. Although the right-of-ways provide some wildlife habitat, usually they are planted with only a few species of grass, are mowed regularly, and in general provide limited cover for most wildlife. Fortunately, a number of counties have recently recognized the potential value of this land and have begun to convert right-of-ways to native vegetation. In addition, tens of thousands of animals are killed in collisions with vehicles each year. About 9,000 deer alone are killed yearly in collisions in Iowa.[21]

The indirect effects of automobiles on wildlife are more subtle but perhaps of equal importance. The automobile (along with trucks and other vehicles) has made travel more rapid and more convenient. Faster transportation means crops can be moved to market rapidly, thereby contributing to the development of more intensive agriculture in the state. Thus, improved transportation has played an indirect but important role in the loss of several habitats described earlier.

Farming

Much of the habitat change in Iowa has involved conversion of original habitats to land uses associated with various agricultural crops. At first, this was done with backbreaking manual labor. An axe, a plow, and a few other simple tools, along with a horse or oxen to supplement the settler's own labor, were often all that was available or needed to start a farm. This was a labor-intensive process, and once the land was cleared or broken, crops were planted and harvested by hand. Farm size typically was limited by the amount of land that a family could plant, tend, and harvest.

During the 1800s, there were a number of technological advances that changed farming from a simple, labor-intensive process to the highly mechanized methods practiced today. These advances had a significant effect on wildlife in Iowa.

An important factor limiting the movement of settlers onto Iowa's prairies was the difficulty of breaking up the thick root masses underlying the virgin tall-grass prairie. In 1837, John Deere developed a plow with a steel cutting-edge that was much better than earlier plows in breaking through the thick mat of roots and heavy soil of the prairie. By the 1850s, Deere was producing large numbers of these plows, just in time for the settlement of Iowa's prairie regions. Often the initial "breaking of the prairie" was done with a special breaking plow, pulled by three to six yokes of oxen and run by a custom crew. A good crew might break only two acres of prairie a day, an indication of the labor involved and the relatively primitive technology available at the time.[22]

Once the sod had been broken, planting, cultivation, and harvesting still were manual, labor-intensive jobs. Gradually, other advances were made that increased the amount of land an individual could farm. In the 1830s and 1840s, a variety of machinery for planting and harvesting various crops was developed, leading to a great increase in productivity. In the post–Civil War era, there were further improvements in farm implements that increased the productivity of farmers, including better harrows, improved corn planters and grain drills, and cultivators. At the same time, there were advances in harvesting machinery: reapers were improved and eventually combines were developed. Although the first tractors were built in the late 1800s, they were not widely available until the 1910s and 1920s. Improvements in technology continued in the early twentieth century. From 1910 to 1940, the replacement of horses with tractors, the advent of mechanical corn pickers, and the development of hybrid corn dominated technological change in the Corn Belt and led to continued gains in productivity on the farm.[23]

Technological advances allowed Iowa's farmers to convert increasing amounts of the state, especially the tall-grass prairie, to farmland. Individual farms also increased in size. In 1860, seventy-two percent of Iowa's 61,000 farms were from 20 to 100 acres in size and only seventeen percent exceeded 100 acres, whereas in 1989 Iowa's farms averaged 319 acres. Although fewer people were directly farming the land, the farming was more intensive and the land-use pattern on farms changed. Tractors did not need pasture land, and they did not eat oats. Thus, land that formerly had been left as pasture for horses and land devoted to growing oats to feed horses could now be planted in other crops, especially corn at first and later soybeans. This shift in land use generally had a detrimental effect on wildlife. Pasture and to some extent oats provide nesting cover for upland game species and in general provide more cover than corn does. Thus, there began a shift toward a less diversified agricultural system in Iowa, one which today is dominated by four commodities— corn, soybeans, beef, pork—and which provides much less habitat for wildlife than the earlier more diversified agricultural system. Also, as farms became larger, field size increased, resulting in fewer fencerows and a decrease in other small patches of "waste" land that formerly were important for wildlife. The recent decline in the number of quail and the disappearance of prairie-chickens from Iowa are good examples of the effect of that change.[24]

A more recent hazard to wildlife populations is the use of various chemicals to increase crop production. Several million tons of various fertilizers and several million pounds of a broad array of herbicides and insecticides are applied annually to a large share of Iowa's land surface. The fate of these chemicals and their effect on wildlife are still poorly understood, but there are enough known deleterious effects to warrant concern. The use of these chemicals is largely a post–World War II phenomenon, and fortunately in recent years their application has been reduced and limits have been placed on some of the more hazardous forms. To minimize their effects on wildlife, the continued use of these chemicals will require better monitoring and understanding than we have had in the past.[25]

Trapping and Hunting

Before 1850, the steel traps used to capture various furbearers were handmade by blacksmiths or people who specialized in their manufacture. In the mid-1800s, the industry began a rapid change in its production methods as it became increasingly mechanized. Machines were used to produce the trap parts, and traps were assembled on an assembly line. As a result, a wide variety of more effective traps were developed and placed on the market. In general, traps became more available to casual trappers, such as many settlers and farmers in Iowa. The increased availability of traps probably was important in the widespread use of traps in Iowa in the late 1800s.

There has been continued improvement in traps in this century, but despite these improvements several of the most heavily trapped mammals in Iowa (e.g., raccoon, coyote, red fox) have managed to thrive and even increase in number. At least for these species, the change has not severely affected their populations.[26]

As with trapping, there have been considerable improvements in the firearms available to hunters over the years. The early explorers and settlers had only muzzleloading muskets and pistols. In the late 1850s, breechloading rifles became available. This improvement, along with better overall design and more reliable ammunition, meant that hunters gradually gained a greater advantage over their prey. While elk and bison were extirpated in the era of the more primitive guns, it is hard to imagine the era of market hunting for waterfowl, shorebirds, and prairie-chickens in Iowa without the shotgun. Firearm improvement has continued up to the present time, with contemporary guns and ammunition more effective than those available a generation or two ago. It is interesting that some modern hunters, in an attempt to turn back time, have returned to using muzzleloaders and bow and arrow to hunt some species.[27]

Social and Political Factors

Legislation Affecting Wildlife

For many years, wildlife was considered a resource to exploit and was given little thought. The first laws affecting wildlife in Iowa concerned bounties paid for killing predators, especially wolves and coyotes. These date back to territorial days and have been discussed in earlier chapters. One of Iowa's first laws to limit hunting was passed in 1878 and set a bag limit of twenty-five per day for a number of upland game species, perhaps the first bag limits passed by any state. For the next twenty years, a variety of game laws, most limiting the number of animals that could be legally taken or the length of the season, were passed. However, there was little attempt to enforce many of these laws, and they generally had little effect on the exploitation of wildlife. In 1897, Iowa established the position of state game warden, the first step toward developing what is now a statewide system of conservation officers. The law also provided for a number of deputy wardens, but it was not until 1909 that the legislature agreed to pay these individuals for their work. In 1900 hunting licenses were required for nonresidents, and in 1909 Iowans were first required to buy a license to hunt, a requirement now considered routine.[28]

Currently, Iowa has laws regulating hunting seasons for a wide variety of species. The timing of the seasons and the bag limits are set annually in an attempt to regulate the exploitation of the species over time. The lack of hunting seasons and limits had a major impact on some species in the pioneer days, but generally game populations are now managed so that hunting does not cause serious effects on the populations.

Land Disposal

Iowa's total land area is about 55,986 square miles, or roughly 35.8 million acres. After Native Americans were displaced, all this belonged to the federal government and was turned over to private ownership very rapidly. By far, the most common means of disposal were grants given to individuals for their service in the military (14.1 million acres) and land sold for cash (11.9 million acres). Another 4.36 million acres were granted to the railroads to spur growth in Iowa; 1.16 million acres were granted to Iowans to try to encourage projects to make the Des Moines River navigable; and another 1.19 million acres were granted under the Swamp Land Act, supposedly so that the state could reclaim the land and make it useful. The Homestead Act, so famous for its encouragement of settlement further west, accounted for only 0.9 million acres in Iowa. By 1890, the federal government owned only about 5,000 acres in Iowa, a testament to the quality and value of Iowa land. Probably few other states matched this record for both the speed and completeness of its settlement.[29]

Human Population Growth

Since virtually all the factors considered so far involve the effect of humans on wildlife, it is important to look at human population growth in Iowa. In 1836, the year Iowa became a U.S. territory, the population, excluding Native Americans, was estimated at 10,531. By 1850 the population was 192,000; ten years later it was 675,000, a phenomenal growth in twenty-four years. Iowa's population continued to grow rapidly, and by 1900 it exceeded two million. At the time, Iowa was the tenth most-populous state in the nation. After a slight dip in the first decade of the 1900s, the population has continued to grow, reaching a peak of 2,913,000 in 1980. The 1980s saw a drop in population for only the second time in the state's history. At its peak, Iowa's population density was about fifty-two per square mile, a moderate density by today's standards. Iowa currently ranks twenty-ninth among the states in population.

Of equal importance is the distribution of Iowa's population. The original settlement pattern was based on an agrarian society, and people were spread out, most living on small farms; six or eight farms per square mile was not unusual. This pattern reached its peak in the late 1800s; since then there has been a continuing population shift, with people moving into the towns

Table 2. Iowa's Population Growth, 1836 to 1990

Year	Total Population	Percent Urban
1836	10,531	
1846	96,088	
1860	674,913	<15
1900	2,321,853	25
1950	2,261,041	48
1980	2,913,808	59
1990	2,700,000	>60

Sources: Data from U.S. Census Statistics.

and, more recently, the cities. The number of farms in Iowa has declined from about 213,000 in 1940 to about 105,000 in 1989. Almost certainly, that number will continue to drop in the future. The population shift is apparent in other ways. Although many small towns and county-seat towns continued to thrive economically into the 1950s and 1960s, in recent years they have lost businesses, schools, and population as people have continued to move to larger cities (see table 2). A few figures amplify this shift. In the 1980s, only seven of Iowa's ninety-nine counties gained population, while an astounding fifty counties lost ten percent or more of their population. From a longer-term perspective, sixty-four counties have fewer people now than they did in 1900.[30]

The population shift has had a number of effects on Iowa's wildlife. The most obvious is that farm units have become larger, and there has been a shift from many small farms with a variety of land uses to fewer farms with larger fields and less variety in their use. In addition, most of the land is now devoted to just a few crops. In most years, somewhat over half of Iowa's surface area is planted in two crops, corn and soybeans. In addition, the shift of humans away from the rural areas has probably contributed to a gradual decline in the number of hunters and trappers in recent years. Although the long-term effect of such a shift on wildlife in general and on hunted and trapped populations in particular is not clear, it may cause some alteration in the societal value of wildlife.

In sum, Iowa has changed dramatically since Europeans first ventured into the region in the 1600s, and the changes have affected the state's wildlife in many ways. Some species have disappeared and probably will never return. Others dwindled and disappeared, only to thrive again when reintroduced into the state. Still others have changed little in number and continue to thrive in Iowa. Probably the safest prediction is that there will be more changes in the future, just as there have been in the past. Only time will provide us the details.

20. The Future of Wildlife in Iowa

W hat does the future hold for Iowa's wildlife? I have discussed about thirty species of birds and mammals native to Iowa that have been exploited in various ways by humans and for which there is some record of population changes since settlement. I have not discussed the 300 or so other species of birds and mammals that regularly occur in the state. Many of these were not hunted or trapped, but virtually all have in some way been affected by humans. Perhaps sometime their story will also be told. But for the species that I have discussed, what future do they have in Iowa?

One species, the passenger pigeon, has no future because it is extinct, and another, the eskimo curlew, is so close to extinction that many people already have written it off as a hopeless cause. Another ten species (bison, elk, black bear, mountain lion, lynx, swift fox, gray wolf, long-billed curlew, marbled godwit, and whooping crane) no longer have breeding populations in Iowa, and the prospects that they will reoccupy the state in the future are remote. Some would argue that two of these, swift fox and lynx, never existed in Iowa or that at best probably only the periphery of their range reached Iowa. One species, marbled godwit, still occurs as a regular migrant in Iowa, and three others, black bear, whooping crane, and long-billed curlew, occasionally wander to Iowa. However, I believe that it is unlikely that any of these ten species will reestablish a stable population in Iowa; certainly not in the near future. Not surprisingly, six of the ten species were primarily inhabitants of prairies and their associated wetlands, the habitat that has been most altered in Iowa.

A few years ago, two other species, sandhill crane and greater prairie-chicken, would have been on that list, too, but in the past several years there has been a glimmer of hope for them. Sandhill cranes, as noted earlier, have expanded their range dramatically in recent years and nested in Iowa in 1992. I believe that there is a reasonable chance that a small breeding population of sandhill cranes might be reestablished in Iowa in the next decade or two. The most recent attempt, in Ringgold County in 1987–89, to reestablish prairie-chickens in the state has had some success and provides some hope for that species. The newly established Walnut Creek National Wildlife Refuge near Prairie City may provide another opportunity to restock prairie-chickens in Iowa. Several thousand acres of prairie-savanna habitat will be restored on the central Iowa refuge, which is about twenty-five miles east of Des Moines. The key to prairie-chicken survival at either site will be providing enough good-quality grassland habitat.

Another eight species seem to be holding their own in Iowa, albeit at reduced numbers from the past. These include the bobcat, red and gray foxes, ruffed grouse, northern bobwhite, American woodcock, common snipe, and American golden-plover. The snipe is mainly a migrant and the plover is strictly so, but both are fairly common in Iowa. The bobcat occurs in very small numbers but seems to be doing about as well as can be expected. The northern bobwhite also seems to be doing reasonably well, although its numbers certainly are reduced from what they were a century ago. Ruffed grouse are holding their own in their northeastern Iowa stronghold and have had moderate success at some of the sites where they have been restocked.

Only a few species seem to be really thriving, including white-tailed deer, coyote, beaver, muskrat, Canada goose, wood duck, and wild turkey. Four of these—deer, beaver, Canada goose, and wild turkey—once were extirpated from Iowa, so their return is especially encouraging. In addition, two introduced species, ring-necked pheasant and gray partridge, continue to do well; the gray partridge has expanded its range rapidly in the last decade or so. These nine species are among the most intensively managed species in Iowa. All seem to be quite adaptable and able to survive near humans and on human-altered landscapes. It is premature to evaluate the success of the recent releases of river otter, but preliminary indications suggest that at least some of the releases have been successful.

Despite the recent success of wood ducks and Canada geese in the state, breeding populations of other nesting waterfowl continue to be much reduced from the past. In Iowa, only mallard and blue-winged teal nest in any numbers, although half a dozen other species—northern pintail, northern shoveler, gadwall, redhead, hooded merganser, and ruddy duck—nest in small numbers, and a few others nest sporadically.

The rapid decline in numbers of many species of waterfowl in the 1980s does not bode well for the future of waterfowl in North America. The North American Waterfowl Management Plan has a goal of providing enough habitat to sustain a breeding population of sixty-two million ducks in North America by the year 2000. This plan emphasizes developing cooperative ventures among the federal governments of the United States, Canada, and Mexico, and also between the federal governments and numerous private, state, and provincial organizations. In Iowa, the goal is to preserve or restore 30,000 acres of wetlands and associated uplands by 2000. If successful, this could ensure that Iowa would continue to support at least remnant populations of mallards, blue-winged teal, and several other nesting species. Such habitat might also support sandhill cranes. The trumpeter swan, a species that disappeared from Iowa in the 1880s, has been restocked in Minnesota, and it could conceivably return. In the early 1990s, the Iowa Department of Natural Resources and several other organizations began developing a plan to release trumpeter swans in Iowa.[1]

Thus, in the 160 years since Iowa was opened to European settlers, there have been tremendous changes in the wildlife found in the state. The net change has been a loss of wildlife. Some species, especially several of the largest predators and hooved mammals, are gone for good. Others, such as the bobcat, are so reduced in number that few people in Iowa will ever see one in the wild. Yet such species as white-tailed deer, wild turkey, and Canada goose have returned to an abundance probably matching their presettlement populations.

Prospects for the Future

There will undoubtedly be further changes for Iowa's wildlife, some positive and some negative. Only about two percent of the state's surface area is publicly owned and in a somewhat natural state. This ranks Iowa about forty-sixth among all states. However, the amount of land in public ownership in Iowa has increased quite rapidly in the past decade. Increasingly, various conservation organizations are preserving or restoring prairies, wetlands, and woodlands. Although the total land area covered by such habitats is still relatively small, it is a promising trend as far as the future of the state's wildlife is concerned.[2]

The future of Iowa's wildlife is also affected by political and economic decisions, many of which are made in Des Moines and Washington, D.C. Just as the removal of the native prairies, woodlands, and wetlands and their replacement with tens of thousands of farms meant major changes for wildlife in the 1800s, so too will changes in agriculture in the 1990s have their effect. A continued decline in the number of farms in Iowa, the removal of the farmsteads themselves, and the trend toward larger cultivated fields, all pushed by economic forces, will probably mean less "waste" land and field edges and thus less habitat for most wildlife species. However, federal programs like the Conservation Reserve Program, which has taken more than two million acres of erodible land in Iowa out of production (at least temporarily), have probably had a positive effect on some wildlife species. Likewise, the reduction in the amount of agricultural chemicals applied to the landscape and the increasing adoption of various conservation practices by farmers generally are positive trends.

Personally, I am cautiously optimistic about the future of Iowa's wildlife. To be sure, some species are gone for good. However, who would have predicted, fifty years ago, that deer would someday be a pest in Iowa or, thirty years ago, that wild turkeys and Canada geese would be nesting statewide and also considered a pest in some areas? Perhaps in twenty years we will look back and wonder why there was so much pessimism in the 1990s about the future of the sandhill crane and greater prairie-chicken in Iowa.

The other reason for my optimism rests with the people of Iowa. Iowa has produced a host of individuals—John Lacey, Aldo Leopold, Ira Gabrielson, and J. N. "Ding" Darling are just a few examples—who have gone on to become leaders in conservation efforts, both in Iowa and nationally. Certainly, with its strong education system and a growing concern for the environment, Iowa will continue to produce leaders who will find innovative ways to balance a concern for natural resources with the need to sustain the state's leading industry, agriculture. Perhaps the information provided in this book will remind these future leaders of what we have lost and prod them to find ways for a brighter future.

Notes

1. Wildlife and the Settlement of Iowa

1. Van der Zee, J. 1915. The Neutral Ground. Iowa Journal of History and Politics 13:321.

2. Bowles, J. B. 1981. Iowa's mammal fauna: an era of decline. Proceedings of the Iowa Academy of Science 88:38–42. Christiansen, J. L. 1981. Population trends among Iowa's amphibians and reptiles. Proceedings of the Iowa Academy of Science 88:24–27. Dinsmore, J. J. 1981. Iowa's avifauna: changes in the past and prospects for the future. Proceedings of the Iowa Academy of Science 88:28–37. Menzel, B. W. 1981. Iowa's waters and fishes: a century and a half of change. Proceedings of the Iowa Academy of Science 88:17–23. Kent, T. H., and C. J. Bendorf. 1991. Official checklist of Iowa birds 1991 edition. Iowa Bird Life 61:101–109. State of Iowa. 1986. Iowa Administrative Code. Section 571, chapter 77.1, pp. 1–4.

3. Wilson, E. O. 1992. The diversity of life. Harvard University Press, Cambridge, Massachusetts.

4. Petersen, W. J. 1952. The story of Iowa (2 volumes). Lewis Historical Publishing Co., New York. Sage, L. L. 1974. A history of Iowa. Iowa State University Press, Ames.

5. Donnelly, J. P. 1968. Jacques Marquette, S. J. Loyola University Press, Chicago, pp. 208–229.

6. Mahan, B. E. 1926. Old Fort Crawford and the frontier. State Historical Society of Iowa, Iowa City, p. 13.

7. Van der Zee, J. 1914. Fur trade operations in the eastern Iowa country under the Spanish regime. Iowa Journal of History and Politics 12:368–369. Scanlan, P. L., and M. Scanlan. 1932. Basil Giard and his land claim in Iowa. Iowa Journal of History and Politics 30:224–225.

8. Moulton, G. E. (editor). 1986. The journals of the Lewis & Clark expedition, volume 2. University of Nebraska Press, Lincoln, pp. 390–499. Thwaites, R. G. (editor). 1959. Original journals of the Lewis and Clark expedition 1804–1806, volume 5. Antiquarian Press, New York, pp. 376–380.

9. Coues, E. 1895. The expeditions of Zebulon Montgomery Pike, volume 1. Francis P. Harper, New York, pp. 13–48. Jackson, D. (editor). 1966. The journals of Zebulon Montgomery Pike, volume 1. University of Oklahoma Press, Norman, pp. 12–28.

10. James, E. (compiler). 1966. Account of an expedition from

Pittsburgh to the Rocky Mountains, volume 1. University Microfilms, Ann Arbor, Michigan, pp. 143–427.

11. Fuller, H. M., and L. R. Hafen (editors). 1957. The journal of Captain John R. Bell. A. H. Clark Co., Glendale, California, pp. 81–88. James, pp. 404–423.

12. Thwaites, R. G. (editor). 1906. Early western travels 1748–1846, volume 22. A. H. Clark Co., Cleveland, pp. 264–278.

13. Kearny, S. W. 1912. An expedition across Iowa in 1820. Annals of Iowa, 3rd series, 10:343–351. Petersen, W. J. 1931. Trail-making on the frontier. Palimpsest 12:298–314.

14. Pelzer, L. (editor). 1909. A journal of marches by the First United States Dragoons 1834–1835. Iowa Journal of History and Politics 7:365–378. Petersen, W. J. 1931. Across the prairies of Iowa. Palimpsest 12:326–334.

15. Van der Zee, J. 1913. Captain James Allen's dragoon expedition from Fort Des Moines, Territory of Iowa, in 1844. Iowa Journal of History and Politics 11:84–108.

16. Audubon, M. R. 1898. Audubon and his journals, volume 1. John C. Nimmo, London, pp. 476–489. Audubon, M. R. 1898. Audubon and his journals, volume 2. John C. Nimmo, London, pp. 170–172.

17. Allen, J. A. 1868. Notes on birds observed in western Iowa, in the months of July, August and September. Memoirs of the Boston Society of Natural History 1:488–502. Allen, J. A. 1871. Notes on the mammals of Iowa. Proceedings of the Boston Society of Natural History 13:178–194. Allen, J. A. 1870. Catalogue of the birds of Iowa. Pp. 419–427 *in* Report on the geological survey of the state of Iowa, volume 2 (C. A. White, editor). Mills and Co., Des Moines.

18. Osborn, H. 1890. Catalogue of the mammals of Iowa. Proceedings of the Iowa Academy of Science 1:41–44. Van Hyning, T., and F. C. Pellett. 1910. An annotated catalogue of the recent mammals of Iowa. Proceedings of the Iowa Academy of Science 17:211–218. Anderson, R. M. 1907. The birds of Iowa. Proceedings of the Davenport Academy of Sciences 11:125–417.

2. Bison

1. Seton, E. T. 1929. Lives of game animals, volume 3. Doubleday, Doran and Co., Garden City, New York, pp. 647, 654–656.

2. Barsness, L. 1985. Heads, hides & horns. Texas Christian University Press, Fort Worth, pp. 65–85.

3. Hornaday, W. T. 1889. The extermination of the American bison. Report of the U.S. National Museum, 1886–87, p. 487. Schorger, A. W. 1937. The range of the bison in Wisconsin. Transactions of the Wisconsin Academy of Sciences, Arts and Letters 30:128.

4. Hornaday, pp. 492–502, 502–513. Seton, p. 670. Barsness, pp. 158–172.

5. Dablon, C. 1959. Relation of the discovery of many countries situated to the south of New France, made in 1673. P. 99 *in* The Jesuit relations and allied documents, volume 58 (R. G. Thwaites, editor). Pageant Book Co., New York. Marquette, J. 1959. Of the first voyage made by Father Marquette toward new Mexico, and how the idea thereof was conceived. Pp. 111, 113 *in* The Jesuit relations and allied documents, volume 59.

6. Petersen, W. J. 1935. Buffalo hunting with Keokuk. Palimpsest 16:33–49.

7. James, E. (compiler). 1966. Account of an expedition from Pittsburgh to the Rocky Mountains, volume 1. University Microfilms, Ann Arbor, Michigan, pp. 420, 191. Wilhelm, P. 1938. First journey to North America in the years 1822 to 1824. South Dakota Historical Collections 19:343.

8. Kearny, S. W. 1912. An expedition across Iowa in 1820. Annals of Iowa, 3rd series, 10:343–351.

9. Pelzer, L. (editor). 1909. A journal of marches by the First United States Dragoons 1834–1835. Iowa Journal of History and Politics 7:365–369.

10. Van der Zee, J. 1913. Captain James Allen's dragoon expedition from Fort Des Moines, Territory of Iowa, in 1844. Iowa Journal of History and Politics 11:84–108.

11. Anon. 1879. The history of Clinton County, Iowa. Western Historical Co., Chicago, p. 330. Bennett, H. A. 1934. The mystery of the Iowa buffalo. Iowa Journal of History and Politics 32:66–69.

12. Meyers, F. W. 1911. History of Crawford County Iowa. S. J. Clarke Publishing Co., Chicago, pp. 57, 148.

13. Garden, R. I. 1907. Did the buffalo ever inhabit Iowa? Pp. 244–245, 263 *in* History of Scott Township Mahaska County, Iowa. Globe Presses, Oskaloosa, Iowa. Anon. 1883. History of Franklin and Cerro Gordo counties, Iowa. Western Publishing Co., Springfield, Illinois, p. 593. Stuart, I. L. 1914. History of Franklin County Iowa. S. J. Clarke Publishing Co., Chicago, p. 91. Ludington, H. H. 1908. An Iowa buffalo hunt in 1852. Proceedings of the Old Settlers Association of Johnson County 42:31–33. Murray, J. S. 1953. They came to North Tama. Traer Star-Clipper, Traer, Iowa, and Hudson Printing Co., Hudson, Iowa, p. 4. Reed, B. F. 1913. History of Kossuth County Iowa. S. J. Clarke Publishing Co., Chicago, pp. 49, 270–271. Birdsall, B. P. 1915. History of Wright County Iowa. B. F. Bowen and Co., Indianapolis, p. 56. Spurrell, J. A. 1917. An annotated list of the mammals of Sac County, Iowa. Proceedings of the Iowa Academy of Science 24:275. Hastie, E. N. 1938. Hastie's history of Dallas County Iowa. Wallace-Homestead

Co., Des Moines, p. 68. Leaman, B. R. 1971. An early settler in Iowa: westward expansion in microcosm. Annals of Iowa, 3rd series, 41:700. Fisher, K. 1978. In the beginning there was land: a history of Washington County, Iowa. Washington County Historical Society, Washington, Iowa, p. 24. Anon. 1881. History of Fremont County, Iowa. Iowa Historical Co., Des Moines, p. 518. Smith, J. H. 1888. History of Harrison County, Iowa. Iowa Printing Co., Des Moines, pp. 123–124.

14. Spurrell, p. 275. Smith, R. A. 1902. A history of Dickinson County, Iowa. Kenyon Printing and Manufacturing Co., Des Moines, pp. 378–381. Flickinger, R. E. 1904. The pioneer history of Pocahontas County, Iowa. Fonda Times, Fonda, Iowa, p. 221. Leaman, p. 700.

15. James, pp. 206–212.

16. Hornaday, p. 503. History of Franklin and Cerro Gordo counties, p. 593. Pammel, L. H. 1930. Buffalo in Iowa. Annals of Iowa, 3rd series, 17:418.

17. Reed, pp. 269–275.

18. Flickinger, pp. 221–223.

19. Smith, J. H., pp. 123–124.

20. Webster, C. L. 1897. History of Floyd County, Iowa. Intelligencer Print, Charles City, Iowa, p. 14.

21. Ludington, pp. 31–33.

22. History of Franklin and Cerro Gordo counties, p. 593. Garden, pp. 235, 239.

23. Percival, C. S., and E. Percival. 1881. History of Buchanan County, Iowa. Williams Bros., Cleveland, p. 56. Chappell, H. C., and K. J. Chappell. 1914. History of Buchanan County Iowa and its people. S. J. Clarke Publishing Co., Chicago, pp. 32–33.

24. Garden, pp. 238–239, 244–245, 263. Jones, E. L. 1977. Nathan Littler's history of Washington County 1835–1870. Conger House, Washington, Iowa.

25. Tjernagel, N. 1952. Pioneer foods and water supply. Annals of Iowa, 3rd series, 31:292. Pammel, pp. 418, 415.

26. Garden, p. 223.

27. White, E. S. 1915. Past and present of Shelby County Iowa. B. F. Bowen and Co., Indianapolis, p. 75.

28. Felton, O. J. 1931. Pioneer life in Jones County. Iowa Journal of History and Politics 29:250–251. Lesan, Mrs. B. M. 1937. Early history of Ringgold County, 1844–1937. Privately published, p. 189. Wilson, E. E. 1932. Buffalo wallows and trails in Black Hawk County. Annals of Iowa, 3rd series, 18:187. Anon. 1878. The history of Wapello County, Iowa. Western Historical Co., Chicago, p. 394.

29. Knight, L. 1943. Early Iowa resident disputes report that

buffalo never roamed this state. Sioux City Journal, 29 July 1943. Shimek, B. 1910. Geology of Harrison and Monona counties. Iowa Geological Survey Annual Report 20:407–410. Pammel, pp. 403–434.

30. Rorabacher, J. A. 1970. The American buffalo in transition. North Star Press, St. Cloud, Minnesota, p. 17. Ahrendsen, J. Clarion, Iowa, personal communication, April 1993.

31. Seton, p. 670. Rorabacher, pp. 116–117.

32. Leonard, E. J., and J. C. Goodman. 1955. Buffalo Bill: king of the Old West. Library Publishers, New York, p. 28. Trefethen, J. B. 1975. An American crusade for wildlife. Winchester Press and the Boone and Crockett Club, New York, pp. 88–89, 140–141.

3. Elk

1. Lyon, L. J., and J. W. Thomas. 1987. Elk: Rocky Mountain majesty. P. 148 *in* Restoring America's wildlife (H. Kallman, editor). U.S. Fish and Wildlife Service, Washington, D.C.

2. Seton, E. T. 1929. Lives of game animals, volume 3. Doubleday, Doran and Co., Garden City, New York, pp. 14, 20. Murie, O. J. 1951. The elk of North America. Stackpole Co., Harrisburg, Pennsylvania, p. 37. Schorger, A. W. 1954. The elk in early Wisconsin. Transactions of the Wisconsin Academy of Science, Arts and Letters 43:7.

3. Spurrell, J. A. 1917. An annotated list of the mammals of Sac County, Iowa. Proceedings of the Iowa Academy of Science 24: 275. Smith, J. A. 1895. The hegira of the elk. Midland Monthly 4: 177. Flickinger, R. E. 1904. The pioneer history of Pocahontas County, Iowa. Fonda Times, Fonda, Iowa, p. 276.

4. Kearny, S. W. 1912. An expedition across Iowa in 1820. Annals of Iowa, 3rd series, 10:343–352. Van der Zee, J. 1915. The Neutral Ground. Iowa Journal of History and Politics 13:320–321. Pelzer, L. (editor). 1909. A journal of marches by the First United States Dragoons 1834–1835. Iowa Journal of History and Politics 7:365–369.

5. Van der Zee, J. 1913. Captain James Allen's dragoon expedition from Fort Des Moines, Territory of Iowa, in 1844. Iowa Journal of History and Politics 11:79–108.

6. Birdsall, B. P. 1915. History of Wright County Iowa. B. F. Bowen and Co., Indianapolis, p. 56.

7. Brainard, J. M. 1894. The great blizzard of 1856. Annals of Iowa, 3rd series, 1:391–394. Hart, I. H. 1914. History of Butler County Iowa. S. J. Clarke Publishing Co., Chicago, p. 43. Wheeler, J. H. 1910. History of Cerro Gordo County Iowa. Lewis Publishing Co., Chicago, p. 189. Kilburn, L. M. 1915. History of Adair County Iowa and its people. Pioneer Publishing Co., Chicago, pp. 193–

194. Lee, J. W. 1912. History of Hamilton County Iowa. S. J. Clarke Publishing Co., Chicago, p. 200. Smith, J. H. 1888. History of Harrison County, Iowa. Iowa Printing Co., Des Moines, pp. 125–126. Anon. 1881. History of Montgomery County, Iowa. Iowa Historical and Biographical Co., Des Moines, p. 407. White, E. S. 1915. Past and present of Shelby County Iowa. B. F. Bowen and Co., Indianapolis, p. 75. Anon. 1884. History of Cass County, Iowa. Continental Historical Co., Springfield, Illinois, p. 288.

8. Corbit, R. M. 1910. History of Jones County, Iowa. S. J. Clarke Publishing Co., Chicago, p. 296. Anon. 1878. The history of Linn County, Iowa. Western Historical Co., Chicago, p. 334. Evans, S. B. 1901. History of Wapello County, Iowa, and representative citizens. Biographical Publishing Co., Chicago, p. 54. Percival, C. S., and E. Percival. 1881. History of Buchanan County, Iowa. Williams Bros., Cleveland, p. 56.

9. Smith, J. A., p. 178. Spurrell, p. 276. Reed, B. F. 1913. History of Kossuth County Iowa. S. J. Clarke Publishing Co., Chicago, pp. 158, 291–293. White, p. 75. Keck, I. 1925. A. J. Whisman, pioneer. Palimpsest 6:340. Andrews, H. F. 1915. History of Audubon County Iowa. B. F. Bowen and Co., Indianapolis, p. 41. Flickinger, pp. 276–277, 603. Spurrell, p. 275. Anon. 1889. Biographical history of Cherokee County, Iowa. W. S. Dunbar and Co., Chicago, p. 300. Smith, J. A., p. 177. Smith, R. A. 1902. A history of Dickinson County, Iowa. Kenyon Printing and Manufacturing Co., Des Moines, p. 382. Monlux, G. 1908–1909. Early history of Lyon County. Privately published, Rock Rapids, Iowa, p. 24. Perkins, D. A. W. 1892. History of Osceola County, Iowa. Brown and Saenger, Sioux Falls, South Dakota, p. 70. Wegerslev, C. H., and T. Walpole. 1909. Past and present of Buena Vista County Iowa. S. J. Clarke Publishing Co., Chicago, p. 110. Stillman, E. B. 1907. Past and present of Greene County, Iowa. S. J. Clarke Publishing Co., Chicago, p. 56.

10. Allen, J. A. 1871. Notes on the mammals of Iowa. Proceedings of the Boston Society of Natural History 13:185. Percival and Percival, p. 56. Reed, pp. 292–293, 154. Flickinger, p. 277. Anon. 1904–05. Compendium of history, reminiscence and biography of Lyon County, Iowa. G. A. Ogle and Co., Chicago, p. 24. Anon. 1981. Grundy County remembers, volume 2. Graphic Agri-Business, Alden, Iowa, p. 109.

11. Reed, pp. 155–158.

12. Anon. 1883. History of Franklin and Cerro Gordo counties, Iowa. Union Publishing Co., Springfield, Illinois, p. 219.

13. Moorehead, G. C. 1928. Historical collections of Ida County. Pioneer Record Press, Ida Grove, Iowa, p. 26.

14. Wheeler, pp. 188–189. Hartman, J. C. 1915. History of

Black Hawk County Iowa. S. J. Clarke Publishing Co., Chicago, p. 70.

15. Bennett, H. A. 1926. Fish and game legislation in Iowa. Iowa Journal of History and Politics 24:394–395, 406.

16. McCarty, D. G. 1910. History of Palo Alto County Iowa. Torch Press, Cedar Rapids, Iowa, p. 19. Mueller, H. A. 1915. History of Madison County Iowa and its people. S. J. Clarke Publishing Co., Chicago, p. 177. Stillman, pp. 24–25. Newhall, J. B. 1841. Sketches of Iowa. J. H. Colton, New York, pp. 28–29. Spurrell, p. 275. Anon. 1901. The history of Humboldt County. Historical Publishing Co., Chicago, p. 334. Reed, p. 154. History of Franklin and Cerro Gordo counties, p. 220. Anon. 1884. History of Kossuth, Hancock and Winnebago counties, Iowa. Union Publishing Co., Springfield, Illinois, p. 642. Andrews, p. 41. Dyke, C. L. 1942. The story of Sioux County. Verstegen Printing Co., Orange City, Iowa, p. 49.

17. Anon. 1879. The history of Dallas County, Iowa. Union Historical Co., Des Moines, p. 299. Chappell, H. C., and K. J. Chappell. 1914. History of Buchanan County Iowa and its people. S. J. Clarke Publishing Co., Chicago, pp. 32–33. Garden, R. I. 1907. History of Scott Township Mahaska County, Iowa. Globe Presses, Oskaloosa, Iowa, p. 223.

18. The history of Dallas County, pp. 299–300. Percival and Percival, p. 56. Thompson, F. O. 1937. Hunting in northwestern Iowa. Iowa Journal of History and Politics 35:85.

19. Reed, p. 154. The history of Dallas County, p. 300.

20. Anon. 1882. History of Floyd County, Iowa. Inter-State Publishing Co., Chicago, pp. 258–259. The history of Dallas County, p. 300.

21. Percival and Percival, p. 56. Chappell and Chappell, pp. 32–33. History of Cass County, pp. 245–246. Ingham, W. H. 1919. Ten years on the Iowa frontier. Privately published. Webster, C. L. 1897. History of Floyd County, Iowa. Intelligencer Print, Charles City, Iowa, p. 40. Reed, p. 49.

22. Andrews, p. 43. White, p. 75.

23. Anon. 1982. Quite a herd down at the Seehusen place. Des Moines Register, 26 September 1982, p. 1B. Anon. 1982. Untitled. Iowa Wildlife Notes (Iowa Conservation Commission) 1(3):5. Norman, J. 1984. Rogue elk roams in Lee County. Des Moines Register, 28 November 1984, p. 6M. Kingsley, L. 1988. All alone am I, bemoans Iowa's ramblin' kinda elk. Des Moines Register, 24 October 1988, p. 1A. Appleby, B. 1978. Let rare elk wander Iowa in peace, hunters asked. Des Moines Register, 2 December 1978, p. 15A. Anon. 1983. Untitled. Iowa Wildlife Notes (Iowa Conservation Commission) 2(9):1. Anon. 1986. Untitled. Iowa Wildlife Notes

(Iowa Conservation Commission) 5(4). Anon. 1989. Iowa hunter charged with killing elk. Ames Tribune, 4 December 1989, p. A6. Anon. 1990. Ida Grove hunter is acquitted in shooting of elk. Des Moines Register, 17 May 1990, p. 1M.

24. Bryant, L. D., and C. Maser. 1982. Classification and distribution. P. 1 *in* Elk of North America (J. W. Thomas and D. E. Toweill, editors). Stackpole Books, Harrisburg, Pennsylvania. Lyon and Thomas, p. 149. Potter, D. R. 1982. Recreation. Pp. 532–533 *in* Elk of North America.

4. White-tailed Deer

1. Seton, E. T. 1929. Lives of game animals, volume 3. Doubleday, Doran and Co., Garden City, New York, pp. 241, 246, 251.

2. Brainard, J. M. 1894. The great blizzard of 1856. Annals of Iowa, 3rd series, 1:393–394. Osborn, H. 1905. The recently extinct and vanishing animals of Iowa. Annals of Iowa, 3rd series, 6: 565. Reed, B. F. 1913. History of Kossuth County Iowa. S. J. Clarke Publishing Co., Chicago, pp. 158–159. Spurrell, J. A. 1917. An annotated list of the mammals of Sac County, Iowa. Proceedings of the Iowa Academy of Science 24:276. Van Hyning, T., and F. C. Pellett. 1910. An annotated catalogue of the recent mammals of Iowa. Proceedings of the Iowa Academy of Science 17:216.

3. Anon. 1882. History of Scott County, Iowa. Inter-State Publishing Co., Chicago, p. 552. Anon. 1878. The history of Delaware County, Iowa. Western Historical Co., Chicago, p. 411. Payne, W. O. 1911. History of Story County Iowa. S. J. Clarke Publishing Co., Chicago, p. 118. Anon. 1884. History of Cass County, Iowa. Continental Historical Co., Springfield, Illinois, p. 276. Anon. 1880. The history of Washington County, Iowa. Union Historical Co., Des Moines, p. 334. Smith, J. H. 1888. History of Harrison County, Iowa. Iowa Printing Co., Des Moines, p. 122. Anon. 1904–05. Compendium of history, reminiscence and biography of Lyon County, Iowa. G. A. Ogle and Co., Chicago, p. 24.

4. Donnel, W. M. 1872. Pioneers of Marion County. Republican Steam Printing House, Des Moines, p. 341. Brainard, pp. 391–394. Bowles, J. B. 1970. Historical record of some Iowan mammals. Transactions of the Kansas Academy of Science 73:425.

5. Hickenlooper, F. 1896. An illustrated history of Monroe County, Iowa. Walsworth Publishing Co., Marceline, Missouri, p. 185. Fisher, K. 1977. In the beginning there was land: a history of Washington County, Iowa. Washington County Historical Society, Washington, Iowa, p. 24. White, E. S. 1915. Past and present of Shelby County Iowa. B. F. Bowen and Co., Indianapolis, p. 76. Andrews, H. F. 1915. History of Audubon County Iowa. B. F. Bowen and Co., Indianapolis, p. 41. Scott, T. G. 1937. Mammals of Iowa.

Iowa State College Journal of Science 12:83. Percival, C. S., and E. Percival. 1881. History of Buchanan County, Iowa. Williams Bros., Cleveland, pp. 56–57. Orr, E. 1971. Reminiscences of a pioneer boy. Annals of Iowa, 3rd series, 40:617. Wegerslev, C. H., and T. Walpole. 1909. Past and present of Buena Vista County Iowa. S. J. Clarke Publishing Co., Chicago, p. 110. Anon. 1917. History of Emmet County and Dickinson County Iowa. Pioneer Publishing Co., Chicago, p. 408. Flickinger, R. E. 1904. The pioneer history of Pocahontas County, Iowa. Fonda Times, Fonda, Iowa, p. 277. Spurrell, p. 276.

6. Bennett, H. A. 1926. Fish and game legislation in Iowa. Iowa Journal of History and Politics 24:394, 397, 399, 406.

7. Murray, C. A. 1839. Travels in North America, volume 2. Richard Bentley, London, pp. 120–129. Anon. 1883. History of Butler and Bremer counties, Iowa. Union Publishing Co., Springfield, Illinois, p. 243. Anon. 1882. History of Floyd County, Iowa. Inter-State Publishing Co., Chicago, p. 318. Hedge, M. 1906. Past and present of Mahaska County, Iowa. Privately published, p. 57. Bonebright-Closz, H. 1921. Reminiscences of Newcastle, Iowa 1848. Historical Department of Iowa, Des Moines, p. 66. Anon. 1881. History of Montgomery County, Iowa. Iowa Historical and Biographical Co., Des Moines, p. 367. Flickinger, p. 235. Anon. 1917. History of Winnebago County and Hancock County Iowa. Pioneer Publishing Co., Chicago, p. 214. Corbit, R. M. 1910. History of Jones County, Iowa. S. J. Clarke Publishing Co., Chicago, p. 296.

8. Reed, p. 158. Phillips. S. A. 1900. Proud Mahaska, 1843–1900. Herald Print, Oskaloosa, Iowa, p. 142.

9. Lee, J. W. 1912. History of Hamilton County Iowa. S. J. Clarke Publishing Co., Chicago, pp. 32–33.

10. Anon. 1907. Past and present of Guthrie County, Iowa. S. J. Clarke Publishing Co., Chicago, pp. 93–94. Merritt, W. W. 1906. A history of the county of Montgomery. Express Publishing Co., Red Oak, Iowa, p. 275. Price, R. E. 1916. History of Clayton County Iowa. R. O. Law Co., Chicago, p. 424. Hart, I. H. 1914. History of Butler County Iowa. S. J. Clarke Publishing Co., Chicago, p. 43. Hartman, J. C. 1915. History of Black Hawk County Iowa and its people. S. J. Clarke Publishing Co., Chicago, p. 106. Fitch, G. W. 1910. Past and present of Fayette County Iowa. B. F. Bowen and Co., Indianapolis, p. 113. Webster, C. L. 1897. History of Floyd County, Iowa. Intelligencer Print, Charles City, Iowa, p. 14. Smith, pp. 125–126. Spurrell, p. 276. Anon. 1890–91. History of the counties of Woodbury and Plymouth, Iowa. A. Warner and Co., Chicago, p. 55.

11. Mueller, H. A. 1915. History of Madison County Iowa and

its people. S. J. Clarke Publishing Co., Chicago, p. 177. Price, p. 424. H. P. U. 1892. Stories of boyhood days. Forest and Stream 38:3.

12. Barrows, W. 1863. History of Scott County, Iowa. Annals of Iowa, 1st series, 1:25–26. History of Scott County (1882), p. 544. Spurrell, p. 276. Brainard, p. 394. Savage, W. 1933. William Savage. Iowa pioneer, diarist, and painter of birds. Annals of Iowa, 3rd series, 19:95, 103–104. Andrews, p. 41.

13. Anon. 1879. The history of Lee County, Iowa. Western Historical Co., Chicago, pp. 589–590.

14. Anon. 1881. The history of Marion County, Iowa. Union Historical Co., Des Moines, p. 321. Merry, J. F. 1914. History of Delaware County Iowa and its people. S. J. Clarke Publishing Co., Chicago, p. 191. History of Winnebago County and Hancock County, p. 214.

15. Scott, pp. 83–84. White, pp. 75–76. Swisher, J. A. 1940. Deer in Iowa. Palimpsest 21:405–409.

16. Scott, p. 84. Madson, J. 1953. Iowa's early deer story. Iowa Conservationist 12:101.

17. Scott, p. 84. Madson, Iowa's early deer story, p. 101.

18. Madson, Iowa's early deer story, p. 101.

19. Speaker, E. B. 1953. Our deer 1936–1952. Iowa Conservationist 12:97. Faber, L. F. 1948. Deer survey, 1948. Iowa Conservationist 7:30. Sanderson, G. C. 1950. Iowa deer herds—1950. Iowa Conservationist 9:25, 31. Anon. 1953. 1953 deer season set. Iowa Conservationist 12:154. Madson, J. 1954. The 1953 Iowa deer season. Iowa Conservationist 13:1. Andrews, R., D. Jackson, L. Jackson, T. Z. Riley, W. Suchy, and G. Zenner. 1991. Trends in Iowa wildlife populations and harvest 1990. Iowa Department of Natural Resources, Des Moines, p. 9. Suchy, W. J. 1990. Playing the numbers game. Iowa Conservationist 49(11):31.

20. Downing, R. L. 1987. Success story: white-tailed deer. P. 48 *in* Restoring America's wildlife (H. Kallman, editor). U.S. Fish and Wildlife Service, Washington, D.C. Hesselton, W. T., and R. M. Hesselton. 1982. White-tailed deer *Odocoileus virginianus*. P. 895 *in* Wild mammals of North America (J. A. Chapman and G. A. Feldhamer, editors). Johns Hopkins University Press, Baltimore.

5. Wild Cats

1. Waller, D. W., and P. L. Errington. 1961. The bounty system in Iowa. Proceedings of the Iowa Academy of Science 68:303–307.

2. Young, S. P. 1958. The bobcat of North America. Stackpole Co., Harrisburg, Pennsylvania, and Wildlife Management Institute, Washington, D.C., p. 8. Bonebright-Closz, H. 1921. Reminiscences of Newcastle, Iowa 1848. Historical Department of Iowa, Des

Moines, p. 70. Babbitt, C. H. 1918. The Missouri Slope fifty years ago. Forest and Stream 88:522. Richman, I. B. 1911. History of Muscatine County Iowa. S. J. Clarke Publishing Co., Chicago, p. 458. Alexander, W. E. 1882. History of Winneshiek and Allamakee counties Iowa. Western Publishing Co., Sioux City, Iowa, p. 344. Orr, E. 1971. Reminiscences of a pioneer boy. Annals of Iowa, 3rd series, 40:619–620. Spurrell, J. A. 1917. An annotated list of the mammals of Sac County, Iowa. Proceedings of the Iowa Academy of Science 24:280.

3. Percival, C. S., and E. Percival. 1881. History of Buchanan County, Iowa. Williams Bros., Cleveland, p. 59. White, E. S. 1915. Past and present of Shelby County Iowa. B. F. Bowen and Co., Indianapolis, p. 77. Anon. 1879. The history of Warren County, Iowa. Union Historical Co., Des Moines, pp. 321–322. Smith, R. A. 1902. A history of Dickinson County, Iowa. Kenyon Printing and Manufacturing Co., Des Moines, pp. 385–386. Orr, p. 620. Donnel, W. M. 1872. Pioneers of Marion County. Republican Steam Printing House, Des Moines, p. 303.

4. Polder, E. 1958. Recent locality records for some Iowa mammals. Proceedings of the Iowa Academy of Science 65:562. Anon. 1947. Numerous bobcats reported. Iowa Conservationist 6:120. State of Iowa. 1986. Iowa Administrative Code. Section 571, chapter 77.1, p. 1.

5. Young, S. P., and E. A. Goldman. 1946. The puma, mysterious American cat. American Wildlife Institute, Washington, D.C., pp. 9–11. Price, R. E. 1916. History of Clayton County Iowa. R. O. Law Co., Chicago, pp. 423–424. Anon. 1878. The history of Delaware County, Iowa. Western Historical Co., Chicago, pp. 411–412. Anon. 1881. History of Montgomery County, Iowa. Iowa Historical and Biographical Co., Des Moines, p. 407. Mueller, H. A. 1915. History of Madison County Iowa and its people. S. J. Clarke Publishing Co., Chicago, p. 176. Anon. 1884. History of Guthrie and Adair counties, Iowa. Continental Historical Co., Springfield, Illinois, p. 830. Anon. 1878. The history of Appanoose County, Iowa. Western Historical Co., Chicago, p. 388. Van Hyning, T. 1913. Additional mammal notes. Proceedings of the Iowa Academy of Science 20:312. Bowles, J. B. 1970. Historical record of some Iowan mammals. Transactions of the Kansas Academy of Science 73:423.

6. Anon. 1878. The history of Monroe County, Iowa. Western Historical Co., Chicago, p. 379. History of Guthrie and Adair counties, p. 830. Jones, E. L. 1977. Nathan Littler's history of Washington County 1835–1870. Conger House, Washington, Iowa, p. 105. Moorehead, G. C. 1928. Historical collections of Ida County. Pioneer Record Press, Ida Grove, Iowa, p. 25.

7. Alexander, pp. 161–169. Marks, C. R. 1904. Past and present of Sioux City and Woodbury County, Iowa. S. J. Clarke Publishing Co., Chicago, pp. 796–797. Meyers, F. W. 1911. History of Crawford County Iowa. S. J. Clarke Publishing Co., Chicago, p. 46. Dyke, C. L. 1942. The story of Sioux County. Verstegen Printing Co., Orange City, Iowa, p. 541.

8. Belden, R. C. 1988. The Florida panther. P. 522 *in* Audubon wildlife report 1988/1989 (W. J. Chandler, editor). Academic Press, San Diego. Klaus, S. 1978. PAWS II: Cougar again sighted in Council Bluffs. Des Moines Register, 29 June 1978, p. 1A. Klaus, S. 1979. Council Bluffs cougar goes south. Des Moines Register, 9 December 1979, p. 5B. Ney, J. 1980. Iowan thinks there's a cougar on prowl. Des Moines Register, 6 November 1980, p. 1A. Turner, R. W. 1974. Mammals of the Black Hills of South Dakota and Wyoming. University of Kansas Museum of Natural History Miscellaneous Publication 60, pp. 133–134.

9. Meyers, p. 67. Richman, p. 458. The history of Warren County, p. 323. History of Montgomery County, p. 407. Stonebraker, B. E. 1915. Past and present of Calhoun County Iowa. Pioneer Publishing Co., Chicago, p. 310. Spurrell, p. 280. Babbitt, p. 522. Mosher, A. A. 1882. The fauna of Spirit Lake. Forest and Stream 18:66.

10. Hazard, E. B. 1982. The mammals of Minnesota. University of Minnesota Press, Minneapolis, p. 151. Rasmussen, J. L. 1969. A recent record of the lynx in Iowa. Journal of Mammalogy 50: 370–371. Van Hyning, p. 312.

11. Knauth, O. 1979. Oklahoma bobcats not delivered, and will live in cages when they are. Des Moines Register, 10 January 1979, p. 7A. Young, pp. 16–20, 68. Anon. 1979. Scared of bobcats. Des Moines Register, 14 January 1979, p. 1B.

12. Rolley, R. E. 1987. Bobcat. P. 679 *in* Wild furbearer management and conservation in North America (M. Novak, J. A. Baker, M. E. Obbard, and B. Malloch, editors). Ontario Trappers Association, North Bay, Ontario. Koehler, G. 1987. The bobcat. Pp. 403, 406–407 *in* Audubon wildlife report 1987 (R. L. Di Silvestro, editor). Academic Press, Orlando, Florida. Quinn, N. W. S., and G. Parker. 1987. Lynx. P. 688 *in* Wild furbearer management and conservation in North America. DeStefano, S. 1987. The lynx. Pp. 414–418 *in* Audubon wildlife report 1987.

6. Black Bears

1. Smith, J. H. 1888. History of Harrison County, Iowa. Iowa Printing Co., Des Moines, pp. 122–123. Petersen, W. J. 1958. Wild game everywhere. Palimpsest 39:560. Percival, C. S., and E. Per-

cival. 1881. History of Buchanan County, Iowa. Williams Bros., Cleveland, p. 61.

2. Percival and Percival, p. 57. Anon. 1879. The history of Lee County, Iowa. Western Historical Co., Chicago, pp. 589–590. Merry, J. F. 1914. History of Delaware County Iowa and its people. S. J. Clarke Publishing Co., Chicago, pp. 191, 198. Throne, M. 1960. Iowa farm letters, 1856–1865. Iowa Journal of History 58: 71–72.

3. Price, R. E. 1916. History of Clayton County Iowa. R. O. Law Co., Chicago, p. 424. Phillips, S. A. 1900. Proud Mahaska, 1843–1900. Herald Print, Oskaloosa, Iowa, pp. 142–143.

4. Percival and Percival, p. 61.

5. Anon. 1879. The history of Warren County, Iowa. Union Historical Co., Des Moines, p. 320.

6. Fitch, G. W. 1910. Past and present of Fayette County Iowa. B. F. Bowen and Co., Indianapolis, pp. 101–102.

7. Anon. 1884. History of Kossuth, Hancock and Winnebago counties, Iowa. Union Publishing Co., Springfield, Illinois, pp. 750–751.

8. Anon. 1879. The history of Dallas County, Iowa. Union Historical Co., Des Moines, pp. 299–300.

9. Smith, pp. 122–123.

10. Bonebright-Closz, H. 1921. Reminiscences of Newcastle, Iowa 1848. Historical Department of Iowa, Des Moines, pp. 73–74.

11. Merry, pp. 197–198.

12. Anon. 1876. Iowa items. Sioux City Daily Journal, 29 November 1876, p. 2.

13. Percival and Percival, pp. 60–61. Schorger, A. W. 1949. The black bear in early Wisconsin. Transactions of the Wisconsin Academy of Science, Arts and Letters 39: 168–173.

14. Anon. 1965. Sheriff kills bear at Tipton. Des Moines Register, 25 May 1965, p. 4. Bowles, J. B. 1975. Distribution and biogeography of mammals of Iowa. The Museum, Texas Tech University, Special Publication 9, pp. 117–118. Benning, V. 1987. Couple reports sighting bear on Iowa farm. Des Moines Register, 9 October 1987, p. 7M.

15. Jackson, H. H. T. 1961. Mammals of Wisconsin. University of Wisconsin Press, Madison, pp. 313–314. Hazard, E. B. 1982. The mammals of Minnesota. University of Minnesota Press, Minneapolis, p. 125. Schwartz, C. W., and E. R. Schwartz. 1959. The wild mammals of Missouri. University of Missouri Press, Columbia, p. 268. Petersen, W. J. 1941. Iowa. The rivers of her valleys. State Historical Society of Iowa, Iowa City, p. 77.

16. Pelton, M. 1987. The black bear. Pp. 524–526 *in* Audubon wildlife report 1987 (R. L. Di Silvestro, editor). Academic Press, Orlando, Florida.

7. Wolves and Coyotes

1. Young, S. P., and E. A. Goldman. 1944. The wolves of North America. American Wildlife Institute, Washington, D.C., pp. 10, 414.

2. Young, S. P., and H. H. T. Jackson. 1951. The clever coyote. Wildlife Management Institute, Washington, D.C., p. 29. Allen, J. A. 1871. Notes on the mammals of Iowa. Proceedings of the Boston Society of Natural History 13:181–182. Van Hyning, T., and F. C. Pellett. 1910. An annotated catalogue of the recent mammals of Iowa. Proceedings of the Iowa Academy of Science 17:218.

3. Anon. 1878. The history of Monroe County, Iowa. Western Historical Co., Chicago, p. 358. Donnel, W. M. 1872. Pioneers of Marion County. Republican Steam Printing House, Des Moines, p. 134. Flickinger, R. E. 1904. The pioneer history of Pocahontas County, Iowa. Fonda Times, Fonda, Iowa, p. 273.

4. Pellett, F. C. 1911. The prairie wolf in Iowa. Forest and Stream 76:452. Mueller, H. A. 1915. History of Madison County Iowa and its people. S. J. Clarke Publishing Co., Chicago, p. 176. Spurrell, J. A. 1917. An annotated list of the mammals of Sac County, Iowa. Proceedings of the Iowa Academy of Science 24:279–280. Andrews, R. D., and E. K. Boggess. 1978. Ecology of coyotes in Iowa. P. 257 *in* Coyotes, biology, behavior, and management (M. Bekoff, editor). Academic Press, New York. Boggess, E. K., R. D. Andrews, and R. A. Bishop. 1978. Domestic animal losses to coyotes and dogs in Iowa. Journal of Wildlife Management 42:364–368. Schaefer, J. M., R. D. Andrews, and J. J. Dinsmore. 1981. An assessment of coyote and dog predation on sheep in southern Iowa. Journal of Wildlife Management 45:885, 888.

5. Anon. 1907. Past and present of Guthrie County, Iowa. S. J. Clarke Publishing Co., Chicago, p. 88.

6. Lee, J. W. 1912. History of Hamilton County Iowa. S. J. Clarke Publishing Co., Chicago, p. 188.

7. Kaloupek, W. E. 1939. The plight of Fiddlin' Jim. Palimpsest 20:310–312.

8. Glazier, W. 1900. Ocean to ocean on horseback. Edgewood Publishing Co., Philadelphia, pp. 433–434.

9. Petersen, W. J. 1940. Wolves in Iowa. Iowa Journal of History and Politics 38:65–69. Merry, J. F. 1914. History of Delaware County Iowa and its people. S. J. Clarke Publishing Co., Chicago, pp. 205–206.

10. Negus, C. 1870. The early history of Iowa. Annals of Iowa,

1st series, 8:204–205. Garland, H. 1961. Boy life on the prairie. University of Nebraska Press, Lincoln, pp. 392–400.

11. Anon. 1879. The history of Warren County, Iowa. Union Historical Co., Des Moines, pp. 320–321.

12. James, E. (compiler). 1966. Account of an expedition from Pittsburgh to the Rocky Mountains, volume 1. University Microfilms, Ann Arbor, Michigan, pp. 172–173. Anon. 1880. The history of Keokuk County, Iowa. Union Historical Co., Des Moines, p. 332. Anon. 1878. The history of Appanoose County, Iowa. Western Historical Co., Chicago, p. 467.

13. Anon. 1883. History of Johnson County, Iowa. Iowa City, pp. 572–573.

14. Payne, W. O. 1911. History of Story County Iowa, volume 1. S. J. Clarke Publishing Co., Chicago, p. 171. Moorehead, G. C. 1928. Historical collections of Ida County. Pioneer Record Press, Ida Grove, Iowa, pp. 24–25.

15. Mueller, p. 176. Spurrell, p. 280. Allen, p. 181. Flickinger, p. 273. Hart, I. H. 1914. History of Butler County Iowa. S. J. Clarke Publishing Co., Chicago, p. 43.

16. Osborn, H. 1905. The recently extinct and vanishing animals of Iowa. Annals of Iowa, 3rd series, 6:566. Van Hyning and Pellett, p. 218. Anon. 1914. Wolves in Lee County. Saturday Evening Post of Burlington, 2 May 1914. Andrews and Boggess, p. 250. Scott, T. G. 1937. Mammals of Iowa. Iowa State College Journal of Science 12:66.

17. Pellett, p. 452. Spurrell, pp. 279–280. Brown, H. C. 1917. Preliminary list of the mammals of Floyd County, Iowa. Annual Report Califor Naturalist Club of Iowa 3:29. Ruthven, A. G., and N. A. Wood. 1912. Notes on a collection of mammals from northwestern Iowa. Proceedings of the Iowa Academy of Science 19:204. Scott, p. 65.

18. Waller, D. W., and P. L. Errington. 1961. The bounty system in Iowa. Proceedings of the Iowa Academy of Science 68:303–307.

19. Ibid., pp. 308–310.

20. Petersen, pp. 85, 88–91. Mathwig, H. J. 1973. Food and population characteristics of Iowa coyotes. Iowa State Journal of Research 47:178–179.

21. Andrews and Boggess, p. 250.

22. Voigt, D. R., and W. E. Berg. 1987. Coyote. Pp. 345–346 *in* Wild furbearer management and conservation in North America (M. Novak, J. A. Baker, M. E. Obbard, and B. Malloch, editors). Ontario Trappers Association, North Bay, Ontario.

23. Andrews and Boggess, pp. 250–251.

24. Ibid., p. 263. Andrews, R., J. Hansen, G. Hanson, D. Jackson, W. Suchy, and J. Kienzler. 1989. Trends in Iowa game populations

and harvest 1988. Iowa Department of Natural Resources, Des Moines, pp. 40–41.

25. Carbyn, L. N. 1987. Gray wolf and red wolf. P. 362 *in* Wild furbearer management and conservation in North America. Peterson, R. O. 1986. Gray wolf. P. 951 *in* Audubon Wildlife Report 1986 (R. L. DiSilvestro, editor). National Audubon Society, New York.

8. Foxes

1. Churcher, C. S. 1959. The specific status of the New World red fox. Journal of Mammalogy 40:514. Sargeant, A. B. 1982. A case history of a dynamic resource—the red fox. Pp. 122–128 *in* Midwest furbearer management (G. C. Sanderson, editor). North Central Section, Central Mountains and Plains Section, and Kansas Chapter of the Wildlife Society, Office of Printing Services, University of Illinois at Urbana-Champaign.

2. Sargeant, pp. 128–133.

3. Allen, J. A. 1871. Notes on the mammals of Iowa. Proceedings of the Boston Society of Natural History 13:182. Smith, R. A. 1902. A history of Dickinson County, Iowa. Kenyon Printing and Manufacturing Co., Des Moines, p. 385. Stephens, T. C. 1922. Mammals of the lake region of Iowa. Bulletin of the Okoboji Protective Association 18:58. Spurrell, J. A. 1917. An annotated list of the mammals of Sac County, Iowa. Proceedings of the Iowa Academy of Science 24:278–279. Moorehead, G. C. 1928. Historical collections of Ida County. Pioneer Record Press, Ida Grove, Iowa, pp. 24–25. Webster, C. L. 1897. History of Floyd County, Iowa. Intelligencer Print, Charles City, Iowa, p. 14. Webster, C. L. 1898. Changes in Iowa fauna and flora. Forest and Stream 50:426. Anon. 1910. Hunting in Iowa. Forest and Stream 74:736.

4. Fisher, K. 1978. In the beginning there was land: a history of Washington County, Iowa. Washington County Historical Society, Washington, Iowa, p. 24. Mueller, H. A. 1915. History of Madison County Iowa and its people. S. J. Clarke Publishing Co., Chicago, p. 176. Nutting, C. C. 1895. Report of the committee on state fauna. Proceedings of the Iowa Academy of Science 2:43. Scott, T. G. 1937. Mammals of Iowa. Iowa State College Journal of Science 12:64. Van Hyning, T., and F. C. Pellett. 1910. An annotated catalogue of the recent mammals of Iowa. Proceedings of the Iowa Academy of Science 17:217. Stout, D. 1975. Skunks to foxes through the years. Cedar County Historical Review 1975:62.

5. Scott, p. 64. Andrews, R., D. Jackson, L. Jackson, T. Z. Riley, W. Suchy, and G. Zenner. 1991. Trends in Iowa wildlife populations and harvest 1990. Iowa Department of Natural Resources, Des

Moines, p. 41. Andrews, R. D. 1981. The red fox in Iowa. Iowa Conservation Commission, Des Moines, pp. 15–16.

6. Voigt, D. R. 1987. Red fox. P. 389 *in* Wild furbearer management and conservation in North America (M. Novak, J. A. Baker, M. E. Obbard, and B. Malloch, editors). Ontario Trappers Association, North Bay, Ontario.

7. Anon. 1881. The history of Marion County, Iowa. Union Historical Co., Des Moines, p. 320. Spurrell, p. 278. Andrews, The red fox, p. 85. Andrews, Jackson, Jackson, Riley, Suchy, and Zenner, p. 43.

8. Waller, D. W., and P. L. Errington. 1961. The bounty system in Iowa. Proceedings of the Iowa Academy of Science 68:305–307. Andrews, The red fox, pp. 18, 19.

9. Andrews, The red fox, pp. 81–88. Andrews, R. 1984. Reynard fox. King of furbearers. Iowa Conservationist 43(1):8–10. Andrews, Jackson, Jackson, Riley, Suchy, and Zenner, p. 39.

10. Andrews, The red fox, pp. 69–74.

11. Ibid., pp. 75–77.

12. Hall, E. R. 1981. The mammals of North America, second edition, volume 2. John Wiley & Sons, New York, p. 944.

13. H. P. U. 1892. Stories of boyhood days. Forest and Stream 38:3. Allen, p. 182. Spurrell, p. 279. Chappell, H. C., and K. J. Chappell. 1914. History of Buchanan County Iowa. S. J. Clarke Publishing Co., Chicago, p. 36. Bowles, J. B. 1975. Distribution and biogeography of mammals of Iowa. The Museum, Texas Tech University, Special Publication 9, pp. 115–116. Webster, History of Floyd County, p. 14. Webster, Changes in Iowa fauna and flora, p. 426. Brown, H. C. 1917. Preliminary list of the mammals of Floyd County Iowa. Annual Report Califor Naturalist Club of Iowa 3:29. Stephens, p. 58. Scott, p. 65. Polder, E. 1958. Recent locality records for some Iowa mammals. Proceedings of the Iowa Academy of Science 65:561.

14. Polder, pp. 560–561. Bowles, p. 115. Andrews, Jackson, Jackson, Riley, Suchy, and Zenner, p. 41.

15. Fritzell, E. K. 1987. Gray fox and island gray fox. Pp. 411, 416–417 *in* Wild furbearer management and conservation in North America.

16. Hall, pp. 939–941.

17. Allen, p. 182. Van Hyning and Pellett, pp. 217–218. Bowles, p. 155. Stonebraker, B. E. 1915. Past and present of Calhoun County Iowa. Pioneer Publishing Co., Chicago, pp. 59–60. White, E. S. 1915. Past and present of Shelby County, Iowa. B. F. Bowen and Co., Indianapolis, p. 77. Spurrell, p. 279. Flickinger, R. E. 1904. The pioneer history of Pocahontas County, Iowa. Fonda

Times, Fonda, Iowa, p. 218. Mosher, A. A. 1882. The fauna of Spirit Lake. Forest and Stream 18:66.

18. Jones, J. K., D. M. Armstrong, R. S. Hoffmann, and C. Jones. 1983. Mammals of the northern Great Plains. University of Nebraska Press, Lincoln, pp. 256–257.

9. Furbearers

1. Van der Zee, J. 1914. Fur trade operations in the eastern Iowa country under the Spanish regime. Iowa Journal of History and Politics 12:355–372. Van der Zee, J. 1916. Episodes in the early history of the Des Moines valley. Iowa Journal of History and Politics 14: 321–347. Robeson, G. F. 1925. Fur trade in early Iowa. Palimpsest 6:14–29. Nasatir, A. P. 1931. The Anglo-Spanish frontier on the Upper Mississippi 1786–1796. Iowa Journal of History and Politics 29:155–232.

2. Van der Zee, J. 1914. Fur trade operations in the eastern Iowa country from 1800 to 1833. Iowa Journal of History and Politics 12:479–567. Mahan, B. E. 1926. Old Fort Crawford and the frontier. State Historical Society of Iowa, Iowa City, pp. 184, 187.

3. Percival, C. S., and E. Percival. 1881. History of Buchanan County, Iowa. Williams Bros., Cleveland, pp. 59–60. Aldrich, C. 1893. Early journalism in Iowa. Iowa Historical Record 9:410. Anon. 1917. History of Emmet County and Dickinson County Iowa. Pioneer Publishing Co., Chicago, pp. 105–106. McCarty, D. G. 1910. History of Palo Alto County Iowa. Torch Press, Cedar Rapids, Iowa, pp. 24, 51. Flickinger, R. E. 1904. The pioneer history of Pocahontas County, Iowa. Fonda Times, Fonda, Iowa, p. 274. Thompson, F. O. 1937. Hunting in northwestern Iowa. Iowa Journal of History and Politics 35:89.

4. Flickinger, p. 275. Thompson, p. 87.

5. Johnson, D. R. 1969. Returns of the American Fur Company, 1835–1839. Journal of Mammalogy 50:837.

6. Bennett, H. A. 1926. Fish and game legislation in Iowa. Iowa Journal of History and Politics 24:399.

7. Stillman, E. B. 1907. Past and present of Greene County, Iowa. S. J. Clarke Publishing Co., Chicago, p. 25. Bonebright-Closz, H. 1921. Reminiscences of Newcastle, Iowa 1848. Historical Department of Iowa, Des Moines, pp. 80, 82.

8. Anon. 1879. The history of Lee County, Iowa. Western Historical Co., Chicago, p. 589. White, E. S. 1915. Past and present of Shelby County Iowa. B. F. Bowen and Co., Indianapolis, p. 77. Flickinger, pp. 236, 275. Spurrell, J. A. 1917. An annotated list of the mammals of Sac County, Iowa. Proceedings of the Iowa Academy of Science 24:281. Bonebright-Closz, p. 82. Chappell, H. C., and K. J. Chappell. 1914. History of Buchanan County Iowa and its

people. S. J. Clarke Publishing Co., Chicago, p. 36. Gavitt, B. H. 1948. Eighty years in Iowa. A. T. DeGroot, Los Angeles, pp. 78–79. Hastie, E. N. 1938. Hastie's history of Dallas County Iowa. Wallace-Homestead Co., Des Moines, p. 52.

9. Richman, I. B. 1911. History of Muscatine County Iowa. S. J. Clarke Publishing Co., Chicago, p. 259. Flickinger, p. 274. Spurrell, p. 281. Birdsall, B. P. 1915. History of Wright County Iowa. B. F. Bowen and Co., Indianapolis, p. 354.

10. Flickinger, p. 275. Spurrell, p. 281.

11. Flickinger, p. 275.

12. Ibid., p. 274.

13. Buchan, D. 1966. Pioneer tales. Annals of Iowa, 3rd series, 38:478. Settle, W. A. 1966. Jesse James was his name. University of Missouri Press, Columbia, p. 43.

14. Stillman, p. 25. Flickinger, p. 274. Kimball, D., and J. Kimball. 1969. The market hunter. Dillon Press, Minneapolis, p. 109.

15. Flickinger, p. 275.

16. Bennett, p. 426.

17. Andrews, R., D. Jackson, L. Jackson, T. Z. Riley, W. Suchy, and G. Zenner. 1991. Trends in Iowa wildlife populations and harvest 1990. Iowa Department of Natural Resources, Des Moines, pp. 41, 43.

18. Boutin, S., and D. E. Birkenholz. 1987. Muskrat and round-tailed muskrat. P. 321 *in* Wild furbearer management and conservation in North America (M. Novak, J. A. Baker, M. E. Obbard, and B. Malloch, editors). Ontario Trappers Association, North Bay, Ontario.

19. The history of Lee County, p. 590. Spurrell, p. 277. White, p. 77. Flickinger, p. 236. Percival and Percival, p. 57. History of Emmet County and Dickinson County Iowa, p. 105. Bonebright-Closz, p. 83.

20. Flickinger, p. 273. Mosher, A. A. 1882. The fauna of Spirit Lake. Forest and Stream 18:66. Osborn, H. 1905. The recently extinct and vanishing animals of Iowa. Annals of Iowa, 3rd series, 6:567–568. Scott, T. G. 1937. Mammals of Iowa. Iowa State College Journal of Science 12:61.

21. White, p. 77. Chappell and Chappell, p. 36. Webster, C. L. 1900. Some notes on Iowa game. Forest and Stream 54:7. Anon. 1910. Hunting in Iowa. Forest and Stream 74:736. Brown, H. C. 1917. Preliminary list of the mammals of Floyd County, Iowa. Annual Report Califor Naturalist Club of Iowa 3:30. Spurrell, p. 277. Van Hyning, T. 1913. Additional mammal notes. Proceedings of the Iowa Academy of Science 20:311–312.

22. Percival and Percival, pp. 57–58. Bonebright-Closz, p. 82.

23. Sanderson, G. C. 1954. Recent records of the otter in Iowa.

Iowa Conservationist 13:52, 55. Polder, E. 1958. Recent locality records for some Iowa mammals. Proceedings of the Iowa Academy of Science 65:560. Bowles, J. B. 1970. Historical record of some Iowan mammals. Transactions of the Kansas Academy of Science 73: 422.

24. State of Iowa. 1986. Iowa Administrative Code. Section 571, chapter 77.1, p. 2. Washburn, L. 1987. River otters return. Iowa Conservationist 46(2):26. Jackson, L. S. 1989. An Iowa victory. Iowa Conservationist 48(1):15. Bishop, R. 1990. Trading turkeys, bartering birds—a benefit to all. Iowa Conservationist 49(1):31. Jackson, L. S. 38 more river otters released. Nongame News (Iowa Department of Natural Resources) 6(2):1.

25. Melquist, W. E., and A. E. Dronkert. 1987. River otter. P. 638 *in* Wild furbearer management and conservation in North America.

26. Hill, E. P. 1987. Beaver restoration. P. 281 *in* Restoring America's wildlife (H. Kallman, editor). U.S. Fish and Wildlife Service, Washington, D.C. Hill, E. P. 1982. Beaver. P. 265 *in* Wild mammals of North America (J. A. Chapman and G. A. Feldhamer, editors). Johns Hopkins University Press, Baltimore.

27. The history of Lee County, p. 589. James, E. (compiler). 1966. Account of an expedition from Pittsburgh to the Rocky Mountains, volume 1. University Microfilms, Ann Arbor, Michigan, p. 181. Durham, S. W. 1898. Another chapter of pioneer history. Annals of Iowa, 3rd series, 3:442.

28. Reed, B. F. 1913. History of Kossuth County Iowa. S. J. Clarke Publishing Co., Chicago, pp. 160–162. Hunting in Iowa, p. 736. Allen, J. A. 1871. Notes on the mammals of Iowa. Proceedings of the Boston Society of Natural History 13:190. Bennett, p. 399. Orr, E. 1971. Reminiscences of a pioneer boy. Annals of Iowa, 3rd series, 40:621. Anon. 1883. History of Johnson County Iowa. Iowa City, p. 562. Mosher, p. 66. Stephens, T. C. 1922. Mammals of the lake region of Iowa. Bulletin of the Okoboji Protective Association 18:54. Spurrell, p. 282. Scott, p. 73. Osborn, p. 567. Nutting, C. C. 1893. Report of committee on state fauna. Proceedings of the Iowa Academy of Science 1(3):40. White, p. 77. Van Hyning, T., and F. C. Pellett. 1910. An annotated catalogue of the recent mammals of Iowa. Proceedings of the Iowa Academy of Science 17:214. Stoner, D. 1918. The rodents of Iowa. Iowa Geological Survey Bulletin 5, p. 51. Flickinger, p. 276.

29. The history of Lee County, p. 589. James, p. 220. Bonebright-Closz, p. 83. Reed, p. 161. History of Emmet County and Dickinson County Iowa, p. 105. Flickinger, p. 236. Spurrell, p. 282. Percival and Percival, p. 58.

30. Sanderson, G. C. 1953. Recent status of the beaver in Iowa.

Proceedings of the Iowa Academy of Science 60:746–747, 750. Aitken, W. W. 1937. Beaver in Iowa. Proceedings of the Iowa Academy of Science 44:176. Pietsch, L. R. 1956. The beaver in Illinois. Transactions of the Illinois State Academy of Science 49:195. Andrews, Jackson, Jackson, Riley, Suchy, and Zenner, p. 41.

31. Novak, M. 1987. Beaver. Pp. 302–303 *in* Wild furbearer management and conservation in North America.

32. Ibid., p. 302.

33. Moorehead, G. C. 1928. Historical collections of Ida County. Pioneer Record Press, Ida Grove, Iowa, p. 25. Orr, p. 622. Savage, W. 1933. William Savage. Iowa pioneer, diarist, and painter of birds. Annals of Iowa, 3rd series, 19:87, 193, 220. Flickinger, p. 236. Webster, C. L. 1897. History of Floyd County, Iowa. Intelligencer Print, Charles City, Iowa, p. 40. Bonebright-Closz, p. 83. Aldrich, p. 410. Thompson, p. 89. Osborn, p. 567. White, p. 80.

34. Andrews, Jackson, Jackson, Riley, Suchy, and Zenner, p. 41. Obbard, M. E., J. G. Jones, R. Newman, A. Booth, A. J. Satterthwaite, and G. Linscombe. 1987. Furbearer harvests in North America. P. 1,023 *in* Wild furbearer management and conservation in North America. Linscombe, G., N. Kinler, and R. J. Aulerich. 1982. Mink. P. 640 *in* Wild mammals of North America.

35. The history of Lee County, p. 589. Bonebright-Closz, p. 11. White, p. 80. Andrews, Jackson, Jackson, Riley, Suchy, and Zenner, pp. 43, 41, 42.

36. Obbard, Jones, Newman, Booth, Satterthwaite, and Linscombe, pp. 1,019–1,020.

10. Passenger Pigeons

1. Schorger, A. W. 1955. The passenger pigeon. Its natural history and extinction. University of Wisconsin Press, Madison, pp. 231–233.

2. Wilson, A. 1829. American Ornithology, volume 3. Collins and Co., New York, pp. 5–7. Bent, A. C. 1932. Life histories of North American gallinaceous birds. U.S. National Museum Bulletin 162:384, 400–402. Blockstein, D. E., and H. B. Tordoff. 1985. Gone forever—a contemporary look at the extinction of the passenger pigeon. American Birds 39:846. Schorger, pp. 91–92, 28–30.

3. Schorger, p. 272. McGee, W. J. 1910. Notes on the passenger pigeon. Science 32:960. Anon. 1910. Hunting in Iowa. Forest and Stream 74:735.

4. Nauman, E. D. 1933. Iowa's vanished hosts. Iowa Bird Life 3:47. Bond, F. 1921. The later flights of the passenger pigeon. Auk 38:524–525. McGee, p. 959. The Captain. 1907. Pigeon shooting in early days. Forest and Stream 68:656.

5. Blockstein and Tordoff, p. 846. McGee, p. 960. Schorger, p. 272.

6. Orr, E. 1936. The passenger pigeon in northeastern Iowa. Iowa Bird Life 6:22–26.

7. Chappell, H. C., and K. J. Chappell. 1914. History of Buchanan County Iowa and its people. S. J. Clarke Publishing Co., Chicago, p. 35. Spurrell, J. A. 1917. Annotated list of the water birds, game birds and birds of prey of Sac County, Iowa. Wilson Bulletin 29:157.

8. McGee, pp. 960–961.

9. Schorger, pp. 129–131. Seerley, H. H. 1924. In retrospect. Palimpsest 5:259.

10. Kimball, D., and J. Kimball. 1969. The market hunter. Dillon Press, Minneapolis, p. 106. Orr, p. 23.

11. Orr, p. 26. Kimball and Kimball, pp. 107–108.

12. The Captain, pp. 656–657.

13. Orr, pp. 23–25.

14. Schorger, pp. 177–179.

15. Anon. 1932. Pioneer recalls pigeon catches. Kanawha Report, 7 July 1932. Anon. 1940. Pests 70 years ago, passenger pigeons now believed extinct. Cedar Rapids Gazette, 28 April 1940. The Captain, pp. 656–657.

16. Schorger, pp. 144–155, 156.

17. Orr, p. 23.

18. The Captain, p. 656. Allbee, E. A. 1911. Passenger pigeons in eastern Iowa, in 1856–1860. Auk 28:261. Merry, J. F. 1914. History of Delaware County Iowa. S. J. Clarke Publishing Co., Chicago, p. 201. Osborn, H. 1905. The recently extinct and vanishing animals of Iowa. Annals of Iowa, 3rd series, 6:569.

19. LePrevost, E. 1930. Clinton County history. Allen Printing Co., Clinton, Iowa, p. 118. Bond, pp. 523–524. McGee, p. 961. Harlan, J. R. 1942. The Iowa game book of George E. Poyner. Annals of Iowa, 3rd series, 23:198. Nauman, p. 48.

20. Anderson, R. M. 1907. The birds of Iowa. Proceedings of the Davenport Academy of Sciences 11:239. Webster, C. S. 1899. The wild pigeon in Iowa. Forest and Stream 52:305. DuMont, P. A. 1933. The passenger pigeon as a former Iowa bird. Proceedings of the Iowa Academy of Science 40:210. Schorger, pp. 218–222, 290, 26–30.

21. Bucher, E. H. 1992. The causes of extinction of the passenger pigeon. Current Ornithology 9:1–36.

11. Prairie-Chickens

1. Johnsgard, P. A. 1973. Grouse and quails of North America. University of Nebraska Press, Lincoln, p. 278. Bent, A. C. 1932. Life

histories of North American gallinaceous birds. U.S. National Museum Bulletin 162:265–269. Anon. 1990. Regional news. Endangered Species Technical Bulletin 15(10):13.

2. Johnsgard, P. A., and R. E. Wood. 1968. Distributional changes and interaction between prairie chickens and sharp-tailed grouse in the midwest. Wilson Bulletin 80:173–180. Johnsgard, p. 278.

3. Quick, H. 1925. One man's life. Bobbs-Merrill Co., Indianapolis, p. 80. Stempel, M. E., and S. Rodgers. 1961. History of prairie chickens in Iowa. Proceedings of the Iowa Academy of Science 68:317.

4. Keagle, L. S. 1890. Migration of prairie chickens. Forest and Stream 35:88. Williams, H. S. 1884. Seasons and birds of the prairie. Forest and Stream 22:403. Cooke, W. W. 1888. Report on bird migration in the Mississippi valley in the years 1884 and 1885. U.S. Department of Agriculture, Division of Economic Ornithology, Bulletin 2, pp. 105–106. Thompson, F. O. 1937. Hunting in northwestern Iowa. Iowa Journal of History and Politics 35:83.

5. Williams, p. 403.

6. Nauman, E. D. 1924. Birds of early Iowa. Palimpsest 5:136. Anon. 1873. Untitled. Forest and Stream 1:268.

7. Nethken, W. V. 1912. A prairie chicken hunt. Forest and Stream 79:683–684. Loyd, A. T. 1890. Prairie chicken shooting. Forest and Stream 34:408. Hough, E. 1896. Chicken shooting past and present. Forest and Stream 47:264–265. Smith J. G. 1880. Dogs for prairie chicken shooting. Forest and Stream 14:371.

8. Hough, E. 1897. Chicago and the west. Forest and Stream 49:167–168. Loyd, p. 408.

9. Sawyer, W. W. 1960. Mallards for the market. Annals of Iowa, 3rd series, 35:459–460.

10. Merry, J. F. 1914. History of Delaware County Iowa and its people. S. J. Clarke Publishing Co., Chicago, pp. 186–187. Sanford, Mrs. N. 1867. History of Marshall County, Iowa. Leslie, McAllaster and Co., Clinton, Iowa, p. 144. Chappell, H. C., and K. J. Chappell. 1914. History of Buchanan County Iowa and its people. S. J. Clarke Publishing Co., Chicago, p. 25.

11. Rosene, W. M. 1937. The last chicken hunt. Nature Magazine 30:342–343.

12. W. R. H. 1894. About prairie chicken trapping. Forest and Stream 43:560. Sawyer, p. 460.

13. Quick, p. 82. Pierce, F. J. 1922. The prairie chicken in east central Iowa. Wilson Bulletin 34:102. Moorehead, G. C. 1928. Historical collections of Ida County. Pioneer Record Press, Ida Grove, Iowa, pp. 26–27. Battin, W., and F. A. Moscrip. 1912. Past and present of Marshall County Iowa. B. F. Bowen and Co., Indi-

anapolis, p. 110. Greene, S. H. 1897. Recollections of Iowa. Forest and Stream 48:222.

14. Greene, p. 222.

15. H. P. U. 1892. Stories of boyhood days. Forest and Stream 38:3. Leaman, B. R. 1971. An early settler in Iowa: westward expansion in microcosm. Annals of Iowa, 3rd series, 41:699.

16. The Captain. 1907. Iowa fifty years ago. Forest and Stream 68:494. Peck, J. L. E., and O. H. Montzheimer. 1914. Past and present of O'Brien and Osceola counties, Iowa. B. F. Bowen and Co., Indianapolis, p. 489. Seerley, H. H. 1924. In retrospect. Palimpsest 5:259.

17. Anon. 1879. The history of Jackson County, Iowa. Western Historical Co., Chicago, p. 417. Newhall, J. B. 1841. Sketches of Iowa. J. H. Colton, New York, pp. 32–33. Usher, I. L. 1922. Letters of a railroad builder. Palimpsest 3:26. Petersen, W. J. 1958. Wild game everywhere. Palimpsest 39:561. Greene, p. 222. Chappell and Chappell, p. 25. Battin and Moscrip, p. 110. Hunt, C. W., and W. L. Clark. 1915. History of Harrison County Iowa. B. F. Bowen and Co., Indianapolis, p. 47. Pierce, p. 103. Ransom, H. 1941. Pioneer recollections. Historical Publishing Co., p. 190. Hartman, J. C. 1909. Habits of the prairie chicken. Des Moines Register and Leader, 15 March 1909, p. 4.

18. Merritt, H. C. 1904. The shadow of a gun. F. T. Peterson Co., Chicago, pp. 61, 153–160, 167–169.

19. Ibid., pp. 191–192.

20. Smith, J. G. 1887. Iowa game and fish. Forest and Stream 28:514. Webster, C. L. 1898. Prairie chicken shooting in Iowa. Forest and Stream 50:44. Hartman, p. 4.

21. W. F. A. 1891. Prairie chickens for market. Forest and Stream 36:107. Hough, E. 1900. Chicago and the west. Forest and Stream 55:226.

22. Pierce, p. 105.

23. Ibid., pp. 104–105. Quick, p. 76. Anon. 1885. Burning prairie chicken eggs. Forest and Stream 25:127.

24. Greene, p. 222. Pierce, p. 104.

25. Bennett, H. A. 1926. Fish and game legislation in Iowa. Iowa Journal of History and Politics 26:394–397.

26. Ibid., pp. 400–401, 418, 420. Anon. 1881. Jottings of a chicken shoot. Forest and Stream 17:290.

27. Fair Play. 1884. Untitled. Forest and Stream 23:125. V. V. S. 1896. Iowa prairie chickens. Forest and Stream 47:186. Hall, W. R., and J. C. Briggs. 1896. Iowa game. Forest and Stream 46:198.

28. W. F. A., p. 107.

29. Stempel and Rodgers, pp. 320–321. Leopold, A. 1932. Preliminary report on a game survey of northern Iowa for the Iowa

Conservation Plan. State Fish and Game Commission and the State Conservation Board, Des Moines, p. 34.

30. Stempel and Rodgers, pp. 320–321. Schaufenbuel, J. 1979. Greater prairie chicken in Harrison County. Iowa Bird Life 49: 26–27. Spengler, R. 1984. Greater prairie chicken in Osceola County. Iowa Bird Life 54:21. Eby, M. 1993. Greater prairie-chicken in Lyon County. Iowa Bird Life 63: 55.

31. Westemeier, R. L., and W. R. Edwards. 1987. Prairie-chickens: survival in the Midwest. Pp. 126–128 in Restoring America's wildlife (H. Kallman, editor). U.S. Fish and Wildlife Service, Washington, D.C.

32. George, R. R. 1981. Prairie boomers. Iowa Conservationist 40(12):7. Wooley, J. 1984. Prairie chicken update. Iowa Conservationist 43(9):10–11.

33. Suchy, W. J., and M. Moe. 1988. The booming ground. Iowa Conservationist 47(6):17. Moe, M. 1990. They're back. Iowa Conservationist 49(6):6–7. Anon. 1991. Watchable wildlife—spring dances. Nongame News (Iowa Department of Natural Resources) 7(1):4.

34. Westemeier, R. L. 1984. Responses and impact by pheasants on prairie-chicken sanctuaries in Illinois: a synopsis. Pp. 117–122 in Perdix III: gray partridge and ring-necked pheasant workshop (R. T. Dumke, R. B. Stiehl, and R. B. Kahl, editors). Wisconsin Department of Natural Resources, Madison. Westemeier, R. L. 1988. An evaluation of methods for controlling pheasants on Illinois prairie-chicken sanctuaries. Pp. 267–288 in Pheasants: symptoms of wildlife problems on agricultural lands (D. L. Hallett, W. R. Edwards, and G. V. Burger, editors). North Central Section of the Wildlife Society, Bloomington, Indiana.

12. Wild Turkeys

1. Schorger, A. W. 1966. The wild turkey. Its history and domestication. University of Oklahoma Press, Norman, pp. 354–376, 42–48, 59–61. Miller, J. E., and H. L. Holbrook. 1983. Return of a native: the wild turkey flourishes again. Yearbook of Agriculture, U.S. Department of Agriculture, p. 170. Mosby, H. S. 1949. The present status and the future outlook of the eastern and Florida wild turkeys. Transactions of the North American Wildlife Conference 14:348.

2. Anderson, T. G. 1882. Narrative of Capt. Thomas G. Anderson. Collections of the State Historical Society of Wisconsin 9: 151–152. Walton, J. P. 1893. Recollections of Muscatine Island. P. 36 in Scraps of Muscatine history. Privately published. Muscatine, Iowa. Savage, W. 1933–37. William Savage. Iowa pioneer, diarist, and painter of birds. Annals of Iowa, 3rd series, 19:83–114, 189–

220; 20:140–150, 459–471, 535–543. Newhall, J. B. 1841. Sketches of Iowa. J. H. Colton, New York, p. 32. Bonebright-Closz, H. 1921. Reminiscences of Newcastle, Iowa 1848. Historical Department of Iowa, Des Moines, p. 77. Keck, I. 1925. A. J. Whisman, pioneer. Palimpsest 6:34. Schorger, pp. 59–61. Bennett, H. A. 1926. Fish and game legislation in Iowa. Iowa Journal of History and Politics 24:394.

3. Thomson, G. W., and H. G. Hertel. 1981. The forest resources of Iowa in 1980. Proceedings of the Iowa Academy of Science 88:2–3.

4. Sherman, A. R. 1913. The extermination of the wild turkey in Clayton County, Iowa. Wilson Bulletin 25:89. White, E. S. 1915. Past and present of Shelby County Iowa. B. F. Bowen and Co., Indianapolis, p. 80. Mueller, H. A. 1915. History of Madison County Iowa and its people. S. J. Clarke Publishing Co., Chicago, p. 177. Babbitt, C. H. 1918. The Missouri Slope fifty years ago. Forest and Stream 88:522–523. Savage, p. 541. Osborn, H. 1905. The recently extinct and vanishing animals of Iowa. Annals of Iowa, 3rd series, 6:568. Garden, R. I. 1907. History of Scott Township Mahaska County, Iowa. Globe Presses, Oskaloosa, Iowa, p. 215. Anon. 1881. History of Montgomery County, Iowa. Iowa Historical and Biographical Co., Des Moines, p. 408. Anon. 1883. History of Johnson County, Iowa. Iowa City, p. 566. Smith, E. R. 1927. When buffalo roamed county. Fairfield Daily Ledger, 17 September 1927. DuMont, P. A. 1933. A revised list of the birds of Iowa. University of Iowa Studies in Natural History, 15(5):58.

5. DuMont, p. 58. Anderson, R. M. 1907. The birds of Iowa. Proceedings of the Davenport Academy of Sciences 11:238. Garden, pp. 215–216. Leopold, A. 1931. Report on a game survey of the north central states. Sporting Arms and Ammunition Manufacturers' Institute, Madison, Wisconsin, p. 197.

6. Audubon, M. R. 1898. Audubon and his journals. John C. Nimmo, London, pp. 488–489.

7. Lee, J. W. 1912. History of Hamilton County Iowa. S. J. Clarke Publishing Co., Chicago, p. 188. Price, R. E. 1916. History of Clayton County Iowa. R. O. Law Co., Chicago, p. 422. Moorehead, G. C. 1928. Historical collections of Ida County. Pioneer Record Press, Ida Grove, Iowa, p. 27. Savage, p. 219.

8. Weaver, J. B. 1912. Past and present of Jasper County Iowa. B. F. Bowen and Co., Indianapolis, p. 288.

9. Barrows, W. 1863. History of Scott County, Iowa. Annals of Iowa, 1st series, 1:26. Usher, I. L. 1922. Letters of a railroad builder. Palimpsest 3:26. Hartman, J. C. 1915. History of Black Hawk County Iowa and its people. S. J. Clarke Publishing Co., Chi-

cago, p. 129. Savage, 19:92. Bartsch, P. 1895. Birds extinct in Iowa and those becoming so. Iowa Ornithologist 2:3.

10. Little, T. W. 1979. History and current status of the wild turkey in Iowa. Iowa Conservation Commission, Research Bulletin 28, p. 3. Klonglan, E. D., G. Hlavka, and H. L. Gladfelter. 1970. Recent wild turkey introductions into Iowa. Proceedings of the Iowa Academy of Science 77:86–90. Little, T. W. 1976. Restoration of the wild turkey to Iowa. Part 2. The Iowa story. Iowa Conservationist 35(8):12–13. Little, T. W. 1980. Wild turkey restoration in "marginal" Iowa habitats. Fourth National Wild Turkey Symposium, pp. 49–50.

11. Klonglan, Hlavka, and Gladfelter, pp. 87–88. Little, Restoration of the wild turkey to Iowa, part 2, p. 13. Jackson, D. 1991. The final chapter. Iowa Conservationist 50(4):7–10. Andrews, R., D. Jackson, L. Jackson, T. Z. Riley, W. Suchy, and G. Zenner. 1991. Trends in Iowa wildlife populations and harvest 1990. Iowa Department of Natural Resources, Des Moines, pp. 21–23, 29, 31, 33, 109–114.

12. Little, T. W. 1983. The wild turkey. Iowa Conservationist 42(3):6–7. Thomson and Hertel, pp. 2–4.

13. Kennamer, J. E., and M. C. Kennamer. 1990. Current status and distribution of the wild turkey, 1989. Proceedings of the National Wild Turkey Symposium 6:2. Lewis, J. B. 1987. Success story: wild turkey. P. 34 *in* Restoring America's wildlife (H. Kallman, editor). U.S. Fish and Wildlife Service, Washington, D.C.

13. Quail

1. Johnsgard, P. A. 1973. Grouse and quails of North America. University of Nebraska Press, Lincoln, p. 413.

2. Leopold, A. 1931. Report on a game survey of the north central states. Sporting Arms and Ammunition Manufacturers' Institute, Madison, Wisconsin, pp. 24–25. Schorger, A. W. 1944. The quail in early Wisconsin. Transactions of the Wisconsin Academy of Science, Arts and Letters 36:77–86.

3. H. P. U. 1892. Stories of boyhood days. Forest and Stream 38:3. Quick, H. 1925. One man's life. Bobbs-Merrill Co., Indianapolis, p. 80. Spurrell, J. A. 1917. Annotated list of the water birds, game birds and birds of prey of Sac County, Iowa. Wilson Bulletin 29:156. Newell, W. 1897. Bob white. Iowa Ornithologist 3:10. W. H. R. 1880. Untitled. Forest and Stream 15:411. Anderson, R. M. 1907. The birds of Iowa. Proceedings of the Davenport Academy of Sciences 11:231.

4. Scott, T. G. 1937. Snow-killing of the bob-white. Wilson Bulletin 49:21–27. Leopold, A. 1932. Report of the Iowa game survey,

chapter two, Iowa quail. Outdoor America (October–November 1932), p. 12.

5. Babbitt, C. H. 1918. The Missouri Slope fifty years ago. Forest and Stream 88:523. Hough, E. 1900. Chicago and the west. Forest and Stream 55:226. Goshorn, A. G. 1891. Iowa game birds. Forest and Stream 36:189. Convis. 1893. The hard winter in Iowa. Forest and Stream 40:135. White, E. S. 1915. Past and present of Shelby County Iowa. B. F. Bowen and Co., Indianapolis, p. 80. Anon. 1912. Quail mortality in Iowa. Forest and Stream 78:208. Stempel, M. E. 1962. Bobwhite quail, winter weather and agriculture. Proceedings of the Iowa Academy of Science 69:261–262, 263–264. George, R. R., J. B. Wooley, and W. Rybarczyk. 1983. Results of long-term direct counts of upland game species on three intensive study areas in Iowa. Iowa Conservation Commission, Iowa Wildlife Research Bulletin 33, p. 17. Rybarczyk, W. 1983. Quail. Iowa Conservationist 42(10):19–20. Spurrell, p. 156.

6. Merritt, H. C. 1904. The shadow of a gun. F. T. Peterson Co., Chicago, pp. 273, 60–61. Leaman, B. R. 1971. An early settler in Iowa: westward expansion in microcosm. Annals of Iowa, 3rd series, 41:699. Richman, I. B. 1911. History of Muscatine County Iowa. S. J. Clarke Publishing Co., Chicago, p. 259. Usher, I. L. 1922. Letters of a railroad builder. Palimpsest 3:26. Petersen, W. J. 1958. Wild game everywhere. Palimpsest 39:561. Hall, W. R., and J. C. Briggs. 1896. Iowa game. Forest and Stream 46:198.

7. Orr, E. 1971. Reminiscences of a pioneer boy. Annals of Iowa, 3rd series, 40:602–603. Newell, p. 11. Bennett, H. A. 1926. Fish and game legislation in Iowa. Iowa Journal of History and Politics 24:401, 418, 419. Stempel, p. 263.

8. The Captain. 1907. Quail and pheasant shooting. Forest and Stream 68:696. Gavitt, B. H. 1948. Eighty years in Iowa. A. T. DeGroot, Los Angeles, pp. 77–78. Savage, W. 1934. William Savage. Iowa pioneer, diarist, and painter of birds. Annals of Iowa, 3rd series, 19:216, 218. Bennett, pp. 397, 399.

9. Webster, C. L. 1897. History of Floyd County, Iowa. Intelligencer Print, Charles City, Iowa, p. 13. Webster, C. L. 1898. Changes in Iowa fauna and flora. Forest and Stream 50:426.

10. Leopold, Report of the Iowa game survey, p. 13. Leopold, Report on a game survey of the north central states, p. 66. Tjernagel, N. 1952. Pioneer foods and water supply. Annals of Iowa, 3rd series, 31:290.

11. Stempel, M. E. 1969. Removal of brushy and wooded quail habitat in three southern Iowa counties in recent years. Proceedings of the Iowa Academy of Science 76:218.

12. Stempel, Bobwhite quail, winter weather and agriculture, pp. 260–264.

13. Andrews, R., D. Jackson, L. Jackson, T. Z. Riley, W. Suchy, and G. Zenner. 1991. Trends in Iowa wildlife populations and harvest 1990. Iowa Department of Natural Resources, Des Moines, p. 76.

14. Crawford, B. T. 1987. Bobwhite quail. Pp. 299–301 *in* Restoring America's wildlife (H. Kallman, editor). U.S. Fish and Wildlife Service, Washington, D.C. Droege, S., and J. R. Sauer. 1990. Northern bobwhite, gray partridge, and ring-necked pheasant population trends (1966–1988) from the North American Breeding Bird Survey. Pp. 8–9 *in* Perdix V: gray partridge and ring-necked pheasant workshop (K. E. Church, R. E. Warner, and S. J. Brady, editors). Kansas Department of Wildlife and Parks, Emporia. Brennan, L. A. 1991. How can we reverse the northern bobwhite population decline? Wildlife Society Bulletin 19:544.

14. Ruffed Grouse

1. Bump, G., R. W. Darrow, F. C. Edminster, and W. F. Crissey. 1947. The ruffed grouse—life history, propagation, management. New York State Conservation Deptartment, Albany, p. 49.

2. Webster, C. L. 1897. History of Floyd County, Iowa. Intelligencer Print, Charles City, Iowa, p. 43. Anderson, R. M. 1907. The birds of Iowa. Proceedings of the Davenport Academy of Sciences 11:232.

3. W. H. R. 1880. Untitled. Forest and Stream 15:411. E. B. B. 1881. Untitled. Forest and Stream 16:210. Spurrell, J. A. 1917. Annotated list of the water birds, game birds and birds of prey of Sac County, Iowa. Wilson Bulletin 29:156. Babbitt, C. H. 1918. The Missouri Slope fifty years ago. Forest and Stream 88:522. Stempel, M. E. 1955. Timber pheasants make comeback. Iowa Conservationist 14:172. Leopold, A. 1932. Preliminary report on a game survey of northern Iowa for the Iowa Conservation Plan. State Fish and Game Commission and the State Conservation Board, Des Moines, map V(c).

4. Leopold, Preliminary report on a game survey of northern Iowa, map V(c). Stempel, p. 172. DuMont. P. A. 1933. A revised list of the birds of Iowa. University of Iowa Studies in Natural History 15(5):56.

5. Savage, W. 1933–37. William Savage. Iowa pioneer, diarist, and painter of birds. Annals of Iowa, 3rd series, 19:102, 104, 107, 199, 207, 210, 212–214, 218; 20:144, 147, 463, 464, 471, 540, 542. Leopold, Preliminary report on a game survey of northern Iowa, map V(c). Leopold, A. 1931. Report on a game survey of the north central states. Sporting Arms and Ammunition Manufacturers' Institute, Madison, Wisconsin, p. 150. Klonglan, E. D., and G. Hlavka. 1969. Recent status of ruffed grouse in Iowa. Proceedings

of the Iowa Academy of Science 76:234. Andrews, R., D. Jackson, L. Jackson, T. Z. Riley, W. Suchy, and G. Zenner. 1991. Trends in Iowa wildlife populations and harvest 1990. Iowa Department of Natural Resources, Des Moines, p. 104.

6. Chappell, H. C., and K. J. Chappell. 1914. History of Buchanan County Iowa and its people. S. J. Clarke Publishing Co., Chicago, p. 33. Garland, H. 1961. Boy life on the prairie. University of Nebraska Press, Lincoln, p. 361. Anderson, p. 232. Orr, E. 1971. Reminiscences of a pioneer boy. Annals of Iowa, 3rd series, 40: 601–602. The Captain. 1907. Quail and pheasant shooting. Forest and Stream 68:696. Little, T. W. 1980. Twelve years of Iowa ruffed grouse hunting. Iowa Conservationist 39(10):8.

7. Bennett, H. A. 1926. Fish and game legislation in Iowa. Iowa Journal of History and Politics 24:401, 416, 404, 410–411, 421. Little, p. 6. Klonglan, E. D., and G. Hlavka. 1969. Iowa's first ruffed grouse hunting season in 45 years. Proceedings of the Iowa Academy of Science 76:226–227. Klonglan, E. D., and G. Hlavka. 1969. Recent status of ruffed grouse in Iowa. Proceedings of the Iowa Academy of Science 76:237–238. Little, T. W. 1984. Ruffed grouse population indices from Iowa. Pp. 10–11 *in* Ruffed grouse management: state of the art in the early 1980's (W. L. Robinson, editor). Proceedings of a symposium held at the 45th Midwest Fish and Wildlife Conference, St. Louis. Andrews, Jackson, Jackson, Riley, Suchy, and Zenner, p. 76.

8. Andrews, Jackson, Jackson, Riley, Suchy, and Zenner, pp. 100–103, 105.

9. Little, T. 1982. The woodland classic—ruffed grouse. Iowa Conservationist 41(9):22. Thomson, G. W., and H. G. Hertel. 1981. The forest resources of Iowa in 1980. Proceedings of the Iowa Academy of Science 88:2–3.

10. Gullion, G. W. 1984. Ruffed grouse management—where do we stand in the eighties? Pp. 169–181 *in* Ruffed grouse management.

11. Atwater, S., and J. Schnell (editors). 1989. Ruffed grouse. Stackpole Books, Harrisburg, Pennsylvania, p. 252.

15. Shorebirds

1. Forbush, E. H. 1912. A history of the game birds, wild-fowl and shore birds of Massachusetts and adjacent states. Massachusetts State Board of Agriculture, Boston, pp. 224–367.

2. Dinsmore, J. J., T. H. Kent, D. Koenig, P. C. Petersen, and D. M. Roosa. 1984. Iowa birds. Iowa State University Press, Ames, p. 155.

3. Anon. 1910. Hunting in Iowa. Forest and Stream 74:734–

735. Merritt, H. C. 1904. The shadow of a gun. F. T. Peterson Co., Chicago, pp. 85–90, 96–97, 122–152, 158–160, 170–174.

4. Moorehead, G. C. 1928. Historical collections of Ida County. Pioneer Record Press, Ida Grove, Iowa, p. 7. Dyke, C. L. 1942. The story of Sioux County. Verstegen Printing Co., Orange City, Iowa, pp. 17–19. Hunting in Iowa, p. 734. Crone, J. V. 1890. Summer residents of Buena Vista Co., Iowa. Oologist 7:45. Quick, H. 1925. One man's life. Bobbs-Merrill Co., Indianapolis. p. 83. Price, N. A. 1881. An Iowa game centre. Forest and Stream 17:89. McCulla, T. 1914. History of Cherokee County Iowa. S. J. Clarke Publishing Co., Chicago, p. 89. Spurrell, J. A. 1917. Annotated list of the water birds, game birds and birds of prey of Sac County, Iowa. Wilson Bulletin 29:155. Shimek, B. 1948. The plant geography of Iowa. University of Iowa Studies in Natural History 18(4):7. Preston, J. W. 1893. Some prairie birds. Ornithologist and Oologist 18:82. H. A. K. 1889. Iowa game notes. Forest and Stream 33:46. Priebe, C. 1990. Long-billed curlew in southwestern Iowa. Iowa Bird Life 60:20. Silcock, W. R. 1991. Long-billed curlew in Pottawattamie County. Iowa Bird Life 61:120–121. Johnsgard, P. A. 1979. Birds of the Great Plains. University of Nebraska Press, Lincoln, p. 155.

5. Dyke, p. 50. McCulla, p. 89. Musgrove, J. W. 1945. Market hunting in northern Iowa. Annals of Iowa, 3rd series, 26:176.

6. Hunting in Iowa, p. 734. Spurrell, p. 155. Preston, p. 82. Musgrove, p. 176. Johnsgard, p. 160.

7. Hough, E. 1890. Plover-shooting. P. 210 *in* Shooting on upland, marsh, and stream (W. Leffingwell, editor). Rand, McNally & Co., Chicago.

8. Crone, p. 45. H. A. K., p. 46. Webster, C. L. 1910. Old times in Iowa. Forest and Stream 74:577. Musgrove, p. 175. Merritt, pp. 285–287.

9. American Ornithologists' Union. 1983. Check-list of North American birds, 6th edition. Allen Press, Lawrence, Kansas, pp. 166–167. Forbush, pp. 341–347. Quick, p. 83. Dacotah, A. 1877. Hunting golden plover. Forest and Stream 8:330. Hunting in Iowa, p. 734. Shimek, p. 7. Spurrell, p. 156. Merritt, pp. 180–181. Musgrove, pp. 175–176. H. A. K., p. 46.

10. Merritt, pp. 282–283.

11. Hough, pp. 202–207.

12. Forbush, pp. 341–347. Dinsmore, Kent, Koenig, Petersen, and Roosa, p. 131.

13. Gollop, J. B., T. W. Barry, and E. H. Iversen. 1986. Eskimo curlew. A vanishing species? Saskatchewan Natural History Society Special Publication 17, pp. 35–36. Hunting in Iowa, p. 734. Hough, E. 1901. Chicago and the west. Forest and Stream 56:

146. Musgrove, p. 176. H. A. K., p. 46. Hallock, C. 1877. The sportsman's gazetteer and general guide. Forest and Stream Publishing Co., New York, p. 56. Hodges, J. 1950. Specimen of the eskimo curlew for Iowa discovered. Iowa Bird Life 20:26. Banks, R. C. 1977. The decline and fall of the eskimo curlew, or why did the curlew go extaille? American Birds 31:128–129. Forbush, pp. 417–432.

14. Forbush, p. 423. Banks, pp. 127–134. Gollop, Barry, and Iversen, p. 15. Gollop, J. B. 1988. The eskimo curlew. Pp. 591–592 *in* Audubon wildlife report 1988/1989 (W. J. Chandler, editor). Academic Press, San Diego.

15. Kimball, D., and J. Kimball. 1969. The market hunter. Dillon Press, Minneapolis, p. 109. Tuck, L. M. 1972. The snipes: a study of the genus *Capella*. Canadian Wildlife Service Monograph Series 5, pp. 359–366. Brooks, D. 1875. Grouse shooting in Iowa. Forest and Stream 5:188. Harlan, J. R. 1942. The Iowa game book of George E. Poyneer. Annals of Iowa, 3rd series, 23:196, 198, 202.

16. Bennett, H. A. 1926. Fish and game legislation in Iowa. Iowa Journal of History and Politics 24:395, 401. Fogarty, M. J., and K. A. Arnold. 1977. Common snipe. Pp. 193, 200 *in* Management of migratory shore and upland game birds in North America (G. C. Sanderson, editor). International Association of Fish and Wildlife Agencies, Washington, D.C. Blohm, B. 1993. Harvest management: sustaining migratory bird populations. Fish and Wildlife News (Winter), p. 12.

17. Sheets, R. 1972. Woodcock—new Iowa game bird. Iowa Conservationist 31(9):10. Martin, E. M. 1979. Hunting and harvest trends for migratory game birds other than waterfowl: 1964–76. U.S. Fish and Wildlife Service Special Scientific Report—Wildlife 218, p. 37. Sauer, J. R., and J. B. Bortner. 1991. Population trends from the American woodcock singing-ground survey, 1970–88. Journal of Wildlife Management 55:302–303.

18. Flickinger, R. E. 1904. The pioneer history of Pocahontas County, Iowa. Fonda Times, Fonda, Iowa, p. 278.

16. Cranes

1. James, E. (compiler). 1966. Account of an expedition from Pittsburgh to the Rocky Mountains, volume 1. University Microfilms, Ann Arbor, Michigan, pp. 344–345. Webster, C. L. 1898. Changes in Iowa fauna and flora. Forest and Stream 50:426. Monlux, G. 1909. Early history of Lyon County. Privately published, p. 20. Greene, S. H. 1897. Recollections of Iowa. Forest and Stream 48:263. Anon. 1884. Game in Iowa. Forest and Stream 22:228. Shimek, B. 1948. The plant geography of Iowa. University of Iowa Studies in Natural History 18(4):7.

2. Flickinger, R. E. 1904. The pioneer history of Pocahontas County, Iowa. Fonda Times, Fonda, Iowa, p. 278. Cunningham, G. W. 1897. Game in central Iowa. Forest and Stream 48:227. Quick, H. 1925. One man's life. Bobbs-Merrill Co., Indianapolis, pp. 84–85. Reed, B. F. 1913. History of Kossuth County Iowa. S. J. Clarke Publishing Co., Chicago, p. 162.

3. Moorehead, G. C. 1928. Historical collections of Ida County. Pioneer Record Press, Ida Grove, Iowa, p. 7. White, E. S. 1915. Past and present of Shelby County Iowa. B. F. Bowen and Co., Indianapolis, p. 79. Spurrell, J. A. 1917. Annotated list of the water birds, game birds and birds of prey of Sac County, Iowa. Wilson Bulletin 29:153. Mosher, A. A. 1882. The fauna of Spirit Lake. Forest and Stream 18:66. Preston, J. W. 1893. Some prairie birds. Ornithologist and Oologist 18:81–82. Crone, J. V. 1893. Hash. Oologist 10:234. Ingalsbe, J. L. 1920. Northwestern Iowa in 1855. Iowa Journal of History and Politics 18:282. Anderson, R. M. 1894. Nesting of the whooping crane. Oologist 11:263–264.

4. Allen, R. P. 1952. The whooping crane. National Audubon Society Research Report 3, pp. 26, 27. Dacotah, A. 1877. Untitled. Forest and Stream 9:14. Anderson, pp. 263–264.

5. Bishop, R. A. 1981. Iowa's wetlands. Proceedings of the Iowa Academy of Science 88:11.

6. Johnsgard, P. A. 1983. Cranes of the world. Croom Helm, London, pp. 172, 185. White, E. S. 1915. Past and present of Shelby County Iowa. B. F. Bowen and Co., Indianapolis, p. 150. Sandpiper. 1877. Sport in Iowa. Forest and Stream 9:288. Chappell, H. C., and K. J. Chappell. 1914. History of Buchanan County Iowa and its people. S. J. Clarke Publishing Co., Chicago, p. 35.

7. Reed, pp. 162, 163. Greene, p. 244. Brooks, D. 1875. Grouse shooting in Iowa. Forest and Stream 5:188. Spurrell, p. 153. Anon. 1904–05. Compendium of history, reminiscence and biography of Lyon County, Iowa. G. A. Ogle and Co., Chicago, p. 168.

8. Burrell, H. A. 1909. History of Washington County Iowa. S. J. Clarke Publishing Co., Chicago, p. 393.

9. Moorehead, p. 7. Garland, H. 1961. Boy life on the prairie. University of Nebraska Press, Lincoln, p. 360.

10. Allen, pp. 52–53. Anderson, pp. 263–264. Dacotah, p. 14.

11. Spurrell, p. 153. Gabrielson, I. N. 1917. A list of the birds observed in Clay and O'Brien counties, Iowa. Proceedings of the Iowa Academy of Science 24:264. Wolden, B. O. 1924. Water birds, fowls and birds of prey observed in Emmet Co. Estherville Vindicator and Republican, 4 June 1924, p. 1. Dinsmore, J. J., T. H. Kent, D. Koenig, P. C. Petersen, and D. M. Roosa. 1984. Iowa birds. Iowa State University Press, Ames, p. 129.

12. Doughty, R. W. 1989. Return of the whooping crane. University of Texas Press, Austin, pp. 23, 111–139, 154. Anon. 1993. Whooper numbers on the rise. Fish and Wildlife News (Winter), p. 35. Logan, T. H., and S. A. Nesbitt. 1987. Status of sandhill and whooping crane studies in Florida. Proceedings of the 1985 Crane Workshop, p. 213.

13. Miller, H. W. 1987. Hunting in the management of mid-continent sandhill cranes. Proceedings of the 1985 Crane Workshop, pp. 43–45.

14. Anon. 1910. Hunting in Iowa. Forest and Stream 74:735. Dinsmore, J. J. 1989. The return of sandhill cranes to Iowa. Iowa Bird Life 59:71–74. Harris, J., and J. Knoop. 1987. The Wisconsin sandhill crane count: a public participation project. Proceedings of the 1985 Crane Workshop, p. 23. Robbins, S. D. 1991. Wisconsin birdlife. University of Wisconsin Press, Madison, p. 249.

15. Poggensee, D. 1992. Nesting sandhill cranes at Otter Creek Marsh, Tama County. Iowa Bird Life 62:112–113.

17. Waterfowl

1. Bennett, L. J. 1938. The blue-winged teal: its ecology and management. Collegiate Press, Ames, Iowa, p. 95.

2. Bishop, R. A. 1981. Iowa's wetlands. Proceedings of the Iowa Academy of Science 88:15.

3. Wolfe, P. B. 1911. Wolfe's history of Clinton County Iowa. 1911. B. F. Bowen and Co., Indianapolis, p. 254. Babbitt, C. H. 1918. The Missouri Slope fifty years ago. Forest and Stream 88:523. Gavitt, B. H. 1948. Eighty years in Iowa. A. T. DeGroot, Los Angeles, p. 11.

4. Moulton, G. E. (editor). 1986. The journals of the Lewis & Clark expedition, volume 2. University of Nebraska Press, Lincoln, pp. 395, 429, 445, 459.

5. Reed, B. F. 1913. History of Kossuth County Iowa. S. J. Clarke Publishing Co., Chicago, p. 163. Shimek, B. 1948. The plant geography of Iowa. University of Iowa Studies in Natural History 18(4):7. Bennett, p. 95.

6. James, E. (compiler). 1966. Account of an expedition from Pittsburgh to the Rocky Mountains, volume 1. University Microfilms, Ann Arbor, Michigan, p. 197. Babbitt, p. 523.

7. Musgrove, J. W. 1945. Market hunting in northern Iowa. Annals of Iowa, 3rd series, 26:174. Thompson, F. O. 1937. Hunting in northwestern Iowa. Iowa Journal of History and Politics 35:74.

8. Musgrove, Market hunting, pp. 173–175, 188, 183, 177.

9. Ibid., pp. 177–184, 180–181.

10. Ibid., pp. 177–178.

11. Bruette, W. A. 1929. Iowa's famous duck passes. Forest and

Stream 99:584–585. Musgrove, J. W. 1949. Iowa. Pp. 201–202 *in* Wildfowling in the Mississippi flyway (E. V. Connett, editor). D. Van Nostrand Co., New York. Anon. 1910. Hunting in Iowa. Forest and Stream 74:735.

12. Musgrove, Market hunting, p. 179.

13. Thompson, p. 76. Musgrove, Market hunting, pp. 181–182, 188.

14. Sawyer, W. W. 1960. Mallards for the market. Annals of Iowa, 3rd series, 35:454–463.

15. Musgrove, Iowa, p. 195.

16. Ibid., pp. 205–206.

17. Ibid., pp. 202–204.

18. Anon. 1983. Iowan recalls day when ducks were plentiful. Des Moines Register, 24 November 1983, p. 1C.

19. Anon. 1874. Untitled. Forest and Stream 2:218. Algona. 1878. Untitled. Forest and Stream 11:369. The Captain. 1907. Duck shooting in early days. Forest and Stream 68:576. Hough, E. 1901. Chicago and the west. Forest and Stream 57:349.

20. Leffingwell, W. B. 1890. Wild fowl shooting. Rand, McNally and Co., Chicago, pp. 204–205.

21. Musgrove, Iowa, pp. 194, 195–196.

22. Anon. 1910. Hunting in Iowa. Forest and Stream 74:735.

23. Musgrove, Iowa, pp. 211–212. Anon. 1880. Spirit Lake. Forest and Stream 15:189.

24. Musgrove, Market hunting, p. 184.

25. Ibid., pp. 192–196.

26. Garland, H. 1961. Boy life on the prairie. University of Nebraska Press, Lincoln, p. 360.

27. H. P. U. 1892. Stories of boyhood days. Forest and Stream 38:4.

28. Bishop, p. 11. Dahl, T. E. 1990. Wetlands losses in the United States 1780's to 1980's. U.S. Department of the Interior, Fish and Wildlife Service, Washington, D.C., p. 6.

29. Bennett, H. A. 1926. Fish and game legislation in Iowa. Iowa Journal of History and Politics 24:401, 404, 409.

30. Andrews, R., D. Jackson, L. Jackson, T. Z. Riley, W. Suchy, and G. Zenner. 1991. Trends in Iowa wildlife populations and harvest 1990. Iowa Department of Natural Resources, Des Moines, p. 55.

31. Ibid., p. 54.

32. Hanson, H. C. 1965. The giant Canada goose. Southern Illinois University Press, Carbondale, pp. viii–ix. Bishop, R. 1978. Giant Canada geese in Iowa. Iowa Conservationist 37(10):6. Zenner, G. G., and T. G. LaGrange. 1991. Land of the giants. Iowa Conservationist 50(6):30.

18. Introduced Species

1. Laycock, G. 1966. The alien animals. Natural History Press, Garden City, New York.

2. Phillips, J. C. 1928. Wild birds introduced or transplanted in North America. U.S. Department of Agriculture Technical Bulletin 61, pp. 9–47.

3. Ibid., pp. 42–43. Einarsen, A. S. 1945. The pheasant in the Pacific Northwest. Pp. 254–255 in The ring-necked pheasant and its management in North America (W. L. McAtee, editor). American Wildlife Institute, Washington, D.C. Faber, L. F. 1946. The history of stocking and management of ringneck pheasants in the state of Iowa. Iowa Conservationist 5:73.

4. Farris, A. L., E. D. Klonglan, and R. C. Nomsen. 1977. The ring-necked pheasant in Iowa. Iowa Conservation Commission, Des Moines, pp. 8–9. Faber, pp. 75, 78. Leopold, A. 1933. Report of the Iowa game survey, chapter three, Iowa pheasants. Outdoor America (December 1932–January 1933), pp. 10–11.

5. Farris, Klonglan, and Nomsen, pp. 11–15, 97–99.

6. Faber, p. 75. Farris, Klonglan, and Nomsen, pp. 114–116.

7. Andrews, R., D. Jackson, L. Jackson, T. Z. Riley, W. Suchy, and G. Zenner. 1991. Trends in Iowa wildlife populations and harvest 1990. Iowa Department of Natural Resources, Des Moines, p. 76.

8. Leopold, Iowa pheasants, p. 31. Westemeier, R. L. 1984. Responses and impact by pheasants on prairie-chicken sanctuaries in Illinois: a synopsis. Pp. 117–122 in Perdix III: gray partridge and ring-necked pheasant workshop (R. T. Dumke, R. B. Stiehl, and R. B. Kahl, editors). Wisconsin Department of Natural Resources, Madison. Westemeier, R. L. 1988. An evaluation of methods for controlling pheasants on Illinois prairie-chicken sanctuaries. Pp. 267–288 in Pheasants: symptoms of wildlife problems on agricultural lands (D. L. Hallett, W. R. Edwards, and G. V. Burger, editors). North Central Section of the Wildlife Society, Bloomington, Indiana.

9. Farris, Klonglan, and Nomsen, pp. 77–78, 121.

10. Ibid., pp. 81–83, 48–49.

11. Dahlgren, R. B. 1987. The ring-necked pheasant. Pp. 305–311 in Restoring America's wildlife (H. Kallman, editor). U.S. Fish and Wildlife Service, Washington, D.C. Dahlgren, R. B. 1988. Distribution and abundance of the ring-necked pheasant in North America. P. 38 in Pheasants.

12. Harrison, C. 1982. An atlas of the birds of the western Palaearctic. Collins, London, p. 111. Phillips, pp. 34–36. Johnsgard, P. A. 1973. Grouse and quails of North America. University of Nebraska Press, Lincoln, pp. 477–481. Vander Zouwen, W. J. 1990.

Recent status of gray partridge in North America. Pp. 22–23 *in* Perdix V: gray partridge and ring-necked pheasant workshop (K. E. Church, R. E. Warner, and S. J. Brady, editors). Kansas Department of Wildlife and Parks, Emporia.

13. Leopold, A. 1933. Report of the Iowa game survey, chapter four, The Hungarian partridge in Iowa. Outdoor America (February–March 1933), pp. 6–7. Spiker, C. J. 1929. The Hungarian partridge in northwest Iowa. Wilson Bulletin 41:25.

14. State Conservation Commission. 1940. Report of the State Conservation Commission for the biennium ending June 30, 1940, p. 37. Klonglan, E. D. 1964. Hungarian partridge population trends in Iowa, 1954–64. Iowa Conservation Commission, Quarterly Biology Reports 16(3):49–50. Bishop, R. A., R. C. Nomsen, and R. D. Andrews. 1977. A look at Iowa's Hungarian partridge. Pp. 18–19, 30 *in* Perdix I: Hungarian partridge workshop (G. D. Kobriger, editor). Minot, North Dakota.

15. Wooley, J. B., and R. R. George. 1980. Huns in southeast Iowa. Iowa Conservationist 39(5):13. Washburn, L. 1990. Iowa's most frustrating gamebird. Iowa Conservationist 49(11):3. Andrews, Jackson, Jackson, Riley, Suchy, and Zenner, p. 76.

16. Vander Zouwen, pp. 24–25, 34.

17. Harrison, p. 112. Christensen, G. C. 1987. The chukar partridge. Pp. 313–314 *in* Restoring America's wildlife.

18. State Conservation Commission. 1938. Report of the State Conservation Commission for the biennium ending June 30, 1938, p. 38. State Conservation Commission. 1940. Report of the State Conservation Commission for the biennium ending June 30, 1940, p. 37. State Conservation Commission. 1942. Report of the State Conservation Commission for the biennium ending June 30, 1942, p. 40. Dinsmore, J. J., T. H. Kent, D. Koenig, P. C. Petersen, and D. M. Roosa. 1984. Iowa birds. Iowa State University Press, Ames, p. 115.

19. Johnsgard, P. A. 1986. The pheasants of the world. Oxford University Press, New York, p. 184. Klonglan, E. D., and G. Hlavka. 1964. Reeves pheasant introduction into Iowa. Iowa Conservation Commission, Quarterly Biology Reports 16(4):9. State Conservation Commission. 1962. Report of the State Conservation Commission for the biennium ending June 30, 1962, p. 93. Klonglan, E. D. 1963. Reeves pheasants—a new experiment. Iowa Conservationist 22:16. State Conservation Commission. 1964. Report of the State Conservation Commission for the biennium ending June 30, 1964, p. 95. Hlavka, G. 1965. Reeves pheasant sightings and stockings, 1963–65. Iowa Conservation Commission, Quarterly Biology Reports 17(3):3–6. Hlavka, G. 1966. Reeves pheasant stockings and observations, 1966. Iowa Conservation Commission, Quarterly Bi-

ology Reports 18(3):71–75. Hlavka, G., and E. D. Klonglan. 1968. "French-strain" Reeves renew stocking experiment in 1968. Iowa Conservation Commission, Quarterly Biology Reports 20(3):5–6.

20. Harrison, p. 111. Oldys, H. 1910. Introduction of the Hungarian partridge into the United States. U.S. Department of Agriculture Yearbook 1909, p. 249.

19. Humans and Wildlife in Iowa

1. Shimek, B. 1911. The prairies. University of Iowa Studies in Natural History Bulletin 6:170–171. Thomson, G. W., and H. G. Hertel. 1981. The forest resources of Iowa in 1980. Proceedings of the Iowa Academy of Science 88:2–3. Dahl, T. E. 1990. Wetlands losses in the United States 1780's to 1980's. U.S. Department of the Interior, Fish and Wildlife Service, Washington, D.C., p. 6. Smith, D. D. 1981. Iowa prairie—an endangered ecosystem. Proceedings of the Iowa Academy of Science 88:8. Pearson, John. Iowa Department of Natural Resources, Des Moines, personal communication, November 1992.

2. Hewes, L., and P. E. Frandson. 1952. Occupying the wet prairie: the role of artificial drainage in Story County, Iowa. Annals of the Association of American Geographers 42:24–50.

3. Kennedy, J. C. G. 1864. Agriculture of the United States in 1860. Government Printing Office, Washington, D.C., p. 50. Iowa Department of Agriculture and Land Stewardship. 1990. 1990 Agricultural statistics. Iowa Department of Agriculture and Land Stewardship and U.S. Department of Agriculture, Des Moines, p. 10.

4. Crane, J. L., and G. W. Olcott. 1933. Report on the Iowa twenty-five year conservation plan. Iowa Board of Conservation and Iowa Fish and Game Commission, Des Moines, pp. 139–140. Hayden, A. 1945. The selection of prairie areas in Iowa which should be preserved. Proceedings of the Iowa Academy of Science 52:127–148. Smith, pp. 8–9.

5. Thomson, G. W. 1980. Iowa's disappearing woodlands. Iowa State Journal of Research 55:129–133. Thomson, G. W. 1987. Iowa's forest area in 1832: a reevaluation. Proceedings of the Iowa Academy of Science 94:116–120.

6. Hewes, L. 1950. Some features of early woodland and prairie settlement in a central Iowa county. Annals of the Association of American Geographers 40:40–57. Thomson and Hertel, p. 3.

7. Thomson, Iowa's disappearing woodlands, pp. 130–133. Thornton, P. L., and J. T. Morgan. 1959. The forest resources of Iowa. Forest Survey Release 22. Central States Forest Experiment Station, U.S. Forest Service, p. 3. Ostrom, A. J. 1974. Forest statis-

tics for Iowa, 1974. U.S. Department of Agriculture, Forest Service Resources Bulletin NC-33. North Central Forest Experiment Station, p. 9.

8. Ostrom, p. 9.

9. Bishop, R. A. 1981. Iowa's wetlands. Proceedings of the Iowa Academy of Science 88:11. Dahl, p. 6.

10. Bishop, p. 11.

11. Lokken, R. L. 1942. Iowa public land disposal. State Historical Society of Iowa, Iowa City, pp. 180–209, 267. Hewes, L. 1951. The northern wet prairie of the United States: nature, sources of information, and extent. Annals of the Association of American Geographers 41:307–323. Gamble, J. M. 1972. The Iowa wet prairie and problems of early settlement. Iowa Geographer 30:51–55.

12. Bishop, p. 15.

13. Ibid., p. 11.

14. Agnew, D. L. 1950. Iowa's first railroad. Iowa Journal of History 48:12–26.

15. Iowa Department of Transportation. 1986. 1985 Iowa railroad analysis update. Iowa Department of Transportation, Ames, p. 24. Association of American Railroads. 1990. Railroad facts. Association of American Railroads, Washington, D.C., p. 45.

16. Oliver, J. W. 1956. History of American technology. Ronald Press Co., New York, p. 383.

17. Thomson and Hertel, p. 5. Braband, L. 1986. Railroad grasslands as bird and mammal habitats in central Iowa. Pp. 86–90 *in* The prairie: past, present and future (G. K. Clambey and R. H. Pemble, editors). Proceedings of the North American Prairie Conference 9.

18. Oliver, pp. 138–139.

19. Hunter, L. C. 1969. Steamboats on the western rivers. Octagon Books, New York, pp. 188–189.

20. Hesse, L. W., A. B. Schlesinger, G. L. Hergenrader, S. D. Reetz, and H. S. Lewis. 1982. The Missouri River study—ecological perspectives. Pp. 287–300 *in* The Middle Missouri River (L. W. Hesse, G. L. Hergenrader, H. S. Lewis, S. D. Reetz, and A. B. Schlesinger, editors). Missouri River Study Group, Norfolk, Nebraska. Hesse, L. W. 1987. Taming the wild Missouri River: what has it cost? Fisheries 12(2):2–9.

21. Iowa Department of Transportation. 1990. Highway mileages in Iowa by surface type. Iowa Department of Transportation, Office of Transportation Inventory, Ames. Kollings, T. 1991. Motorists should be on lookout for deer. Des Moines Register, 15 September 1991, p. 4D.

22. Kendall, E. C. 1959. John Deere's steel plow. Contributions of the Museum of History and Technology Bulletin 218:16–25. Coffin, L. S. 1902. Breaking prairie. Annals of Iowa, 3rd series, 5: 447–452.

23. Miller, M. F. 1902. The evolution of reaping machines. U. S. Department of Agriculture, Office of Experiment Stations, Bulletin 103. Oliver, pp. 224–228, 362–367, 548. Wendel, C. H. 1979. Encyclopedia of American farm tractors. Crestline Publishing Co., Sarasota, Florida. Bogue, A. G. 1983. Changes in mechanical and plant technology: the Corn Belt, 1910–1940. Journal of Economic History 43:1–25.

24. Kennedy, p. 199. Iowa Department of Agriculture and Land Stewardship, p. 4.

25. Kendall, R. J., and J. Akerman. 1992. Terrestrial wildlife exposed to agrochemicals: an ecological risk assessment perspective. Environmental Toxicology and Chemistry 11:1,727–1,749.

26. Gerstell, R. 1985. The steel trap in North America. Stackpole Books, Harrisburg, Pennsylvania, pp. 167–169. Novak, M. 1987. Traps and trap research. Pp. 941–969 *in* Wild furbearer management and conservation in North America (M. Novak, J. A. Baker, M. E. Obbard, and B. Malloch, editors). Ontario Trappers Association, North Bay, Ontario.

27. Bonebright-Closz, H. 1921. Reminiscences of Newcastle, Iowa 1848. Historical Department of Iowa, Des Moines, pp. 58–60.

28. Waller, D. W., and P. L. Errington. 1961. The bounty system in Iowa. Proceedings of the Iowa Academy of Science 68:301–313. Bennett, H. A. 1926. Fish and game legislation in Iowa. Iowa Journal of History and Politics 24:401, 345–347, 407–408, 415–416.

29. Lokken, pp. 266–267.

30. Iowa Department of Agriculture and Land Stewardship, p. 4.

20. The Future of Wildlife in Iowa

1. U.S. Fish and Wildlife Service. 1986. North American waterfowl management plan. U.S. Fish and Wildlife Service, Washington, D.C.

2. Szcodronski, Kevin. Iowa Department of Natural Resources, Des Moines, personal communication, December 1992.

Index

hunting, 153–160; population decline, 163–165; prices for, 154–155, 160; sport hunting, 160, 162–163; at time of settlement, 152–153

Waterloo, Iowa, 108, 109, 124, 161, 174

Waukon, Iowa, 92, 96

Wayne County, 112, 113

weasel, 78

Webster, Clement, 82, 99, 109, 125, 129, 138, 145

Webster City, Iowa, 37, 43, 53, 79, 82, 89

Webster County, 25, 130

Wesley, Iowa, 27

West, Abraham, 103

West Bend, Iowa, 139

West Okoboji Lake, 16, 44, 158

wetlands: in Iowa, 182–183; loss of, 182–183

Whisman, A. J., 116

Whitacre, Joseph, 37

Whitehead, Charles, 144

Wiggins, Billy, 162

Wilhelm, Paul, 13

Williams, H. S., 103

Williams College, 32

Williamson, R. W., 44

Wilson, Alexander, 90–91

Wilson, James, 160

Winnebago County, 37, 39, 52, 170

Winneshiek County, 38, 47, 55, 92, 113, 130

winter of 1856–57, 26, 27, 29–30, 35, 38–39

Winterset, Iowa, 123

Winthrop, Iowa, 110

Wisconsin, 12, 91, 99

wolf, gray: 8, 57–66, 78, 182, 194; bounties, 63–65; food of, 58; hunting, 60–61; incidents with humans, 59–60; poisoning, 62; population decline, 62–63; trapping, 61–62

wolf, great plains, 58

Woodbine, Iowa, 18, 125

Woodbury County, 38, 47, 83, 129

woodcock, American: 135–136, 143, 182, 194; bag limit, 143; harvest of, 143; hunting, 135–136; hunting seasons, 143; market hunting, 136; prices for, 136

Wooster College, 52

Worth County, 130

Wright, John, 31, 53

Wright County, 13, 15, 26, 33, 130, 152

Wyalusing State Park, 100

Yale University, 122

Yellow River, 44, 92

Yellow River Forest, 119

Yellowstone National Park, 22, 23, 33

Bur Oak Books